Politics in Action:
Contemporary sources for students of politics and government

Chris Leeds

Stanley Thornes (Publishers) Ltd

First published 1986 by
Stanley Thornes (Publishers) Ltd,
Old Station Drive,
Leckhampton Road,
CHELTENHAM GL53 0DN,
England.

British Library Cataloguing in Publication Data
Leeds, C.
Politics in action: contemporary sources for students of politics and government
1. World politics – 20th century
I. Title
909'.09812082   D443
ISBN 0-85950-188-4

Typeset by Grafikon nv, Oostkamp, Belgium.
Printed and bound in Great Britain at the Bath Press, Avon.

Contents

Preface

This book is primarily intended to supplement main course texts in an A-level GCE politics course. It can, however, also be used with first examination courses to complement *Politics and Government: a first sourcebook*, as a general or modern studies reader by students taking non-examined courses at school or college, and by anyone beginning the study of politics, whether individually or at undergraduate level.

The aim is to cover the key aspects of the subject that form part of nearly all the A-level syllabuses. Extracts have been chosen that are not easily obtainable by students, and that illustrate some of the wide range of sources of information available for the study of past and present developments in politics and government. Some of the topics selected have been covered in more than one extract, the object being to provide contrasting points of view, or in some cases to provide two or three extracts that reinforce and complement each other. It is hoped that the material in this book will encourage students to search for additional references in the press, magazines, etc. so as to keep up to date with current developments.

The questions are mainly for use in courses at A-level and below, since this is the level at which they are most likely to be helpful. The first series of questions after each group of extracts can be answered from a study of the extracts alone, and vary in difficulty, starting from the simplest, depending on the nature of each source. Questions headed **Class discussion** raise wider issues which are not covered totally by the text, and may perhaps best be tackled in a general discussion in which the teacher or lecturer participates. The **Extension work** section provides questions for individual research through reference to textbooks and other materials, whether done during a class or course or outside. The questions on each extract do not necessarily exhaust all possible issues covered in a particular source, and a group might well want to discuss or investigate other themes or problems raised.

The extracts have been arranged in groups according to their principal subject, but many of them are relevant to more than one area. The index therefore provides a fuller guide, referring to every document that is relevant to a particular topic.

CHRIS LEEDS

Acknowledgements

The author and publishers are grateful to the following for permission to reproduce previously published material or for the provision of material:

Alliance Action for Electoral Reform for the illustration on p. 115; Armament and Disarmament Information Unit for J11; Associated Newspapers Group plc for C7, D11, H2 and H3; Mr R Blackburn for H5B; Basil Blackwell Ltd for C3; Butterworths for D1 and H1B; Cambridge University Press for B7; Jonathan Cope for C5; Conservative Research Department for C4; The Daily Telegraph for D2, D7, E8, G4, J13; The Economist for A2, D3, G3; Electoral Reform Society for F6; Express Newspapers plc for B2; The Fabian Society for B4; Carolyn Faulder for E9; Fontana Paperbacks for D9A; The Freedom Association for A7; Mr A C Geddes for H5B; The Guardian for B10, C2, E4, E7, F2, F5, H5A, H5C, H5D; Her Majesty's Stationery Office for D9B; The House Magazine for G5; D Judge for C6; The Labour Party for D10, F7, F8, G6, H1A, H6, J2, J8B, K5; The Liberal Party for F4; London Review of Books for E10; Longman for J10; Macdonald & Co (Publishers) Ltd for B5; Marxism Today for K6; The Monday Club for K3; NOP for B3; National Council for Civil Liberties for A6, A8, A9; New Society for F1; New Statesman for G1, G2; The Observer for B9, E3, E6, J4, J9; The Parliamentarian for E2; John Patten MP for J1; SDP for G7; The Spectator for A10, J5; Sphere Books Ltd for B8; Elizabeth Stones, Education Officer, House of Commons for C1; Syndication International Ltd for D8, J7; T & G Record for J3A; Thomson Regional Newspapers for B1; Times Newspapers Limited for A1, A3, H4, J8A, J12 and K1; The Western Morning News for H7.

Every attempt has been made to contact copyright holders, but we apologise if any have been overlooked.

Section

A

Basic concepts and principles

Introduction

Until about the mid-1960s many of the British felt that their political system was one of the best and most stable in the world. Certain of its admired features are referred to by David Butler in the opening paragraph of A1. This belief in the soundness of British institutions led to our politicians influencing many newly independent Commonwealth countries to emulate the 'Westminster model', as Britain's form of parliamentary democracy was known.

Broadly speaking, from 1945 until the early 1970s each of the two main parties accepted the changes made by the other party when the latter governed, and did not try to turn the clock back by reversing them. The policies of both parties tended to overlap as they sought to gain the support of electors in the centre, neither strongly left or right. Words such as 'consensus', 'compromise' and 'Butskellism' were often heard in the fifties and early sixties.

From the late 1960s certain commentators and a growing number of the electorate became less confident in the ability of the political system to deal with a variety of social, political and economic problems. To some extent the decline in support for the two major parties reflected this growing public disillusionment (see Section F). Adversary or confrontational politics developed as the differences between the two main parties increased. The collapse of 'consensus politics' was accompanied by a decline in public respect for political institutions and politicians (see A2 and A3) and for the rule of law. People became more assertive about their rights and protest increasingly took a violent or potentially violent form, of which the Brixton riots in 1981 and the miners' strike of 1984–85 are examples.

1

Students of politics used to be primarily occupied with analysing and explaining the nature of our political institutions. Little thought was given to the possibility that anything needed serious reform, with the possible exception of the House of Lords. Then increasingly many of our political institutions and principles came under fire from various opponents (see A1 and A2). Critics have argued that a link exists between Britain's economic decline and our inability to change and modify our political system and attitudes. This is tied to our way of looking at all issues in polarised terms as if only two alternatives existed, derived from the largely two-party system. The only institution that largely escaped any serious criticism, and which if anything became more respected, during this period, was the monarchy, a point stressed in A2.

The broad question of which people and institutions carry the greatest influence or power in politics, make the real decisions, rule or govern, is discussed in A3, A4 and A5. An essential condition of effective participation in democracy is the possession of information, and the ability to obtain and store information and restrict popular access to it is one indicator of political power. This matter is linked to the wider issues of open and closed government, and the secretive nature of British politics, discussed in Sections B, C and D. It is also linked directly with human rights issues (see A6–A9). The article on the referendum (A10) is placed at the end of this section because it is related to the issues of human rights and a bill of rights, though it also represents a form of popular participation in politics (discussed at the end of Section F).

Herbert Marcuse, the American academic, once argued that developments in technology, far from liberating individuals to do what they want, make people dependent on technology for solutions. Developments in telecommunications, which apparently offer freer communication between individuals, can also increase government's access to information and therefore its power; hence the concern for proper standards against such things as telephone tapping (A8). Today people are increasingly dependent on the technological experts, who though skilled may be unscrupulous, like the hackers who can manipulate computers to pirate information from others.

A1

Politics: the vanishing certainties

by DAVID BUTLER

For a quarter of a century I have earned my living as a teacher of British government. I have found myself explaining, and in large measure defending, much of the status quo of the established constitutional machinery. In Britain we have evolved civilised rules that combine democracy with administrative efficiency, and strong government with responsible government; we have had an honest and neutral civil service and a workable party system; and everything has operated without fuss within an unwritten and flexible constitution.

But in the last few years second thoughts have begun to assert themselves. The system is much less stable than we used to think. It has not, over the last decade, given us notably good government and certainly it has not proved very exportable. Outside the Old Commonwealth, few countries have found it convenient, or even possible, to run their affairs on Westminster lines. And in Britain, itself, the old rules of the game seem to be changing fast.

Because we have an unwritten constitution which evolves gradually, through practice, rather than being formally altered, British textbooks on politics are always out of date; they describe what once was plainly true but the precedents they cite tend to be already obsolete. The greatest observer of English government, Walter Bagehot, made a vast impact in 1867 by pointing out that the Crown had no political clout and that every writer on the constitution was still deceived by Blackstone's exposition of the separation of judiciary, legislature and executive. But even Bagehot was already out of date; he did not understand what the coming of mass franchise was already doing to the party and governmental system. Today there are a host of would-be Bagehots but they too fail to spot what is happening and are trapped by dead precedents and obsolescent examples.

Lecturing in the United States fifteen years ago, I could straightforwardly expound some of the simple clarities of the British system: first, an unwritten constitution; second, the supremacy of Parliament; third, responsible government; fourth, a two-party system; fifth, a stable electorate; sixth, first-past-the-post elections; seventh, centralised government (i.e. no element of federation); and eighth, unitary government (i.e. no separation of powers). And when asked about the possibility of change in any of these, I could dismiss the question 'Not a hope. However desirable, it's just not on!'

How different the situation is today. Outwardly British government may go on much the same — apart from entry into Europe, there has been no formal change in our constitutional arrangements. But I could not now discount the chances that each one of these eight principles or practices, once accepted as central to the British way of running affairs, might soon be a thing of the past, an outdated concept.

1 We, alone among advanced nations, still have an unwritten con-

stitution. But when we adhered to the Treaty of Rome in 1972, we became subject over substantial areas to written rules of procedure that are outside our power to change. And devolution would take us in the same direction. Moreover, Lord Hailsham and Lord Justice Scarman are not wholly isolated or eccentric voices when, without reference to Europe or devolution, they now call for a Bill of Rights and even for a comprehensive written constitution.

2 As the beginnings of a written constitution creep in, so the old doctrine of the absolute supremacy of Parliament withers. The idea that no Parliament can pass an Act that binds its successor has been central to British constitutional evolutions. But it has been substantially abridged, *de facto*, and everything in the previous paragraph argues that the process seems set to continue.

3 Britain still has responsible government — ministers individually and collectively answerable to Parliament and, ultimately, to the electorate. But there has been a considerable abridgement of the notion of rule by party Cabinets that stayed united (or concealed their disagreements) and offered themselves at election on an unequivocal defence of their past and their programme. The 1975 referendum provided the most conspicuous example. Not only was a major issue referred from Cabinet and Parliament to the electorate but the Cabinet openly divided.

Last month's events throw a further doubt on the old simplicities of responsible government. The consultative rights (and, in effect, the veto power) now given to the Liberal Party are bound to confuse the elector who wants to use his vote in praise or blame of the Government's action. There are, moreover, some cynics who

believe that with the falling off in official secrecy and the increase in Cabinet leaks, collective responsibility has been sharply on the decline over the past decade.

4 Britain used to have an overwhelmingly two-party system. From 1950 to 1970 all except 2 per cent of MPs elected were Conservative or Labour and 92 per cent of all votes cast were for candidates of those two parties. In 1974 only 94 per cent of MPs and 75 per cent of votes were so confined. Ulster Unionists and Scottish Nationalists account for most of the growth in third-party MPs while English Liberals account for most of the growth in third-party votes. But it is the MPs who make the differences to the working of government and it is the Ulster Unionists and the Scottish Nationalists who are most certain to survive. Thirty minor-party MPs would seem to be the minimum likely complement for any future parliament — and 30 MPs would have been enough to hold the balance of power in six of the last nine Parliaments. Single-party government can no longer be taken for granted.

5 Britain used to have a very stable electorate. In the 1950s, the swings between one general election and another were always under 2 per cent; the monthly opinion polls fluctuated little and hardly any seats changed hands in by-elections. In the last 10 years the electorate has demonstrated a new volatility. The swings in polls and by-elections have been three times as great as a generation ago and people have shown far less attachment to their parties. The electoral loyalties which gave ballast to the political system are weakening. This opens the way on the one hand to electoral landslides, overwhelming victories for the party that happens to be uppermost when a dissolution

occurs. On the other hand, the possibility of the sudden upsurge of a new party becomes far greater, as the Liberal, and even more the SNP, advances in 1974 demonstrated.

6 The first-past-the-post electoral system used to be as totally accepted as the two-party system. The Electoral Reform Society found the greatest difficulty in recruiting a single Labour or Tory MP to its letterhead. The snags in the system were thought a small price for the responsible one-party governments it produced. The major parties would accept full power for half the time and full powerlessness for half the time in preference to the compromises of coalition.

Many would still retain that view — but the question is no longer closed. In this decade Parliament has imposed two proportional representation elections on Northern Ireland. PR, if not adopted by Westminster for the first election to a European Parliament, will certainly be imposed by Strasbourg for the second. It is under serious consideration for an Edinburgh Assembly. And it is even being thought of for Westminster. It was not only Liberals who were shocked in 1974 when 20 per cent of the vote gave them only 2 per cent of the seats. But the real driving force for change comes from those Conservatives who realise that they mind more about preventing Labour getting full power (on perhaps 38 per cent of the vote) than they want full power for themselves.

7 Britain still has centralised government. But the complete dominance of London is under challenge; federalism has entered the political scene in two obvious ways — in the upwards merger into the European community and in the downwards complications of Scottish and Welsh devolution (and even the demands for

English regionalism). The centrifugal forces are strong. We shall never again be so London-focused as we once were.

8 Britain still has unitary government. The confrontations between executive and legislature, and the judiciary's disallowance of the acts of both of them, which so characterises American government, are largely absent. But once again Community membership and internal devolution are changing the British scene, opening up the possibility of formalised conflict between our separate instruments of government. There is also the possibility of a Bill of Rights or a written constitution, subject of course to judicial interpretation. Moreover, quite independently of such developments, the courts are getting more active in political affairs. In the 1950s and 1960s the number of lawsuits which had a significant bearing on the political process were very few. But within the last year the High Court has slapped down Mr Mulley over Tameside comprehensives, Mr Shore over Laker Skytrains and Mr Silkin over the citizen's access to the law in an industrial dispute. Unless Parliament takes drastic action, further loopholes will be found; citizens aggrieved by some action of an ever-more complex state machine will discover legal objections which the judges will sustain.

Nor is it only through the judiciary that the separation of powers may become more significant. The fustian of legislature and executive (through a Cabinet answerable to, but in control of, the Commons) is under challenge. When governments lack assured majorities, Parliament comes into its own. In the current tug-of-war between Downing Street and the Palace of Westminster, there is an echo, albeit a very faint one, of the continuous battle fought out between the White House and Capitol Hill.

It is easy to be too apocalyptic. A few falling stones do not necessarily presage a landslide. This article has been concerned to show that most of the established certainties of the British system of government are far less established than they used to appear.

To say that is not to forecast a revolutionary change. Each one of the trends detected here may stop dead in its tracks. I am not here predicting a multi-party, proportional representation Britain, with a written federal constitution enshrining the separation of powers, governed by a coalition answerable to an assertive Parliament and an ever-more fickle electorate.

But some of these developments are at least on the cards. In the rules of government, as in so many other things, the pace of change has increased faster than we have realised. We must be prepared for future shocks.

[from the *Sunday Times*, 17 April 1977]

Democracy is a device — the best so far invented — for diminishing as much as possible the interference of governments with liberty.
(Bertrand Russell)

A2

A meaning to Jubilee

When Elizabeth II ascended the throne in 1952, to be crowned the following year, real gross world product was a quarter of what it is now. During the brief intervening 25 years man has increased his productive capacity by three times as much as in all the previous aeons of his history. The most optimistic paeans in 1952 and 1953 about a new Elizabethan age did not dare to forecast that things would go one tenth as well for the world as this.

But for Britain . . . for Britain these Elizabethan years of great worldwide advance have been years of relative national decline. In 1952 Britain's gnp per head was $1\frac{1}{2}$

times West Germany's and $4\frac{1}{2}$ times Japan's. Though a Briton today is 69 per cent better off than he was in 1952, he is only between a half and three quarters as prosperous as a Japanese or German. The main reasons are that Britain's society has not proved as well-suited as continental Europe's and Japan's to the great surges of increased productivity that have become possible in the last stages of the manufacturing age, and that the labour shake-out of Britian's steadily less-competitive manufacturing industries has switched mainly into low-productivity white collar (notably government) jobs. The relative decline has not been accompanied by any noticeable drop in that peculiarly British, less and less well deserved, satisfaction with whatever is British.

How far can this British smugness about nothing be blamed on the from-the-top-down pomp now parading itself through the Jubilee streets of London, or how far has the cohesive magic of old loyalties saved British society from disintegrating into something much worse while some of the logical reasons for national self-confidence were disappearing?

There is a sense in which Britain has suffered because its institutions and obsequious reverence for over-government were not ploughed through by defeat in war. The Germans have gained greatly because their previous excessive respect for public servants was wiped out during 12 horrible years after 1933; while in Japan and France the civil service is a body which the successful leave in their 40s in order to enter socially more valuable jobs. There is now a disadvantage for Britain in being a country where judges and Speakers of the House of Commons wear wigs, where conventional treasury advisers and establishment tycoons and trade union leaders get knighthoods, where Parliament meets in a building that looks like a church, and where the upper aisle in that church contains many people of ability who are allowed neither to run for election nor to be the essential constitutional check to the elected power of the lower aisle.

The dignified and the inefficient

Walter Bagehot taught that in the Victorian age the dignified parts of British government captured the lively awe of ill educated men so that the efficient parts could work. Today, in the Elizabethan age, the dignified parts retain the duller awe of much better educated people and thus help to enable the inefficient parts to continue to function unreformed. Ironically, Bagehot's monarchy for the uninstructed has adapted so that it is quietly accepted by a much more highly instructed people today, while the British parliamentary democracy designed by an elite has become an object of cynicism to virtually everybody except the new committee-room elites who are elected under it.

The most inefficient part of British government is the House of Commons. Read Hansard and see how question-time in the Commons is a daily occasion for a jolly adversary schoolboy joust based on amusedly exacerbated class divisions. This expensive amusement then percolates down from Parliament to every factory in the country. In efficient modern foreign countries there is an assumption in each negotiation that contracts can be worked out of mutual benefit to both employers and workers. In British factories, as in British parliamentary debates, there is an implicit assumption during each manoeuvre that workers and employers are engaged in a version of the parliamentary adversary game, so that each £1m of wage increases just means £1m less for the employer even if it drives both workers and employers out of business or into the unwilling tax-payer's pocket.

At this juncture of its history, Britain would be better served by systems (proportional representation, regional assemblies, a Bill of Rights and a supreme court, extensive reprivatisation of local and central government jobs) that forced parties to seek coalitions rather than ping-pong points. But the flummery in and around the near-cathedral at Westminster murmurs with ancestral voices to all the players that this would be 'against Britain's ancient traditions'. The country loses hugely from this. It is natural that some foreign critics associate the Queen, travelling in her golden carriage to speak from the throne with words put in her mouth by hack Westminster politicians, with the flummery. In several important senses they are wrong.

Alone at the head of the dignified part of government, Queen Elizabeth has in these 25 years performed at least three desperately needed services for Britain, even while the dignified appurtenances in the Westminster and Whitehall systems have become consecrated obstructions.

No revolutions, hate or Hitlers

At her accession in 1952 most sensible people foresaw that the Queen's overseas empire would dissolve as quickly as it has done. But few foresaw that Britain would fight so many losing rearguard actions, in the Kenyas and the Adens and the Cypruses, and would, 25 years later, even have on its hands a long civil war in the United Kingdom's own Ulster province. Britain has had so many Algerias, but without so much as a single constitutional, let alone a revolutionary, upheaval. For that thank God and the Queen. But curse, also, our luck.

Three of the Queen's seven Prime Ministers (Eden, Wilson, Heath) happened, although estimable men, to have the unfortunate capacity to be actively disliked by many of those politically opposed to them. Lyndon Johnson and Richard Nixon in America had the same disability. During Vietnam and Watergate many Americans who opposed their President came almost to hate their country too. In Britain, where the Head of State is not the head of erring government, that has not happened. Thank God and the Queen, but curse, also, our luck.

Although the few republicans in Britain belong to the not very amiable left, monarchy in these past 25 years has been mainly a bulwark against the growth in Britain of the nationalist right. In a monarchy a National Front parading behind Union Jacks does not look patriotic to Colonel Blimps, but just inexpressibly vulgar. Winston Churchill once said that Corporal Hitler would not have risen in Germany if the victorious allies of 1918 had not insisted on creating a vacuum by sacking all Kaisers. In Britain a particularly able and happy family of Kaisers, stretching into Prince Charles's generation, has reigned intact. Thank God, the Queen, her father and mother and grandfather, but curse, also, our luck.

Why curse? Because Britain's constitutional system, consecrated by its monarch, is both its chief blessing and its greatest impediment to change. The very restraint and dignity with which the Queen, now the most knowledgeable, certainly the only universal, politician in the United Kingdom, has exercised her job, have provided a golden cloak to cover up the mediocrity of her Commons in Westminster. By preserving, as she so well does, the idea of continuity in the life of the country,

the Queen has unwittingly helped protect those who have used what constitutionally exists to obstruct change.

Served by more imaginative politicians, that same royal continuity, the same mixture of respect and practicality which the British monarchy has created, could provide cover for something very different. It could offer Britain the chance to absorb more radical changes in its political and social order than would otherwise be possible without risk of riot. It is not fanciful to suggest that even were Britain to experience civil disorder the Queen would have enough residual power and respect to restore parliamentary democracy — and on a more representative pattern than today — by a combination of royal decree and public royal appeal.

A stability that should help change

Such future drama is unlikely and unwanted. The point to grasp is that Britain, more than any other democratic country, can run the risk of incurring it precisely because it is so unlikely. A phlegmatic, rather conservative, adequately royalist people could run along the cliff-edge of revolution without even coming near to toppling over it. Very few Britons nowadays stand up still in those few cinemas which any longer play God Save the Queen at the end of the show. But the majority accepts the lady who appears on the television screen each night as the national anthem is played, and would want her to stay the more other political institutions were forced to change.

Thanks very largely to the stability which a constitutional monarchy provides, the Queen's (and Prince Charles's) second quarter century contains many possibilities for change. Her Lord Melbourne was long ago. When Winston Churchill was her first Prime Minister in 1952, her present Principal Secretary of State for Foreign Affairs was presumably putting on his first pair of long trousers. Her most probable next Prime Minister had recently ceased to be an undergraduette. Bagehot said that the most successful years of any constitutional monarch began when he was experienced enough to labour 'in the world of sober fact'. The most sober, if little realised, fact about Britain today is that from its old Parliament stem many of its economic and social ills.

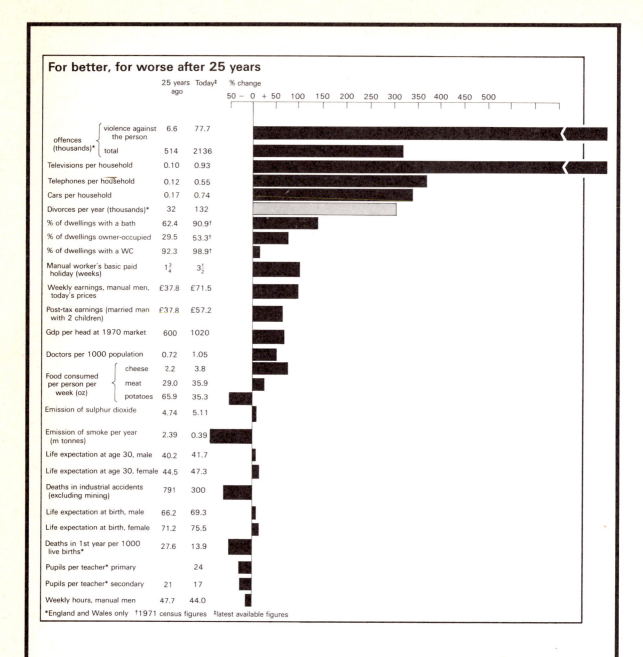

For better, for worse after 25 years

		25 years ago	Today‡
offences (thousands)*	violence against the person	6.6	77.7
	total	514	2136
Televisions per household		0.10	0.93
Telephones per household		0.12	0.55
Cars per household		0.17	0.74
Divorces per year (thousands)*		32	132
% of dwellings with a bath		62.4	90.9†
% of dwellings owner-occupied		29.5	53.3†
% of dwellings with a WC		92.3	98.9†
Manual worker's basic paid holiday (weeks)		$1\frac{3}{4}$	$3\frac{1}{2}$
Weekly earnings, manual men, today's prices		£37.8	£71.5
Post-tax earnings (married man with 2 children)		£37.8	£57.2
Gdp per head at 1970 market		600	1020
Doctors per 1000 population		0.72	1.05
Food consumed per person per week (oz)	cheese	2.2	3.8
	meat	29.0	35.9
	potatoes	65.9	35.3
Emission of sulphur dioxide		4.74	5.11
Emission of smoke per year (m tonnes)		2.39	0.39
Life expectation at age 30, male		40.2	41.7
Life expectation at age 30, female		44.5	47.3
Deaths in industrial accidents (excluding mining)		791	300
Life expectation at birth, male		66.2	69.3
Life expectation at birth, female		71.2	75.5
Deaths in 1st year per 1000 live births*		27.6	13.9
Pupils per teacher* primary			24
Pupils per teacher* secondary		21	17
Weekly hours, manual men		47.7	44.0

*England and Wales only †1971 census figures ‡latest available figures

Little new blood, little liberty

There is no system of primary election, so new blood in Westminster is limited to those who most fawn on, rather than most disturb, the ancient party prejudices of Labour and Tory. There is no separation of powers and no system of popular election of party leaders, so new leadership is restricted, except in time of war, to those party hacks who have most successfully rubbed the backs over 20 years of Westminster party prejudice. Americans, imagine that your choice for President in 1976 had been restricted to Mr Carl Albert and Mr John Rhodes.

There is no system of proportional voting in British general elections, so virtually every British government this century, Tory or Labour, has counted itself elected by a minority of the electorate to do and undo what it wills, regardless of what the three fifths of those who have often voted against it wanted. There is little local sanction to protect a Member of Parliament against party Whips imposed on him by his Prime Minister. There is no effective senate. There is no Bill of Individual Rights against these alternating partisan tyrannies. There is no supreme court. There is a chap called an ombudsman, but nobody much knows who he is; he has some influence but little power.

Britain in the next two decades will be most especially in need of extra-parliamentary thought to make politics less of a constant adversary game, to reduce over-government, to use the dignified as well as the in-efficient parts of the British government system to reduce class divisions and to make contracts more acceptable, to halt the causes of Britain's 25 years of relative decline. It is true that the Queen can do little directly to bring such thinking about, let alone the necessary changes. The monarch's power of veto is gone — last used by Queen Anne in 1707. The power to dismiss a government is probably gone too, last exer-cised in 1834. In normal times it is just imaginable, but not very likely, that the Queen could refuse a dissolution of Parliament — or exercise, in some circumstances, the power to choose a Prime Minister. But her chief,

indefinable residual power is as a bulwark against ab-normal times — and, were they still to occur, as a potential restorer of normality. And that residual power — or rather the knowledge of it — does provide one large assurance that change can be undertaken in Britain with little risk of its getting out of hand.

Her next seven Prime Ministers

A nation has two basic needs, that for stability and that for change. The British monarchy, in the hands of its present, simple, commonsense, upper-crust royal family, is a large weight in the scales of British stability. The British establishment has done much to abuse that stability by making it one of several excuses for not re-forming itself. Given the constitutional monarchy it is lucky enough to enjoy, Britain and its establishment can afford in future to take more risks. Barring the emer-gence of another old Gladstone (Heath? Callaghan? Wilson?), most of Queen Elizabeth's next seven Prime Ministers will be younger than she will be. They should be encouraged, by her in private and by others in public, to use the cloak of dignity that royalty can put upon change to stop Britain's constitutional democracy being so inefficiently undemocratic.

[from *The Economist* (editorial), 4 June 1977]

If all mankind minus one were of one opinion, and only one person were of the contrary opinion, mankind would be no more justified in silencing that one person, than he, if he had the power, would be justified in silencing mankind.
(John Stuart Mill)

Questions

1 Explain the origion of the name 'Parliament'.

2 In what way does Butler suggest that Britain is unique among advanced countries? (A1)

3 Which institution links the legislature and the executive? (A1)

4 Which major principle of government does Butler suggest would disappear if the UK had a written constitution? (A1)

5 How does Butler suggest that Britain's centralised system is under challenge? (A1)

6 List two examples given by Butler to illustrate that the collective responsibility doctrine has weakened. (A1)

7 What details does Butler give to illustrate his description of the modern electorate as volatile and fickle? (A1)

8 What can you establish from A2 are the merits and advantages that the writer attributes to the monarchy today?

9 Illustrate how *The Economist* argues that Britain is fortunate in having a Head of State who is not the head of government as well. (A2)

10 Which one of the changes suggested by *The Economist* has to some extent been implemented since 1979? (A2)

Class Discussion

1 Would you agree with Butler's particular list of the past 'simple clarities of the British system'? What additions and deletions might be made to describe the system today? (A1)

2 How would you define and relate the following concepts: (a) 'strong' government; (b) 'responsible' government; (c) 'good' government?

3 Explain what is meant by a 'workable party system'. Would this be a desirable state of affairs? Does the present (post-1983 election) large Conservative majority really make Parliament more workable? (A1)

4 Is Britain's constitution best described as 'unwritten' or 'uncodified'?

5 Comment on the role played by the monarch today. How true nowadays is the observation made by Bagehot in 1867 that the Crown had no political clout? (A2)

6 Comment on the various suggestions made by *The Economist* for change or reform of the present political system. To what extent are these recommendations based on customs and practices in western Europe or the USA? (A2)

7 Suggest reasons for the continued popularity of the monarchy in Britain and the lack of support for republicanism. (A2)

Extension Work

1   Give detailed explanations of the following: (a) 'a stable electorate'; (b) 'first-past-the-post elections'; (c) separation of powers theory; (d) 'supremacy of Parliament'. (A1)

2   Give details concerning the political significance or career of the following: (a) Walter Bagehot; (b) Blackstone; (c) Lord Hailsham.

3   To what does Butler refer when he says 'Last month's events throw a further doubt on the old simplicities of responsible government'? (A1)

4   Why did Parliament permit two PR elections in Northern Ireland?

5   Under what circumstances today might the monarch have some say in the choice of Prime Minister? (A2)

6   Describe the role a supreme court might play if Britain's political system underwent change. (A2)

7   Explain the meaning or significance of the following phrases: (a) 'jolly adversary schoolboy joust'; (b) 'an implicit assumption during each manoeuvre that workers and employers are engaged in a version of the parliamentary adversary game'; (c) 'Colonel Blimps'; (d) 'her chief, indefinable residual power'. (A2)

A3 – A5   *Power elites and the location of power*

A3

MPs, the untrusted men who don't run Britain

by Hugo Young,
of the even less trusted profession of journalism

MEMBERS of Parliament are generally felt to be less trustworthy than doctors, judges, lawyers, Cabinet Ministers and civil servants. They are also believed to be less influential than either trade unions or the Press.

This doleful verdict has been delivered in an opinion poll conducted by Opinion Research Centre. [. . .]

The 1093 people interviewed were asked to nominate from a list of 12 professions the two they thought the most, and the two they thought the least, trustworthy. By a wide margin doctors, with a 75 per cent vote, led the most trustworthy field, followed far behind by judges (55 per cent) and lawyers (23 per cent). MPs, it seems, enjoy the maximum trust of only 4 per cent of people, and only businessmen and city financiers, with 2 per cent each, are lower than that.

Among least trustworthy figures, trade union leaders and local councillors rate prominently with 31 per cent and 23 per cent of the vote respectively. But neither are quite so heavily stigmatised as journalists, whom more than a third of the country, according to the poll, reckon among the least trustworthy of all people. (Opinion pollsters were not among the professions listed for evaluation.)

Some odd insights are supplied into the public view of how influence is apportioned. Pollsters supplied people with a list of British institutions as power groups and asked them to pick the two which they thought had the greatest effect, plus the two with the least effect, on the way the country is run.

Although the Queen gets much the largest vote (56 per cent) for having least effect on how the country is run, there evidently remain 44 per cent of people (39 per cent, discounting Don't Knows) who think other-wise. These are the people who did not place her in the bottom two of a list which comprised the Civil Service, the Cabinet, the Prime Minister, the electorate, the media, the Commons, the unions, the courts, the parties, the Stock Exchange and large companies.

Trade unions are given a clear lead in effectiveness (40 per cent), followed by the Prime Minister (33 per cent), the Commons (19 per cent) and the Cabinet (18 per cent).

Despite the deep distrust of journalists, the media rate third on this influence list (23 per cent) — far higher than those pillars of rectitude in the Civil Service with 10 per cent. If true, this picture is one of extraordinary cynicism, an interpretation which is possibly corroborated by the fact that the electorate feels it has less influence than any other group apart from the Queen. Twenty-three per cent of people polled put voters in the lowest category of influence.

Exploring political attitudes further, the poll revealed that while about half the country (51 per cent) claim to take some interest in politics, only 18 per cent have ever written or talked to their MP. But there is a generally wary evaluation of MPs' credibility. Asked to say when they were most likely to believe what an MP says, the smallest number (9 per cent) named party political broadcasts while most (40 per cent) chose plans announced when no election is imminent. Most (58 per cent) said that MPs were *least* credible when they spoke just before an election.

Asked how much attention MPs pay to their electors, 48 per cent replied 'not much'. Asked what attention they expected MPs to pay to constituents who wrote or talked to them, 47 per cent said not much or none at all on local issues, and 51 per cent said the same on national issues. Social differences were again striking, with greater scepticism expressed by the youngest respondents and lower income groups.

In keeping with all this scepticism is the fact that 58 per cent of people asked to assess the proposition that most MPs are there for their own gain and ambition, agreed either very or fairly strongly.

[from *The Times*, 15 July 1973]

> *Intolerance among the elderly is sad, but understandable: opinions often harden with the arteries . . . But intolerance among the young is a tragedy, for it represents the closing of minds that have not even had time to open fully.*
> (Editorial, *The Observer*, 12 December 1976)

Britain's Real Men of Power
Special Survey by NOW!

Who are the people who really run this country? You may think you know. You may be wrong. In this special survey, Marplan asked nearly 100 holders of Britain's top jobs to name their choices of those with real influence. Robin Oakley reports.

Who are the most influential figures in the country after the Prime Minister? Where does real power lie in Britain?

According to a poll of top people conducted for *NOW!* by Marplan the leading six are three politicians, two trade unionists and one civil servant — an intriguing measure of the relative authority of the three groups. The most powerful figure in the group after Mrs Thatcher is, according to those in a position to know, her witty and aristocratically independent Foreign Secretary, Lord Carrington. Significantly, the man rated the second most influential figure by the men of influence themselves is TUC General Secretary Len Murray.

After Mr Murray came two more members of the Cabinet in key positions on the economic front: Industry Secretary Sir Keith Joseph, often described as Mrs Thatcher's guru, and Chancellor of the Exchequer Sir Geoffrey Howe. He may have had his critics in Opposition, but clearly the quietly persuasive Sir Geoffrey is a man who counts today.

The remaining two places in the top six were occupied by Whitehall mandarin Sir Robert Armstrong, the Secretary to the Cabinet, and Moss Evans, Jack Jones's successor as General Secretary of the Transport and General Workers Union.

Marplan set out to discover the individuals with the most power and influence in Britain by asking those who actually wield power themselves. Marplan com-

piled a list of widely acknowledged top people in 10 elite groups: the Church, the Armed Services, business, the City, politics, trades unions, the media, the Civil Service, the judiciary and the police. These top people, 358 in all, were then asked to name, in confidence, the three most influential individuals within their own elite. They were also asked to say which they considered the two most powerful elites and whom they considered to be the most powerful and influential figure in those elites.

The response was clearly biased towards top people in business, politics, the unions and the media. It underplays the views of the judiciary, the police and the Civil Service, three groups who were mostly very unwilling to participate. Judges, policemen and civil servants nearly all refused to be interviewed.

But a total of 96 top people agreed to take part in the survey, and 78 of them agreed to be identified as having done so. The result of their collated opinions provides a fascinating insight into power in Britain today, with some considerable surprises.

Not only did politicians and trades unionists jostle in the list of the six most powerful people in the land — the survey showed the trades unions (51 votes) in a clear second place to Government (69 votes) in the list of 'most influential' power elites, followed in order by the Civil Service (28), the media (22), business (14) and the City (8).

In the list of the most influential individuals in the

country the only names to earn more than a single vote who were not politicians, trade unionists or civil servants were CBI Director General Sir John Methven (4), Sir Gordon Richardson, Governor of the Bank of England (3), Dick Francis, Director of Current Affairs/News, BBC (3), Sir Michael Swann, Chairman, BBC (3), Sir Arnold Weinstock, Chairman of GEC (2) and two media men, Editor of *The Times* William Rees-Mogg (2) and Editor of the *Daily Mirror* Mike Molloy (2).

[from *NOW!*, 22 February 1980]

THE MOST INFLUENTIAL
PEOPLE IN UK
excluding Margaret Thatcher

LORD CARRINGTON Foreign Secretary	23	**ARTHUR SCARGILL** Yorkshire NUM President	3
LEN MURRAY TUC General Secretary	19	**Sir GORDON RICHARDSON** Governor, Bank of England	3
Sir KEITH JOSEPH Industry Secretary	17	**RICHARD FRANCIS** Director, Current Affairs/News, BBC	3
Sir GEOFFREY HOWE Chancellor	15	**JOHN BIFFEN** Chief Secretary to the Treasury	3
Sir ROBERT ARMSTRONG Secretary to the Cabinet	12	**Sir MICHAEL SWANN** Chairman, BBC	3
MOSS EVANS General Secretary, T&GWU	11	**WILLIAM WHITELAW** Home Secretary	2
Sir IAN BANCROFT Head of the Civil Service	8	**TERRY DUFFY** President, AUEW	2
DAVID BASNETT General Secretary, G&MWU	5	**WILLIAM REES–MOGG** Editor, *The Times*	2
Sir JOHN METHVEN Director General, CBI	4	**Sir ARNOLD WEINSTOCK** Chairman, GEC	2
Sir DOUGLAS WASS Permanent Secretary, Treasury	4	**FRANK CHAPPLE** General Secretary, EEPTU	2
JOE GORMLEY President, NUM	4	**MICHAEL MOLLOY** Editor, *Daily Mirror*	2

[from *NOW!*, 22 February 1980]

> *All power tends to corrupt and absolute power corrupts absolutely.*
> (Lord Acton)

Is our future all in the past?

James Bellini

About 900 years ago William the Conqueror ordered a survey of his newly-acquired territory. The result was the Domesday Book. The giant volume is a fascinating record of what life was like in the England of 1086 — who was rich, who was poor and who pulled the strings in medieval politics.

Little has changed in nine centuries. The Britain of the Eighties is marked by the same pattern of wealth, privilege, power and poverty that existed all those centuries ago.

The private ownership of land is dominated today, as then, by aristocrats, the Church and the Crown. You cannot do anything unless you have some land to do it on, whether it is to grow crops, build houses or set up industrial complexes. So the man who owns the land is the man with the ultimate power. And an investment in land is as solid as rock.

About 12 million of Scotland's 19 069 440 acres are owned by a small group of landlords, many of them English. The top 10 landowners have more than 1 500 000 acres between them, valued conservatively at more than £2000 million.

Nearly 250 000 of these Scottish acres are in the hands of one family, the dynasty of Lord Cowdray. Ironically, the Cowdray country seat in Sussex is close to the site of the Battle of Hastings of 1066.

But if all land is equal, some is more equal than the rest. The Duke of Westminster's trifling 300 acres in London's Belgravia area would have a price tag of several billion pounds — if they were for sale.

There are, of course, new landowners. But Joe Briton and his wife are not among them. Big Brother State, gearing up for *1984*, now holds some 2 500 000 acres through local authorities and Whitehall departments. And the cash-rich pension funds — made rich through Joe Briton's savings, but run by calculating moneymen — are stuffing cash into farmland with a vengeance.

However, our landowning aristocrats have grown wise in 900 years. In a Britain without industry the key weapon is now information. Without access to up-to-the-minute information the money machine of the City, where the aristocrats make their profits, would soon grind to a halt. As a result, these days the City is crammed with the best computer systems money can buy. And if you can store away money-making information in a bank of computers to which you alone hold the key, then you are in an envied position of great power.

Thus, the owners of the land and information — the 'landfax' (land and facts) aristocracy — will rule Britain in the years to come. And so we turn full circle back to 1086 when the nobles owned the land and knowledge was under the strict control of loyal servants within the Church.

In time, the priests built the universities of Oxford and Cambridge. The rich sent their sons to gain a privileged education. From the 13th century onwards, these temples of knowledge dominated the government of Britain.

Even today, the politicians, princes and civil servants who run the country are Oxbridge at the core. Prime Minister Mrs Margaret Thatcher's government is awash with them. Her new Cabinet included 16 Oxbridge graduates, six more than in class-ridden 1935. Former Labour Prime Minister James Callaghan was little better. His 1976 Cabinet had 10 Oxbridge graduates, seven public school products and a peer of the realm.

The same is true of the ministries in Whitehall. The latest intake of leading civil servants, who will be running things in the year 2000, is dominated by people from Oxford, Cambridge and the public schools. Most of them have degrees in the arts, subjects ridiculously ill-suited to the challenges of the twenty-first century.

And the City's financial institutions are controlled, true to its medieval traditions, by a tight group of top-drawer money-makers.

We have convinced ourselves that old Britain has been overtaken by the new. But a closer look at the shape of the country's society, at who owns the wealth and who runs the centres of power, reveals a different picture. Change the names and Britain is close to what it was in the time of the first King William.

The nobles are still there. The loyal stewards run the Civil Service and keep the trade unions in check — more or less. And the collapse of industry is creating a vast population of landless serfs, without jobs and manipulated by the computer system behind the castle walls. Rule Britannia! Britons never ever ever shall be slaves. I truly wonder?

[from the *TV Times*, 18–24 July 1984]

Questions

1 Identify the six 'most influential' power elites according to the Marplan survey. Compare this with the list of the four most effective groups according to the ORC opinion poll. (A3, A4)

2 Which two groups, according to the ORC poll in 1973, had least effect on how the country was governed? (A3)

3 What reasons does Hugo Young suggest as to why politicians rank low in popularity polls? (A3)

4 Name the person among the top twenty-two most influential people in the Marplan list who was most in the news during 1984. (A4)

5 Suggest one possible reason why the judiciary and the police are not represented in the Marplan list. (A4)

6 What evidence does James Bellini give to indicate that the main centres of power remain broadly the same as they were at the time of William the Conqueror? (A5)

Class Discussion

1 Are politicians, trade unionists and civil servants likely to remain the most influential groups irrespective of individual personalities and roleholders?

2 Why do some people and groups have more political power than others? Why do some groups have virtually no political power or influence?

3 Why do Oxbridge graduates and public school products still play a leading role in politics? Is this situation in the process of changing? (A5)

4 Comment on Bellini's observation that the owners of 'landfax' will rule Britain in the future. (A5)

5 Discuss the view that any list of the most influential people in the UK is determined by the inherent power or importance of the office rather than the particular ability of the individual holding it.

Extension Work

1 A Foreign Secretary, *per se*, does not necessarily have great political influence. For what achievement in 1979 was Lord Carrington noted which may account in part for his high rating in the Marplan poll? (A4)

2 Is it still true that most of the leading civil servants only have arts degrees? Are such qualifications really, as Bellini says, 'ill-suited to the challenges of the twenty-first century'? (See Section C.)

A6

We are pledged to ensure and safeguard these essential rights: *National Council for Civil Liberties charter of civil rights and liberties*

1 to live in freedom and safe from personal harm

2 to protection from ill-treatment or punishment that is inhuman or degrading

3 to equality before the law and to freedom from discrimination on such grounds as disability, political or other opinion, race, religion, sex, or sexual orientation

4 to protection from arbitrary arrest and unnecessary detention, the right to a fair, speedy and public trial, to be presumed innocent until proved guilty, and to legal advice and representation

5 to a fair hearing before any authority exercising power over the individual

6 to freedom of thought, conscience and belief

7 to freedom of speech and publication

8 to freedom of peaceful assembly and association

9 to move freely within one's country of residence and to leave and enter it without hindrance

10 to privacy and the right of access to official information.

[from *1934–1984: Half a century of civil liberties* (NCCL, 1984)]

A7

JOIN THE FIGHT FOR FREEDOM

The Charter of Rights and Liberties

WE believe that in return for allegiance to the Sovereign in Parliament, citizens enjoy the right to be governed according to the rule of law, duly enforced without fear or favour. We believe that the following rights and liberties belong to all and that they should be entrenched through a new constitutional settlement, for which the Association is pledged to work: amendment would thereafter be made only by affirmative vote through a referendum of the entire electorate, assented to by the Sovereign in Parliament.

1 The right to be defended against the country's enemies.
2 The right to live under the Queen's peace.
3 Freedom of movement within the country and in leaving or re-entering it.
4 Freedom of religion and worship.
5 Freedom of speech and publication.
6 Freedom of assembly and association for a lawful purpose.
7 Freedom to withdraw one's labour, other than contrary to public safety.
8 Freedom to belong or not to belong to a trade union or employer's association.
9 The right to private ownership.
10 The right to dispose or convey property by deed or will.
11 Freedom to exercise choice or personal priority in spending, and from oppressive, unnecessary or confiscatory taxation.
12 Freedom from all coercive monopolies.
13 Freedom to engage in private enterprise and pursue the trade or profession of one's choice without harassment.
14 Freedom of choice in the use of State and private services (including education and medicine).
15 The right to protection from invasion of privacy.

[from *Free Nation* (Journal of the Freedom Association)]

A8

PRIVACY

1983 was a year of missed opportunity for the Government in the field of privacy. Parliament debated the Data Protection Bill, the Government's cosmetic 'Privacy Bill', which will be ineffective in safeguarding personal information and inefficient in operation; the Telecommunications Bill which allows widespread telephone tapping uncontrolled by Parliament or the courts; and Parliament discussed in Committee — to which NCCL gave evidence — the introduction of identity cards. Public debate on all these issues was yet again hampered by official secrecy.

The Data Protection Bill purports to allow individuals access to information held about them and to regulate the transfer of that information to third parties — aims for which NCCL has been campaigning since the launch of the Right to Know campaign in 1978 and which are of increasing importance with the prolifera-

tion of records held by others concerning each area of our lives. Yet the Bill is inadequate: it only covers computers and not the sensitive information which is held on manual records; it fails to establish an efficient system of regulation and enforcement — one registrar with only 20 staff will have the job of registering and regulating an estimated 300 000 to 400 000 computer systems.

The inadequacies of the Bill led to widespread opposition from computer professionals, doctors, lawyers and consumer groups as well as civil libertarians. Even the Lindop Committee, the Home Office appointed committee on whose report the Bill is based, described as a 'palpable fraud on the public' the provision of the Bill which allows transfer of confidential information collected, for example, by doctors or social workers, to the police or Inland Revenue, without the knowledge or consent of the doctor or patient. It was the widespread opposition in the House of Lords which defeated the proposal in the Bill to allow unregulated transfers of information to the immigration authorities.

The expanding computer capacity of the police, Inland Revenue and DHSS computers, and the co-ordination of information-sharing, will lead to a growth of police and government records whose accuracy cannot be ascertained as the Bill already excludes most police records from subject access and allows government ministers to exclude central government records.

While purporting to protect personal privacy the Bill will not prevent monitoring and intelligence gathering about political beliefs and opinions. The Telecommunications Bill will allow surveillance through telephone tapping which is not subject to scrutiny by either Parliament or the courts. At present the Government maintains that the public interest is safeguarded by the High Court judge who reports on the number and relevance of telephone taps — yet his reports are themselves secret. Yet in 1983 the European Commission of Human Rights made a preliminary finding in the case of *Malone v. United Kingdom* that the British procedures which allow telephone tapping by warrant of the Home Secretary with no safeguards on when, how often, and in respect of whom warrants are issued was a breach of individual rights. Mr Malone, a Surrey antiques dealer, first tried to obtain recompense for the police tapping of his telephone from the English courts. Although the judge told him that the matter was one which 'cries out for legislation' Mr Malone's action failed and the case is now awaiting consideration by the European Court.

NCCL has drafted over 70 amendments to the Data Protection Bill, lobbied in support of amendments to the Telecommunications Bill to make wiretapping subject to the rule of law, and briefed members of both Houses of Parliament on these issues. Some of our amendments have been accepted in principle and the arguments have been widely discussed both inside and outside Parliament. Time and again in our work we are faced with the 'British disease' of official secrecy. For 50 years we have campaigned against the refusal to disclose official information and the wide provisions of Section 2 of the Official Secrets Act and shall continue to do so during 1984.

[from *NCCL Annual Report 1983*]

A9

Contents of a Bill of Rights

INTRODUCTION

In principle there should be no difficulty in sitting down and writing out a list of the rights that should be protected as fundamental, and the situations in which these rights could be curtailed in the interests of the State, or of others. In practice, this is by no means straightforward. If it is accepted that a Bill of Rights should be based on a reasonable consensus of opinion, some rights immediately become controversial. Ought there to be a right not to belong to a trade union as in the Universal Declaration of Human Rights, which Britain has endorsed? How should the right to own property be balanced against the claims of compulsory purchase or of nationalisation measures? Ought freedom of speech to be curbed in the interests of 'territorial integrity' (as in the European Convention on Human Rights), with all that could imply for the expression of Republican sentiments over Northern Ireland? How far should the notion of democratic government be spelled out? Free elections and universal suffrage, clearly; but how about proportional representation and restrictions on minority governments; or a duty imposed on the executive to disclose full information about its proposals and deliberations, so that public debate and participation can be properly conducted? It would be easy to multiply the examples of potential difficulties. If it were possible to draft a Bill of Rights that would satisfy the demands of civil liberties activists, it would most likely be too strong meat for a proportion of the population. Conversely a Bill satisfactory to the Whitehall axis would seem small beer in the quest for adequate protection of civil liberties.

The dilemma is compounded by the thought that a delicate and carefully constructed balance in the Bill as drafted could so easily be upset by parliamentary amendment. MPs would be pressed by sectional interest groups to seize the opportunity of championing a wide range of causes, and it has to be admitted that some MPs have rather unlikely hobbyhorses. This is one occasion when it would be difficult for the party machines to stop MPs from advancing their own proposals. This is not to say that the proposals individually would be objectionable (though some might be). But the cumulative effect of a sprinkling of amendments might well be to make the Bill much less clear, much less generally palatable (and so less effective) and more a charter of sectional liberties. If the party which happened to be in the majority at the time took the opportunity to force through some doctrinally-inspired amendment, the minority party could well become hostile to the spirit of the Bill; and irrespective of the merits this could only damage the long term prospects of its acceptance. Even if amendments were unsuccessful, a process of party political bickering would tend to diminish the credibility of the Bill of Rights, as a generally agreed framework for the future conduct of government.

Advantages of the European Convention

Many of these potential difficulties could be avoided by the use of the text of the European Convention on Human Rights. This is a document the substance of which has been accepted as a basis for legislation by most of the proponents of a Bill of Rights. It has been ratified by a Labour government and supported by a Conservative one. It can therefore be taken to have the initial advantages of a wide basis of support.

[from *Civil liberties and a bill of rights* by Peter Wallington and Jeremy McBride (Cobden Trust, 1976)]

A10

When should the people decide?

Vernon Bogdanor

The strongest tendencies displayed by the popular vote were, according to Lecky, 'a dislike to large expenditure, a dislike to centralisation, a dislike to violent innovation'. The referendum, accordingly, is commonly believed to be a conservative rather than a radical weapon. Indeed, when in 1972 Mr Roy Jenkins resigned from Labour's Shadow Cabinet in protest against the decision to support a referendum on Britain's entry into the EEC, he warned that the referendum would prove the most powerful barrier to progress that Britain had seen since the unreformed House of Lords.

Yet the Conservative party has never, despite occasional flirtations, been able to accomodate itself to the regular use of the referendum; and Mr Nicholas Edwards MP, the chairman of a Conservative party committee on *The Referendum and the Constitution*, which has just reported, was given an unenviable task. For leading Conservatives had raised expectations which it would prove hard to fulfil. Mr Teddy Taylor had advocated a referendum on capital punishment; but would MPs be willing to surrender their consciences to the electorate on such an issue? Should they be required to do so? Mrs Thatcher had suggested that a referendum could be used in a situation of industrial conflict such as brought down the Heath government in 1974. Yet a referendum in such a situation might be akin to a game of Russian roulette. What if the government won, but the trade union concerned refused to acknowledge the verdict?

Nevertheless the referendum has already been invoked by a Conservative government (the border poll in Northern Ireland) and a Labour government (the EEC and the Scotland and Wales Acts). It is likely to be used again. Therefore, instead of becoming involved in a sterile argument about the pros and cons of referenda, Mr Edwards's committee rightly sought to discover how the referendum could be used to improve the quality of government in Britain.

The committee came to the conclusion 'that it was as a constitutional safeguard that the referendum was most urgently needed and where its use could be most easily reconciled with our existing system of parliamentary democracy'. For it was vital to provide an insurance against the introduction of fundamental changes in the constitution which the majority of electors did not want. The committee accordingly proposed the introduction of a Constitution (Fundamental Provisions) Bill to provide for a referendum before any such fundamental change, and the setting up of a Referendum Commission 'to draft the question and to supervise the conduct of the referendum'.

But what is to count as a 'fundamental change in the constitution' in a country such as Britain which lacks a written constitution? For if there is no clear dividing line between what is constitutional and what is not, then it will be left to the government of the day to decide what issues are to be referred to the people. This would add enormously to the powers of the executive. For the government could then use the referendum as a tactical device to overcome back-bench opposition, as the present government has done with the Scotland and Wales Acts. Opposition to government legislation in the Commons will be disarmed since MPs will be told that they are denying the people their right to express an opinion. Far from acting as an instrument of constitutional protection, therefore, the use of the referendum in such circumstances would destroy one of the already flimsy barriers to the omnicompetence of British governments.

The committee was of course aware of this problem, and sought to evade it by enumerating what was to count as 'constitutional' legislation. Protection would be given to the continued existence of the House of Lords, and a referendum would be necessary before it could be abolished. The unity of the realm would be protected by requiring referenda before either devolution or independence was conceded to any of the constituent parts of the United Kingdom, and any alteration in the electoral system would also need to be ratified by a referendum.

Yet is is doubtful if this list really provides a sufficient check upon government to alleviate the condition which Lord Hailsham has called 'elective dictatorship'. It certain-
[from the *Spectator*, 30 September 1978]

ly excludes many issues which Conservatives might regard as having constitutional importance, such as the legislation adding to the privileges of the trade unions, the bill abolishing pay beds in National Health hospitals, the bill removing the disqualification on the Clay Cross councillors, or, in the Sixties, the use of retrospective legislation to deprive the Burmah Oil Company of its war damage compensation awarded by the courts.

All of these measures were introduced by governments elected on a minority vote, and would probably have been rejected by the electorate in a referendum; perhaps they would probably have been rejected by the referendum confined to Labour party voters. Yet the committee's proposals would do nothing to protect the public against them. Admittedly, the committee advocated that the proposed Bill should include provision for the government of the day to hold referenda on 'non-constitutional matters'. But it is hardly likely that governments will willingly submit measures which they know to be unpopular to the electorate: here, also, they will use the referendum to increase their power by appealing over the heads of dissident MPs.

If the referendum is to become part of British constitutional practice, therefore, some authority other than the government must be found to decide when a Bill is to be referred to the people. The committee, however, found it 'extraordinarily difficult to devise a satisfactory triggering mechanism if the referendum is to be used as a defence against arbitrary government or as an expression of popular will'. For in the absence of a written constitution, such a triggering mechanism can only be found if the referendum is introduced as part of an overall constitutional settlement.

The referendum could play a genuinely constitutional role in Britain only in the context of a directly elected Second Chamber, as advocated by Lords Carrington and Hailsham, which could compel the government of the day to submit controversial measures to the people before they become law. The government would have the right to submit any bill to referendum in the case of deadlock between the two Houses. Such occasions would be unlikely to occur frequently. For governments would not have recourse to the referendum unless they believed that they would win: while the Lords would compromise if they realised that public opinion was not behind them. The Commons would thus retain its supremacy, and the government would be able to secure its legislation provided that it could obtain either the acquiescence of the Lords or the support of the people.

Questions

1   On which three basic rights and liberties do the National Council for Civil Liberties (NCCL) and the National Association for Freedom (NAF) seem basically agreed? (A6, A7)

2   Mention an important point absent from the NAF list but in the NCCL list which deals with minority rights. (A6, A7)

3   What does the NCCL describe in A8 as the 'British disease'?

4   What are the chief weaknesses of the Data Protection legislation discussed in A8?

5   For what reason did the Conservative party committee on *The Referendum and the Constitution* (A10) think that a referendum was urgently needed?

6   What other political changes have been suggested as necessary if the referendum device became a regular part of Britain's system of government? (A10)

7   Under what conditions does Vernon Bogdanor suggest that governments are quite keen to submit matters to a referendum? (A10)

8   Why do Wallington and McBride suggest that a Bill of Rights might be difficult to implement? (A9)

9   Why would it not be easy to draft a list of generally accepted basic rights? (A9)

Class Discussion

1   Is the NAF mainly concerned with economic rights and the NCCL with legal protection against government, the police and the judiciary?

2   Which rights mentioned in either of the lists (NAF or NCCL) do you think should not be entrenched in a constitutional settlement?

3   Which rights advocated by the NAF suggest that it is a right wing organisation?

4   Should the right exist for an individual not to belong to a trade union if he or she so wishes?

5   Could it be true to say that in one sense George Orwell's *1984* has already arrived as a result of developments in computing and telecommunications?

Extension Work

1   What developments have taken place concerning the promotion or infringement of personal information as a result of legislation or government measures since 1983?

2   *Malone v. United Kingdom* (A8) involved telephone tapping. Find other information concerning the controversial issue of telephone tapping.

3   Which party promised in an election manifesto (1983) to introduce a Bill of Rights Act?

4   Suggest reasons for the growing demand for a Bill of Rights during the 1970s.

5   When, and for what reasons, have referendums been held in the UK before? (A1)

The Prime Minister and the Cabinet

Introduction

The first three documents (B1–3) discuss some of the qualities of leadership. James Margach in *The Anatomy of Power* (1979), pp. 2–3, gives ambition, courage, ruthlessness, character, judgement, patience and stamina as essential qualities after a person has attained leadership but argues that luck is the most precious asset beforehand. He refers to the Conservative leadership election in 1975 when Margaret Thatcher 'could not have been luckier both in timing and in her rivals'.

B4–7 analyse recent developments in the power of the Prime Minister. The 'presidential school' is supported by those who argue that the powers of the office have so increased that they set the Premier above other ministers, as more than *primus inter pares* (first among equals). John Mackintosh's *The British Cabinet* (1962) exalted the power of the Prime Minister, as did Richard Crossman in his introduction to Bagehot's *The English Constitution*. The 'chairmanship school' (or 'Prime Ministerial model' of 'Cabinet government', as it is called in B5) stresses the Prime Minister's dependence upon others within the government and the party. Harold Wilson argued in *The Governance of Britain* (1976), p. 11, that Crossman had failed to take account of the new checks qualifying the power of the leader, such as the greater independence of Cabinet committees. In addition one can also note the vulnerability of a leader to other pressures, such as the Cabinet revolt against Wilson's planned trade union reform in 1969, Edward Heath's experience of 1972–4 and James Callaghan's defeat by the House of Commons in 1979.

In B5 Thatcher is accused of using a *dirigiste* approach in her handling of the Cabinet (in other words, conforming to the presidential school), and it is evident that, even if Thatcher has suffered several defeats in full Cabinet, she was able to impose a 'monetarist' economic policy on the country which only had minority support among Cabinet colleagues. Thomas Mackie and Brian Hogwood (B7) illustrate how various Prime Ministers overcame opposition when necessary. Basically the power of the Prime Minister depends on the personalities, the circumstances and the relationships involved. Some leaders assume a dominant position (as Churchill did as war leader), others are content to be merely *primus inter pares*, while yet again one leader might conform to both models at different times or when faced with different situations.

The importance and continued application of the principles of individual and collective ministerial responsibility (reference to the 'collective' aspect is made in B6 and B10) can be assessed by the reader in the context of sources given in Sections C, D and F of this book, which refer to Cabinet committees, the closed nature of much of British government, the workload of senior ministers, and the various ploys of civil servants to get ministers to follow departmental policy.

B1

The Iron Lady who won't give in

Maggie's decade at the helm . . .

Ten years ago Margaret Thatcher became leader of the Conservatives and since then has stamped her mark on her party and the country more than any leader in recent times. PETER WOODIFIELD examines what has been achieved.

Ten years ago today Mrs Thatcher hijacked the Conservative Party and the shock waves are still being felt.

For the difference between the Prime Minister and her predecessors is that, unlike them, she is not the champion of the 'haves' or 'have nots'. Mrs Thatcher's heart lies with the 'want to haves'.

A passionate supporter of the enterprise culture, her instinctive sympathies lie with the people who want to own their own homes, who want to give their children a better start than they had, who are prepared to make sacrifices so that they can provide for their families rather than having to rely on the State.

That was the sort of background her Grantham grocer's shop upbringing gave her and it helps to explain why increasingly large numbers of trade union voters have turned to the Conservatives.

Another important strand in her make-up is that Mrs Thatcher has little time for the Establishment and all it stands for. To her the Establishment represents much of what is wrong with British society as she sees it and is responsible for much of Britain's economic decline. She has said that none of the self-made millionaires she knows went to university.

Dislike

Mrs Thatcher is an Oxford chemistry graduate who then qualified as a barrister. So while she has a respect for learning she does not regard it as a substitute for doing or making things.

Equally the Establishment has little time for her. They dislike her refusal to look for the compromise and the fact that she is not one of 'them'. Above all what they dislike is the way Britain has become more politicised and polarised than at any time since the war, when what they stand for is a search for the widest possible consensus at the expense of any radical change.

But what has Mrs Thatcher actually changed over the past 10 years and, indeed, what has she achieved? The economic record, as Labour continually remind her and she reminds them, is like a record stuck in a groove where everyone knows the lyrics.

Inflation down to 4–5 per cent, productivity improving, investment up, output up, retail spending up. That is offset by remorselessly rising unemployment, officially at 3.3 million but in reality much higher.

To Labour and the Alliance, as well as an increasingly vocal number of Tory critics, the scourge of unemployment outweighs on the scales the other gains and demands urgent action to tackle it.

It is a symptom of the third industrial revolution into which Britain is heading that while recovery has now been under way for four years according to all the traditional statistics it has had absolutely no impact on the dole queues.

Explanations like the baby boom in the early 1960s, a higher proportion of women at work, the lack of conscription, all fail to persuade people that the Government could not do more to fight unemployment.

But then of course conventional wisdom said that no Government could possibly win a general election with more than three million unemployed. That theory was stood on its head in June 1983 when Mrs Thatcher swept back to Downing Street with a massive 143 majority.

That victory owed as much to her perceived qualities of leadership, heightened by the Falklands War, as it did to Labour's massive problems, which led the voters to see them as unfit to govern whatever they thought of the Iron Lady.

Her courage and determination (stubbornness if you disapprove of her) were highlighted by the way she snatched the leadership of the Conservative Party back in 1975. Regarded as no more than a competent Cabinet Minister when at Education, Mrs Thatcher saw the Heath years of office as a time when the Tories were beginning to lose their way and failing to appeal to their natural electorate.

When her mentor Sir Keith Joseph decided he could not run against Heath following reaction to two controversial speeches, Mrs Thatcher stepped into the breach rather than let her leader have a free run.

Her willingness to pick up the gauntlet at the right moment contrasted with her rivals like Willie Whitelaw. Being a party leader requires ruthlessness, and Whitelaw's great attribute is his loyalty, which is why he was not prepared to strike the first blow against Heath.

As opposition leader Mrs Thatcher gradually brought in the people she felt comfortable with, but nevertheless the only heavyweights of the Heath era to get off the bus before 1979 were Geoffrey Rippon and Robert Carr who stepped off voluntarily.

By the time of the 1979 General Election Labour's position was so bad after the Winter of Discontent that Mrs Thatcher only had to avoid any serious mistakes in the campaign to be sure of becoming the western world's first woman leader.

But in the Commons she had already made her mark in the twice weekly exchanges at Prime Minister's Question Time, helped by her Gang of Four, which included Norman Tebbit, who spent their time plotting how to trip up Jim Callaghan.

The radical nature of her first administration became apparent very quickly. In Sir Geoffrey Howe's first budget VAT shot up to 15 per cent to pay for a reduction in income tax to 30 per cent and a big increase in personal allowances.

On the legislative side the piece of legislation which will probably do more in the long run to help the Tories hang on to power also came early. That was the bill to allow council tenants to own their own homes. Since then 600 000 people have become homeowners under the Act. The first seeds of the privatisation programme were also visible with the legislation to sell off British Aerospace.

Recession

Nevertheless the economy was going horribly wrong for the Government. Inflation rocketed to 21 per cent before starting its long decline but more importantly the Government's shift in economic policy had hurtled Britain quicker into the world's deepest recession for 50 years than anyone else.

By the summer of 1981 the Government was at its all-time low in popularity with just 25 per cent of the vote, while the newly born SDP/Liberal Alliance had around half the vote according to the polls.

But it was the 1981 budget that underlined Mrs Thatcher's nickname of TINA (There Is No Alternative). Under immense pressure to change course she and Sir Geoffrey decided instead to batten down the hatches and reef in the sails a few notches. He produced a budget that froze personal tax allowances and froze the hearts of some of his supporters.

The economy did, however, start to pick up and by the spring of 1982 the Government was back in the lead in the opinion polls for the first time in a very long time.

Then came the Falklands, a testing time for any leader. Her determination to press ahead in the face of what many considered to be dangerous odds showed that she was a leader who led from the front. That was a chord that seemed to strike home with a nation that knew deep down Britain could not go on the way it had been.

After the 1983 election the only traditional land-owning Tory grandee left in the Government was Whitelaw, who was made a Viscount and shoved upstairs to the Lords. Of the others the only one whose departure she regretted was Lord Carrington who resigned over the Falklands invasion.

The others, like Lord Thorneycroft, Lord Soames and Sir Ian Gilmour, who all went in 1981, were not in tune with her way of thinking. She sacked Francis Pym as Foreign Secretary after the election, but she had never got on with him.

Of the 'wet' heavyweights Jim Prior had been safely neutralised in Ulster while Peter Walker was out of the way in Agriculture. As usual her instincts had told her who it was safe to get rid of and who it was wiser to keep in government.

Since the election the path has been rockier. The trouble started when Cecil Parkinson had to resign from the Cabinet after his mistress became pregnant. Since then things have rarely been on an even keel, even though the sell-off of British Telecom saw two million individuals become shareholders — most for the first time.

British Telecom in a way epitomises the Thatcher dream of a property and share-owning democracy. Since its monopoly powers were relaxed it has become much more competitive, but people will be watching closely to see that the private monopoly does not start displaying all the bad habits of a public one.

But of course the post-election period has been dominated by the 11-month miners' strike.

Even without the three rounds of legislation clipping the unions wings, with Arthur Scargill as the miners' leader conflict was inevitable. Mrs Thatcher backed down in 1981 when she knew she could not win.

[from *The Journal*, 11 February 1985]

Last March she was better prepared for a fight to the finish with mountainous coal stocks at power stations.

Radical

People seem to forget that the stakes are so high. If she had lost this strike Thatcherism and all it stands for would have been finished, and she knew it. On the other hand victory would see history portraying the strike as the dying spasm of an old economy, based on major industrial conflict, being replaced by Silicon Glen and no-striking agreements.

As it looks at the moment the irresistible force is foundering on the immoveable object.

Mrs Thatcher claims she is as radical as ever and is full of ideas but there does not seem to be quite so much evidence of them as there used to be.

Nevertheless after 10 years as party leader and nearly six as Prime Minister it is clear that her main achievement has been to grab British politics by the scruff of the neck and shift it, often almost single-handed, a long way to the right (she would prefer to say back to the centre). That can best be judged by the fact that Mrs Thatcher sets the terms of the political debate. The starting point is her assumptions and her attitudes.

Whether one likes it or not more voters prefer them to the others on offer. How much longer she stays in power depends on how the other parties react to that fact.

[from *The Observer*, 10 February 1985]

WHAT ARE THE MOST IMPORTANT QUALITIES IN A PM?

1.	25%	Good at leading whole country	Callaghan wins 40—19
2.	20%	Person of sound judgement	Callaghan wins 40—27
3.	14%	Person you can trust	Callaghan wins 28—27 (women 26—31)
4.	13%	Person who keeps promises	Callaghan wins 29—24 (women 27—27)
5.	9%	In touch with ordinary people	Callaghan wins 36—28
6.	7%	Able to deal with TU leaders	Callaghan wins 56—12
7.	6%	Strong personality	Thatcher wins 46—28
8.	4%	Good at leading party	Callaghan wins 37—24
9.	1%	Good on television	Callaghan wins 31—38 (women 27—30)

DO YOU RATE CALLAGHAN OR THATCHER MORE HIGHLY AS GOOD AT LEADING THE WHOLE COUNTRY?

	All %	Men %	Women %
Callaghan	40	42	37
Thatcher	19	18	21
Both equal	18	18	18
Don't know	23	22	24

The NOP survey was taken of nationally representative samples of men and women aged 18 and over. In all, 1567 interviews were conducted between June 17 and 23 in 90 parliamentary constituencies in England, Scotland and Wales.
Copyright National Opinion Polls Ltd, 1978

[from the *Daily Mail*, 11 July 1978]

> *I have no politics, but I always vote Conservative because I think it is safer for the country.*
> *(Dr Warre, one-time headmaster of Eton)*

HOW THE POLITICAL LEADERS MEASURE UP
What people think of political leaders . . . in percentages

	THATCHER	PYM	OWEN	FOOT	JENKINS	REAGAN
Capable leader	44	14	18	9	13	10
Good in crisis	47	29	8	4	5	4
Grasps world problems	28	24	21	17	21	13
Talks down	39	12	10	8	11	16
Narrowminded	17	9	5	24	8	17
Inflexible	22	7	6	13	6	15
Sound judgement	25	21	18	9	16	4
More honest	29	17	19	17	13	7
Trustworthy	19	17	12	9	19	6
Grasps home problems	38	35	22	19	18	12
Down to earth	18	16	11	16	9	6
Good personality	24	8	19	9	13	22
Inexperienced	7	12	11	17	8	36
Out of touch	42	17	9	22	17	28

[from the *Daily Express*, 3 June 1982]

Questions

1   Which particular qualities of Thatcher does Peter Woodifield refer to which equip her for the task of Prime Minister? (B1)

2   What justification does Woodifield give for his claim that Thatcher represents the 'want to haves'?

3   Why has Thatcher been called the 'Iron Lady' and 'TINA'? (B1)

4   What examples does Woodifield give to illustrate the qualities of Thatcher's policies and beliefs (Thatcherism)? (B1)

5   How does Woodifield assess the Thatcher government's record in dealing with economic problems since 1979?

6   What evidence does Woodifield provide that 'the path has been rockier' for Thatcher since the 1983 election?

7   Mention one obvious advantage that Callaghan would have over Thatcher in dealing with trade union leaders. (B3)

29

Class Discussion

1   What do you think are the most important qualities in a Prime Minister? Do you think the NOP survey recorded in B3 asked the right questions?
2   According to the survey summarised in B2, which of the six people named appears to be the best political leader?
3   Explain what Woodifield means by his comment that 'Mrs Thatcher hijacked the Conservative Party.' (B1) What arguments can be presented in support of or in opposition to this view?

Extension Work

1   Give details of the events which led to Thatcher's winning the election to become Conservative leader in 1975.
2   Explain the meaning of the following phrases or concepts: (a) 'the Establishment'; (b) 'the third industrial revolution'; (c) 'Gang of Four'; (d) 'the "wet" heavyweights'; (e) 'Silicon Glen'. (B1)
3   If Callaghan had a high rating as a Prime Minister in July 1978, why did his party, as the Labour government, lose the election in March 1979?

B4 – B7   *The powers of the Prime Minister*

B4

The key issue is whether or not the powers of the Prime Minister should be increased or reduced relative to those of his (or her) senior Cabinet colleagues.

However, it is impossible to discuss the issue in the abstract. The power of the Prime Minister is inextricably linked to the personality of each individual incumbent and the political circumstances surrounding his or her position. Some Prime Ministers acquire almost presidential control over certain aspects of government (such as Ted Heath and the EEC negotiations in 1971), while others are content to interfere relatively little with the work of their departmental ministers (for example, Harold Wilson, 1975–6). Nevertheless, there are certain characteristics common to all Prime Ministers and Cabinets, which are the parameters within which each individual is required to perform. Several of these characteristics can tend to hinder rather than assist the efficient implementation of a political programme.

The Prime Minister is much more than *primus inter pares*.

The present system

The Prime Minister has the power to appoint all ministers; to dismiss ministers without warning or explanation; to dissolve parliament; to determine the Cabinet agenda, and to control Cabinet conclusions through his or her position as Chairman and through an increasingly powerful Cabinet Office; to commit the government to changes in policy simply by making a public pronouncement; to rally public opinion, and initiate public debate; to issue instructions (Prime Ministerial 'memos') to any minister on any subject; to control the security services; and to have access (in theory) to any item of information known to the British government.

This battery of powers makes most Prime Ministers much more than *primus inter pares* inside the Cabinet. The power of appointment is crucial. It can be used to block a minister seeking to push through a particular policy (for example, the transfer of Tony Benn from the Department of Industry to the Department of Energy in 1975 marked the effective end of the industrial strategy contained in *Labour's Programme, 1973*). More generally, the Prime Minister's power of dismissal ensures that no Cabinet Minister can safely ignore a directive from Number 10. The practice of appointing political allies to the lesser positions in Cabinet tends to ensure that the Prime Minister commands a Cabinet majority.

While the power of appointment is at the root of the Prime Minister's power, the control of Cabinet procedure is also vital. The Prime Minister can use the position as Cabinet Chairman to prevent issues from being raised in Cabinet (such as devaluation in the early months of the 1964–70 Labour government, and pay policy in 1974–5). Alternatively, potentially dissenting ministers can be excluded from consideration of an issue by careful use of the Cabinet committee system, which is entirely within the Prime Minister's sphere of control.

On occasions, certain issues can be removed from the Cabinet system altogether. A bilateral meeting between the Prime Minister and a departmental minister (particularly the Chancellor) can often be the forum where the real decisions are taken. Sometimes the Prime Minister will establish *ad hoc* groups of ministers and officials to take key decisions.

The Prime Minister is able to operate a system of 'divide and rule' mainly because of the tradition of secrecy which permeates the entire system of British government. The 'need to know' principle applies not only to outsiders and officials, but also to Cabinet Ministers themselves. The Prime Minister will often regard the disclosure of economic information to, say, the Secretary of State for the Environment as a 'leak'. Treasury submissions to Cabinet on economic policy (which would often be agreed in advance by the Prime Minister) only rarely tell the whole truth as the Treasury sees it. Normally, these documents are designed to limit discussion, and to ensure that the Treasury line wins the day. The Prime Minister will almost always support the Chancellor on matters of economic policy in Cabinet (usually because a joint line has been agreed beforehand) and the rest of the Cabinet can be virtually powerless in the face of a united front between Number 10 and Treasury. Even the physical proximity of the two and the existence of a connecting door between Number Ten and Number Eleven Downing Street reinforces this axis.

This system means that Cabinet Ministers are frequently bound by the doctrine of collective responsibility to support decisions over which they have little say. It also means that the Cabinet is often not the body which actually takes the real decisions on major strategic issues.

Limits on Prime Ministerial power

Despite all this, the power of the Prime Minister is very far from absolute. The power of appointment is, in practice, severely restricted by the need to retain 'party balance' in Cabinet. Many ministers are 'unsackable', and carry a resignation threat which is almost as potent as that of the Prime Minister. Furthermore, after making an initial appointment, the Prime Minister simply does not have the time or resources to retain control over ministers' decisions. Within their own provinces, individual ministers wield great power, often almost entirely independent of Prime Ministerial or Cabinet control.

In addition, the Prime Minister's powers are obviously circumscribed by outside influences — the Parliamentary Party, the Party, pressure groups and public opinion. If the Prime Minister loses the support of one or more of these groups, his or her position inside Cabinet can become extremely weak or even untenable. A wise Prime Minister will therefore be careful to carry the support of Cabinet in adopting policies which are likely to prove politically contentious.

One further factor which can restrict the Prime Minister's power is the fact that his or her sources of advice can become monolithic. The Number 10 Private Office plays a varied role, which includes the processing of the Prime Minister's papers, the transmission of information, the control of the Prime Minister's diary, speech-writing and policy advice. But the main source of policy advice open to the Prime Minister is the Cabinet Office, which will automatically brief him or her on each issue raised at Cabinet (including advance warning about the views likely to be expressed by ministers) and will provide draft conclusions for the meeting in advance. Cabinet Office advice, augmented as necessary by the Number 10 Private Office, will normally be well informed, subtle, accurate and perceptive. But it will tend to be *mainstream* Civil Service advice which will reflect the predominant official view. Since the Cabinet Office and Number 10 officials will always be 'on loan' from another department, it is likely that they will more often than not reflect departmental thinking in their briefing. For all its strengths, the Civil Service is not very good at producing imaginative alternatives to its own conventional wisdom.

The last four British Prime Ministers have recognised the dangers of single source advice, and have attempted to establish institutions (such as the CPRS and the Number 10 Policy Unit) which can provide extra options and more politically oriented ideas. But this effort has never been on the required scale, and with the necessary conviction, to provide an effective *long term* counterweight to the slow but sure advance of Civil Service influence on ministerial thinking. Over a period of years, it is almost inevitable that a Prime Minister, and his or her Cabinet colleagues, will have their attitudes moulded by the sheer persistence of Civil Service thinking and the absence of options. While this may on many occasions be a good thing, it does not increase the chances of implementation of a radical, reforming political programme.

[from 'Making Government Work' ed. David Lipsey (Fabian Society, 1982)]

B5

Under the model of Prime Ministerial government established by Attlee, and followed, more or less, by every Prime Minister since, the Prime Minister is no more than *primus inter pares* and it has been assumed that it is necessary for him to carry a majority of the Cabinet with him on all major planks of policy. There are no votes in Cabinet, and Prime Ministers traditionally asked the opinion of each minister in turn, then summed up the collective Cabinet view. This did not mean that every major issue was decided at the Cabinet table. Every Prime Minister has attempted to settle the major issues before a decision comes to Cabinet. But the Cabinet has remained the principal policy-endorsing body and any Prime Minister who did not carry the day in Cabinet would be considered to have lost the confidence of his colleagues. Sometimes, as in the Cabinet discussions over the 1977 IMF loan, Cabinet meetings have been essential policy-forging meetings in which genuine, substantial issues are decided. In Thatcher's Cabinet, the opposite was the case. With such a large majority of her Cabinet opposed to the dogma which governed her economic policy, she kept discussions as far away from the Cabinet as possible, never raising the central direction of the policy at Cabinet level. The core of Cabinet government — that a majority of the Cabinet is needed to maintain the principal elements of the government's policy — was intentionally avoided.

She ignored the well-established precedents for Prime Ministerial chairing of Cabinet meetings in favour of a more *dirigiste* approach. She would sound the views of each colleague in turn, but would argue loudly with each who dared to raise a dissenting voice. Although it is true that she enjoys an argument, she does not enjoy losing them, particularly at a full Cabinet meeting. The distance between the Cabinet and the Cabinet committee which formulates economic policy — the 'E' Committee, which used to meet each Tuesday — was substantial and there was considerable resentment among Cabinet Ministers who had views on economic policy but who were excluded from the policy-making, decision-taking process.

[from *Thatcher — the major new biography* by Nicholas Wapshott and George Brock (Macdonald, 1983)]

We think your cabinet is wonderful

Is cabinet government dead? Yes, says the political editor of the *Sunday Times*, Mr Hugo Young, dead at the hands of Mrs Margaret Thatcher. Witness her brutal dismissal of her navy minister, Mr Keith Speed, and her high-handed and secretive style of chairmanship. But wait, the corpse is stirring.

Cabinet government has always been more real in the eye of the observer than in the rough and tumble of Downing Street (see Walter Bagehot, Professor John Mackintosh, et al). It has never possessed any constitutional significance and Cabinet Ministers stand publicly by their joint decisions for the simple and practical reason that a house divided against itself will fall. 'Collective responsibility' is the tool of the British system of party government, not its master.

But many observers clearly feel more comfortable with it around — not least when faced with such stern and potentially authoritarian personalities as Mrs Thatcher and Mr Tony Benn. So what of the charges laid against the former?

Mrs Thatcher came to office as the most determinedly 'outsider' Prime Minister since Mr Clement Attlee. Her first Cabinet received rave notices as being impeccably balanced — indeed some argued she had gone overboard in generosity to the Heathites (if not to Mr Edward Heath himself).

Since then Cabinet government has performed to the book. Despite deep splits — understandable in view of the state of the nation — no senior minister has resigned 'in protest'. There has been no public or parliamentary breaking of ranks on the central course of Cabinet strategy. Leaks, rows, subterranean explosions there have been aplenty, but no Cabinet has been without these. Indeed, ministers have on occasions performed truly breathtaking feats of political self-abnegation in the cause of Cabinet responsibility — witness Sir Keith Joseph on British Leyland, Mr James Prior on the budget, Mr Michael Heseltine *passim*.

But what of Mrs Thatcher's style of Cabinet management? Is that not notoriously dictatorial and uncollective? Cabinet meetings on Thursday are only the tip of any Cabinet's iceberg. Full Cabinet only debates those items forced on to its agenda by disagreements in committee, apart from formal Prime Ministerial reports. All British Cabinets are therefore by definition about conflict and debate. And by all accounts the present Prime Minister has, whether through temperament or inexperience, been worsted in this conflict more often than any of her recent predecessors.

The list of Cabinet decisions which have gone against Mrs Thatcher's better judgement or explicit pleading is already awesome: trade union reform, energy pricing, aid to industry, cuts in pensions, MPs' pay, the whole conduct of successive cuts packages. From the early discussions over Rhodesia, through the Wet Ascendancy of 1980, to the coal debacle of this spring, Mrs Thatcher has allowed herself to be steered, pushed, occasionally bludgeoned, by her senior colleagues.

The two instances cited of her desire to circumvent her Cabinet — the Trident decision last year and this year's budget 'judgement' — were precisely according to Cabinet precedent. Neither defence procurement decisions, however costly, nor the budget preliminaries have ever been matters for full Cabinet debate. Indeed the remarkable thing about Mrs Thatcher is that she has kept disaffected Mr Prior in the job of employment secretary, with a seat on the main economic committee and a very definite voice on economic policy. Now she is to be the first Prime Minister to concede to her Cabinet (as a result of its pressure) a greater say in budget decisions.

Indeed Mrs Thatcher has quite deliberately loaded the dice against herself in her supposed bid for presidentialism. Not for her the Wilsonian 'kitchen Cabinets' — which sparked the last round of Cabinet government obituaries. She has kept her Downing Street staff small and relatively weak on the explicit grounds that 'my Cabinet are my political advisers'. As a direct result, the various organs of Cabinet government — the committee system, inter-departmental groups, bilaterals and 'meetings with the Prime Minister' — are probably seething with as much collective argument and dissent as they have been for years. Contact between Mrs Thatcher and her colleagues may often be peremptory, bossy, even downright rude, but officials are constantly aware of its frequency. 'Madame' may love the sound of her own voice and be convinced of the initial rectitude of her prejudices. But that does not mean she gets her own way. Cabinet government is alive and kicking. You can tell by the kicking.

B7

The appointment of the committee chairman is particularly important in the British system given the lack of formal votes and the key role of the chairman in summing up the decision of the committee. For example, in 1978 the Cabinet committee on energy (ENM) was chaired not by the left-wing energy Minister, Tony Benn, but by the more right-wing industry Minister, Eric Varley. More generally, Page alleges:

> given Benn's following, there could be no question of his exclusion from the publicly-appointed Cabinet, but within the secret system of committees the Premier can register disfavour by excluding Benn from chairmanships, which are reserved for trusties like Varley and Rees.[1]

A former British permanent secretary has argued that the allocation of departmental and Cabinet committees' responsibilities enabled the 'monetarists' to dominate the 1979 Thatcher Government on economic matters:

> The monetarist minority nevertheless prevailed in economic and industrial policy because they had strategic control of the key Departments and *Cabinet committees*; as in previous administrations, only the Prime Minister and Treasury Ministers were effectively involved in taxation policy and, in conjunction with the Bank of England, in interest rates and exchange policy. *The doubters and dissenters were either given no opportunity to mount a challenge in full Cabinet or were unable to do so effectively.*[2]

The key decision to proceed with a British atomic bomb was taken in a Cabinet committee reconstituted to exclude ministerial opponents of the bomb. At a meeting of the relevant Cabinet committee (GEN 75) on 25 October 1946 Dalton, the Chancellor of the Exchequer, and Cripps, the President of the Board of Trade, voiced opposition to developing the bomb, doubting whether the economy could afford it or whether it was needed. They were defeated on that occasion, but only by the late arrival of Bevin, the Foreign Secretary. When the time approached to take a final decision, Dalton and Cripps were excluded from the relevant committee by the device of replacing GEN 75 by a new committee, GEN 163, which met without them on 10 January 1947.[3] This again illustrates the ability of the British Prime Minister to skew membership of Cabinet committees.

[from 'Decision arenas in executive decision making: Cabinet committees in comparative perspective' by Thomas T. Mackie and Brian W. Hogwood (*British Journal of Political Science*, Vol. 14, part 3, July 1984)]

[1] Bruce Page, 'The Secret Constitution', *New Statesman*, 21 July 1978, p. 74.
[2] Sir Leo Pliatzky, *Getting and spending: public expenditure, employment and inflation* (Oxford: Basil Blackwell, 1981), p. 178, emphasis added.
[3] Peter Hennessy, 'How Bevin saved Britain's bomb', *The Times*, 30 September 1982.

Questions

1. What sort of power helps to make most Prime Ministers more than *primus inter pares* inside the Cabinet? (B4)

2. What constraints or checks exist on the powers and influence of the Prime Minister? (B4)

3. Explain the function of the Prime Minister's Private Office. (B4)

4. Why does the Prime Minister need sometimes to widen the sources of advice that he or she receives? (B4)

5. How does the tradition of secrecy in government enable the Prime Minister to dominate his or her Cabinet colleagues? (B4, B7)

6. Suggest other sources for policy decisions in addition to the full Cabinet or Cabinet committees. (B4, B5)

7. What techniques can a Prime Minister employ to prevent dissenters mounting a challenge to his or her policies in full Cabinet? (B4–7)

8. Compare and comment on the differing interpretations of Thatcher's style of Cabinet government given in B5 and B6.

9. Why does the committee chairman play such a decisive role in Cabinet government? (B5, B7)

10. Why did the minority 'monetarist' view eventually prevail in the Thatcher government from 1979? (B5, B7)

11. Are British Cabinet committees discussion or decision-making committees?

12. Explain how the decision was taken in 1947 to make an atomic bomb. (B7)

Class Discussion

1. Does the system of allowing Cabinet committees to make major decisions conflict with the principle of collective responsibility?

2. Comment on the sentence '"Collective responsibility" is the tool of the British system of party government, not its master.' (B6)

Extension Work

1. When did Cabinet committees originate and why?

2. When and why was the CPRS created? What did it do? Give reasons for its abolition, and mention when this occurred. (B4)

3. Briefly explain the nature of the industrial strategy contained in *Labour's Programme, 1973*. What event contributed to the end of this policy? (B4)

4   Is it possible to distinguish between two styles of leadership: presidential and prime ministerial?

5   Explain or give further details on the following: (a) 'Wet Ascendancy of 1980'; (b) 'Wilsonian "kitchen cabinets"'; (c) 'feats of political self-abnegation in the cause of Cabinet responsibility' (d) 'Trident decision' and 'defence procurement decisions'. (B6)

B8 – B10 *Cabinet Ministers: their role and efficiency*

B8

The Prime Minister forming his Cabinet, no less in appointing ministers of State and Parliamentary under secretaries of State, has to use all the qualities he is presumed to have in order to have reached the position he holds.

First, he needs a good memory of his colleagues' specialisations and past experience, or any tendencies to weakness in a crisis. Even more, he needs a good 'forgettory'. Forming a Cabinet is no time for settling old scores, or bearing grudges or associating a first class potential minister with some groupings during some best-forgotten party argument. It is as likely to have been your fault as his, and in some past party row he had his loyalties, as you had yours. Second, the Prime Minister must pay full regard to preserving a real balance in the Party, in Parliament, and in the country. The Labour Party, and this is, I would think, equally true of the Conservative and Liberal Parties, is, as I have said, a broad church. No government should be based on a faction, still less a clique. It should embrace and reflect the whole Party, though the Prime Minister can be forgiven if he disregards a few idiosyncratic extremists at the margins, where membership of his Party seems to be asymptotic to the views of right and left groupings, owing little loyalty to the basic tenets of his Party — in my own case to democratic socialism. A modern government claims, with whatever justification, to represent something like half the country: its spread of individual views may range even more widely than that. So should the government. 'What you cannot afford is a Government of cronies and like-minded people, who can be relied on for their loyalty in Cabinet, but who, for that very reason, cannot deliver a corresponding strength, whether in backbenchers or in popular support in the country.'[1]

Third, he must concentrate on the doctrine of horses for courses, not only in using the specialist knowledge of individual ministers, but also in reflecting the changing priorities of national and international relationships. A 'priority' ministry may become less important as old problems and challenges give way to new.[2] 'Horses for courses' includes the great and unteachable quality of being able to handle the House of Commons. In the first resort, as in the last, a government survives, and deserves to survive, in proportion to its success in understanding Parliament, in reflecting, and sometimes knowing when to resist, its changing moods; to its accountability to Parliament, and at times of crisis to its collective ability to lead Parliament.

Fourth, Cabinet and other ministerial appointments should reflect a real rapport with the Party nationally, and above all in the country. Every member of the administration — regardless of which party is in office — must remember that he is not where he is, not even in Parliament, as a result of his own transcendent qualities: he is there because people believe in him, and work for him, not primarily as an individual but as a standard-bearer. As a member of the Cabinet, particularly, he needs them more than they need him. Whatever may have been the situation in the spacious days of the Edwardians, political inspiration comes from the country, not from the dinner tables of the elite,[3] or the hot-house atmosphere of London's political fringe. Members of Parliament, and ministers, may be less prone than some of the fringe to believe that as soon as you are north of Watford the Arctic Circle begins; or that when you pass Basingstoke the natives paint themselves with woad. Inspiration comes from the country.

[1]   The present writer in an address before the British Academy (25 April 1975).
[2]   Shortly before he died, I invited Clement Attlee to Chequers where he had spent the happiest days of his life (having first ensured that Chequers without his wife would not be too upsetting). Following his stroke, he found speaking difficult, so I put questions to him. 'If you were in this chair', I asked him, 'what subject would you put higher in the system of priorities than it appears to occupy today?' Immediately he answered, 'Transport'. I moved Barbara Castle there from Overseas Development within a very short period. (In a different context I asked him, parties and politics apart, whom he regarded as the best Prime Minister *qua* Prime Minister since he first took an interest in politics. He had no hesitation — 'Salisbury'.)
[3]   When I was elected leader of the party in February 1963, I immediately received dining invitations from certain leading Labour MPs. In my first speech to Party meeting I said that I should reject them all: instead of spending three or four hours with one or other Labour MP, the time saved would be spent in my room at the House, with the door open to any Labour member who wanted to see me.

[from *The Governance of Britain* by Harold Wilson (Sphere, 1977)]

Why do we have to have so many ministers?

In an echo of Dunning's famous resolution, JOHN GRIGG argues that the size of successive British governments has increased, is increasing and ought to be diminished.

MRS THATCHER is widely credited with being a politician of more or less inflexible principle, unlike all those dreadful opportunists and compromisers who preceded her in the office of Prime Minister. For instance, she is supposed to be dead against overmanning, the waste of public money, and everything covered by the term 'Big Government'. But has she lived up to her reputation where her control is most immediate and direct, i.e. in the use of her patronage and, more especially, in the construction of her ministry? The short answer is that the Government today is substantially larger than under Mr Heath, and only a fraction smaller than under Mr Callaghan.

For the past quarter-century British governments have been getting far too big, and Mrs Thatcher has made no significant attempt to reverse the trend. In 1900, when Britain was a superpower ruling much of the world, Lord Salisbury's Government numbered in all 64 — a misleading figure for comparison, since it included 17 Court appointments, many of which soon ceased to be filled by political nominees. In 1922, with fewer courtiers on the books, the Bonar Law Government had only 60 members, despite the recent creation of new ministers (such as Air, Labour, Transport and Health) by Lloyd George. Two years later the first MacDonald ministry was, with 57 members, the smallest of modern times, and in general the size of governments was kept within reasonable bounds until the Second World War.

But Churchill then began the process of ministerial inflation, and in the post-war period Attlee's regime of austerity did not apply to politicians. His 1945 government was 81-strong, but even that seems modest compared with Sir Harold Wilson's 98 in 1970. Mr Heath at the end of his time had a Cabinet of 21, and a total ministry of 99. For Mr Callaghan the relative figures were 24 and 109. For Mrs Thatcher they are 22 and 108.

A most undesirable new form of ministerial life is the minister of State, who is neither one thing nor the other. The precedent was set in 1943 when Richard Law (later Lord Coleraine) was appointed minister of State at the Foreign Office. Previously even that important and busy Department had only a secretary of State and an under secretary. In the circumstances of the time the change seemed justified, because the Foreign Secretary, Anthony Eden, was working under extraordinary pressure, being also a member of the War Cabinet and leader of the House of Commons. But by 1960 the number of ministers of State had risen to eight, and by 1970 to 22. Today it stands at 27.

One does not need to be unduly cynical to suggest that the intermediate tier is useful to Prime Ministers as a means of bringing more politicians on to the payroll, and of giving them higher status and pay without making them top ministers. Since at the same time not fewer, but more, under secretaries have been created, it is hardly surprising that the net inflationary effect has been so great. And while the number of ministers has been going up, so of course have their salaries. Today the basic pay of a Cabinet Minister is £28 950, that of a minister of State £20 575, and that of an under secretary £15 700, compared with the basic MP's salary of £14 510 (and no doubt the Top Salaries Review Body will soon be recommending further increases).

There is no evidence that the larger establishment of politicians in each department has significantly improved the efficiency of government. Civil servants will say, privately, that they often have to invent work for their ministers to do. One of the most talented — and candid — men appointed to junior office since the war, C. M. Woodhouse, has written of his year as parliamentary secretary to the Ministry of Aviation that he had 'little to do' but 'splendid quarters to do it in'.

Anyway, even the efficiency of Government matters less than the capacity of Parliament to do its proper job, and there can be no doubt that the really sinister aspect of what has been happening has been the increased domination of Parliament by the executive. Since most members of the Government are recruited from the House of Commons — a much larger proportion, incidentally, than earlier in the century — the present size of ministries can only have a corrupting effect upon the governing party in the elected House. Quite apart from the large number of MPs who are silenced by being actually given jobs, there is the outer penumbra of those who serve ministers as PPSs or who merely hope for office in the next reshuffle.

As if this were not bad enough, Mrs Thatcher has also revived the practice, prodigally used by Mr Macmillan, but spurned (to his cost) by Mr Heath, of bestowing knighthoods, etc., upon MPs who might otherwise be disaffected. Not since the eighteenth century has Government maintained itself so shamelessly, or have placemen been so much in evidence in our political system. If the Alliance wins the next election it will have a duty to give the country not only better ministers, but fewer, and also in other ways to restrict the scope of Prime Ministerial patronage, which has become a serious menace to our parliamentary democracy.

[from *The Observer*, 27 March 1983]

B10

The nine lives of a Cabinet minister

Malcolm Dean

The third question raised by [*Tony Benn's*] paper is whether any Cabinet Minister can do justice to the separate jobs he is expected to perform. In intimidating statistical detail, Mr Benn has produced a diary of a year in the life of a Cabinet Minister: a Crossman without the gossip. He has identified nine separate categories of work.

In the sequence with which they came into play, the groups to which Mr Benn believes he is accountable are: his local constituency party's general management committee which adopted him; the voters of Bristol who elected him; the Parliamentary Labour Party which elects its Leader and Shadow Cabinet when in Opposition; the constituency Labour Parties across the country whose delegates voted him a member of the party's National Executive Committee; and its Prime Minister, who appointed him Secretary of State for Energy. [. . .]

Mr Benn writes: 'Most of the day, from the time of arrival in the Department at about 9 a.m. until leaving for the House of Commons in the late afternoon, is occupied with discussions with other ministers, political advisers or officials, or in meetings with outside groups.

At about eight o'clock every evening my private secretary packs one — and sometimes more — official red boxes with papers to be dealt with overnight. These include papers requiring positive decisions (policy submissions, letters to ministers, drafts of parliamentary answers or appointments), papers for information, invitations and engagements plus general reading matter. Work on these boxes may take from one to three hours each night and weekend boxes about the same. [. . .]'

Mr Benn adds: 'As the Crossman diaries revealed, there is a great deal of tension between ministers and officials in the formulation of policy. Open government allows those outside Whitehall to know what the issues are, allowing them to feed in a stream of advice representing alternative views which may help ministers in their task. Any Labour minister will want to maintain the closest contact with the Labour and trade union movement as part of this process. This strengthens his hand both in developing policy and in winning support for its implementation.' [. . .]

Mr Benn writes that the task of preparing his report, and of drawing together many different strands of his experience, point to some issues for discussion. These are:

(1) 'The case for a clearer understanding of how parliamentary democracy really works. Modern British government and politics are in fact run collectively through a huge network of interlocking committees, consultations, and conferences. This means that few, if any, policy decisions can be attributed to one person.

Even though they originate in the mind of an individual, they have to be argued out with others and agreed by them and will not be accepted until they have gone through that process. This, combined with the House of Commons' control and the final power of the electorate at general elections, constitutes important safeguards on the abuse of power. It also makes public presentation of politics, by the media, in terms of personalities, increasingly irrelevant and misleading.

[from *The Guardian*, 11 February 1978]

(2) The case for a better flow of information. The extent to which the work of government is still conducted in secret makes the safeguards mentioned above far less effective than they would be and should be. A major shift in the balance of political power in favour of the people and Parliament must now be seen as urgent. Greater openness, backed up by a full "Freedom of Information" Act would greatly help. It is equally important that there should be wider access by the people to each other through the mass media. [. . .]

(8) The case for replacing ministerial patronage by an open appointment system based on the following possibilities: (a) public advertisement followed by a proper appointments board procedure; (b) the scrutiny of candidates by Select Committees with power to confirm or reject; (c) the progressive introduction of industrial democracy providing for appointments to be made after election as within the nationalised industries.

(9) The case for a redefinition of the principle of collective Cabinet responsibility, which, combined with tight official secrecy, now has the effect of obstructing the democratic process.

It should be made clear that collective Cabinet responsibility does not extend back to previous administrations: nor can it be projected forward to cover policy for future Parliaments.

It should also be accepted that it does not require a pretence of non-existent unanimity but is solely to protect collective decisions already taken, and not even to preclude the advocacy of policy changes in the future.

In addition, the acceptance of dissent, where circumstances justify it, should be seen as a strength and not a weakness. If an interpretation along these lines were to become widely understood, it would restore credibility to the processes of government, because it would recognise the existence of an ongoing debate about policy within the Cabinet.'

Questions

1 What criteria, according to Wilson, does a Prime minister consider when choosing ministers and selecting Cabinet members? (B8)

2 Briefly define the doctrine of 'horses for courses' as used for selecting ministers. (B8)

3 Which few words does Wilson use to describe the idea that a government should embrace and reflect the whole Party? (B8)

4 Wilson refers to a government's accountability to Parliament. List ways in which government can be made accountable to the House of Commons. (See Section D.)

5 How does Grigg illustrate the practice of Prime Ministerial patronage? (B9)

6 How does Benn explain the difficulty of pinpointing precise responsibility for many political decisions? (B10)

Class Discussion

1   Why is it important that a minister should be able to 'handle the House of Commons'? What exactly does this phrase mean? (B8)

2   What political significance, if any, is there in the belief that 'as soon as you are north of Watford the Arctic Circle begins'? (B8)

3   'Civil servants will say, privately, that they often have to invent work for their ministers to do.' (B9). Can you reconcile the comment above with the evidence produced by Benn, as described in B10?

4   Does the heavy workload of some senior ministers, as indicated by Benn, tend to erode the principle of individual ministerial responsibility? (B10)

5   Is it inevitable that with the growth of the functions of government in the last hundred years, the size of governments should have grown correspondingly? Or do you agree with Grigg's view that the size of governments should be reduced? (B9)

6   Explain clearly Grigg's phrase 'MPs who are silenced by being actually given jobs.' (B9)

7   Comment on Benn's suggestions relating to: (a) ministerial patronage; (b) redefining the principle of collective Cabinet responsibility. (B10)

Extension Work

1   What would you say are the 'priority' ministries today? (B8)

2   Describe the function of: (a) a minister of State; (b) a PPS. (B9)

3   Identify organisations other than ministries or Civil Service departments which also perform important State activities or government functions.

4   Cite cases when the principle of collective Cabinet responsibility has been waived temporarily and Cabinet Ministers have agreed to differ openly.

Section
C

Whitehall: Government – Civil Service relations

Introduction

An aspect of the traditional theoretical view of minister–Civil Service relations is presented in C1; in contrast to this, C3 describes some of the difficulties faced in practice by a minister in trying to manage a department. One of the few recent major reforms or reorganisations in central government was carried out with regard to the Civil Service, following the recommendations of the Fulton Report. C2, however, suggests that the reforms never had the desired effect.

Sir John Hoskyns, head of Thatcher's policy unit at Number 10 from 1979 to 1982, expresses a critical view of civil servants and the competence of ministers in C4. He wants to reduce the workload of ministers and to politicise the Civil Service at the top. To some extent Thatcher has tried to do this (as described in C6). The ideal objective, Hoskyns believes, is to have temporary heads at the top who will rapidly and efficiently execute government policies, instead of powerful permanent heads who are able to obstruct government policies and projects. The *Daily Telegraph* has mentioned that the introduction of educational vouchers 'was frustrated by skilled civil servant tactics, using administrative subterfuges to defeat ideas'[1]. Examples of such tactics at local government level are given in C8.

C7–9 look at aspects of the problem of secrecy and security and public access to information. Benn claimed in January 1980 that 'manipulating' civil servants kept him in the dark when he was a Cabinet Minister, and he supports open government as one means of democratising Britain. The Labour Party Manifesto of 1983 stated that it would introduce freedom of information legislation which would place the onus on the authorities to justify withholding information.

C5 discusses the influence of Whitehall official committees. In his *Diaries*, Crossman comments that it was difficult for a minister or a Cabinet committee to oppose the decision hammered out by an official committee in an interdepartmental policy paper. In addition he mentions that officials within a department try to make the minister see things along departmental lines. (See C3 and C8.)

The doctrine of individual ministerial responsibility implies that the civil servants are answerable to a minister, that the advice they give remains confidential and is not available to the public, and that the minister (the political head) takes responsibility for any major errors or blunders, being prepared to resign if necessary. This is supposed to promote good government (C6, paragraph 1), but is at the cost of considerable secrecy concerning what actually goes on in Whitehall, which critics argue inhibits efficient government.

The problem is that since few ministers have the time or knowledge to become acquainted with much of what happens in a large department, many decisions not of major political significance are taken by civil servants. Rarely does a minister resign voluntarily today unless personally involved in a particular decision, or for misconduct or socially unacceptable behaviour, as in the case of Cecil Parkinson in 1983. In addition, as Benn points out (B10), few policy decisions can be attributed to any one person, as many are involved over a period of time, and this gives ample scope for passing the buck. This means that when some major error is eventually exposed civil servants can escape blame by hiding behind a veil of anonymity and secrecy, and it is difficult to pin the blame fairly on any one minister. Examples are the De Lorean Affair (see the introduction to Section D) and the Crown Agents' Affair (1969–77). In the latter, though certain politicians and civil servants knew there was cause for concern at an early stage in the handling of public funds by the Crown Agents, investigations were half-hearted and reports were not made available to relevant ministers or the House of Commons. In the end civil servants, government and Parliament all bore part of the blame for the loss of at least £212 million. Thanks to a vigilant press many of the details eventually became available to the public.[2]

Sometimes ministers leak sensitive proposals on certain legislation in advance to the media and later adjust the intended legislation according to the way the public reacts. Civil servants may also leak information (C3), but this violates the doctrine of the neutral or non-political Civil Service.

C8 advocates civil servant loyalty to the minister at the head of the department but implies that civil servants are not helpful enough when called before House of Commons committees, and criticises Sir Ian Bancroft's guidelines to senior civil servants. However rightly or wrongly, civil servants feel conflict of loyalty or duty here, since the price for their offer of frank advice to their minister is that such advice will not be publicly exposed whether in Parliament or elsewhere. The other problem is the considerable influence of Whitehall official committees or even the 'departmental line' in certain cases; hence the interest of Commons Select Committees and others in getting the right information from which to draw conclusions and make decisions.

The relative scarcity of outsiders in Whitehall is attributed by Hoskyns in C4 to the reluctance of top officials to admit 'strangers', but Lord Bancroft argues against this, saying it is difficult 'to persuade outsiders to cross the threshold'[3]. In the same article he also states that 'government needs to be more open', that everyone needs to know 'what is decided and why'. However, government would become even more difficult, he implies, if it became public knowledge 'how decisions are reached — who gave what advice to which minister and whether it was taken'.

There are always various pros and cons to be considered in assessing opposing goals; for example, under different circumstances a case can be made for saying that either closed or open government makes for better administration and leadership. Thus there are no easy answers, as government is a complex business with many interlocking variables involved.

[1] Editorial, 21 January 1984.
[2] One source is 'Whitehall's cover-up', the *Sunday Times*, 4 December 1977.
[3] 'In defence of the mandarins', *The Observer*, 2 October 1983.

C1

The two main parties have very different ideas, e.g. about education, housing and industry. In order to maintain continuity within the departments, each department is staffed by permanent officials, known as **civil servants**. Civil servants are politically neutral and serve each government, regardless of which party is in power. Many ministers only stay in a post for about two years before moving elsewhere. Civil servants, on the other hand, may spend over 40 years in one department, and they, therefore, have the time to become experts in the work of their department. In fact, they may know far more about it than the minister does, although they will look to him for political direction. Because of this, ministers have to rely on civil servants for advice and information. When, for example, a minister is required to answer Questions in the House on the work of his department, he will rely heavily on the information supplied by the department's civil servants. [. . .] Of course, the research work done by the Civil Service is not only designed to help the minister during Question Time. Civil servants will also provide information which will help the minister to work out his policies. They present him with the full facts of a situation to enable him to make a decision. Without this assistance a minister might, for example, accidentally harm one section of the community while trying to help another. You can, therefore, see how important the Civil Service is.

Only a small number of civil servants are, however, engaged in research work. Many civil servants have professional and technical skills. They may for example be scientists, computer experts or librarians. Others perform a variety of office duties like filing or typing. The Civil Service employs people with a wide range of skills because it is not only concerned with offering advice and information to ministers. A minister also relies on the Civil Service to carry out his instructions. As these instructions will involve a variety of tasks, you can see why a variety of skills and abilities are required in order to carry them out. This diagram shows the relationship between a Minister and his civil servants.

[from *Education Sheets 1*, 'Parliament & Government', by Elizabeth Stones (House of Commons, May 1982)]

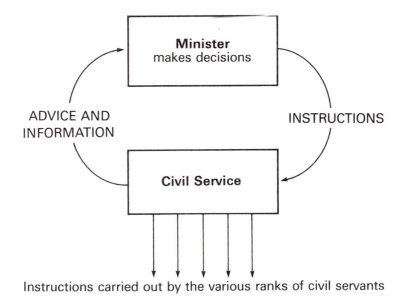

Minister
makes decisions

ADVICE AND INFORMATION

INSTRUCTIONS

Civil Service

Instructions carried out by the various ranks of civil servants

C2

Royal road to the top for the brilliant few

John Garrett

THE PROPOSITION set out by Sir Kenneth Clucas ('Agenda', 22 August) is that most of the reforms which have aimed to make the higher Civil Service more managerial and technocratic and less administrative in style have failed to recognise the political environment in which it operates. Even the Fulton Report, he said, simply considered the Civil Service as if it were like any other organisation. In fact, Volume II of the Fulton Report, the management consultancy study, which has come to be seen as the most valuable part of the report, heavily emphasised the effects of 'public accountability and political direction' on the management of the service. It went on to say that new structures and procedures aimed at making the Civil Service more effective would have to be devised for that unique environment and proposed a number of them.

Sir Kenneth failed to mention the weaknesses of the administrative style which the higher Civil Service has developed, and still continues to apply, in response to its environment. The Civil Service studied by the Fulton Committee and its consultants was one in which a top cadre of Oxbridge arts graduates not only regarded the management of departments as none of their concern but as an inferior occupation for the executive and specialist grades.

They saw their job as 'the awareness of ministerial responsibility'; that is, they were a political secretariat, politicians' politicians, looking up to the minister and not down to the organisation. A deputy secretary, at the head of a huge executive division with thousands of staff, would say that his job was to anticipate, and deal with, the policy and other problems facing his minister, not to plan and control his department's operations, nor to be concerned with its personal or organisational development.

In the consultancy group, we found that an institution based on the primacy of the generalist administrator used people very poorly, worked very slowly, except in a parliamentary crisis, and could not effectively mobilise the specialist skills needed to address the complex social, economic and technological issues facing the nation. It placed a low valuation on, and could not use, quantitative analysis and research.

The consultancy group said that the management of the service should 'be able to handle more variables than can be expressed in the traditional essay by which the top echelons of the service now usually analyse and judge policy options'. This style permeated the whole organisation so that promotion at lower levels, for example, depended not on proven competence but on impressing a panel of generalists in interview: being able to discourse on that day's *Daily Telegraph* editorial counted for more than a ten-year record of efficient management.

It led to a career structure which provided a royal road to the top for the 'best' graduates (as defined in a specification by Sir Cyril Burt, no less), namely, top flight Oxbridge classicists and historians, and ensured that, for example, a brilliant accountant or engineer could never get into top general management. It created elaborate and wasteful organisation structures to ensure that professionally qualified 'specialists' were always kept in separate advisory divisions where they could not make management or financial decisions but could only explain the issues to transient generalist administrators.

The generalists changed jobs every couple of years or so in order to maintain their generalism and not get to know too much about any subject: if they stayed any longer they might cease to be dispassionate.

Sir Kenneth did not acknowledge the disappointment and frustration of the specialists who were shut out of a managerial role, often in highly technical policy areas. This fed back into the universities where the best specialist graduates did not like the sound of a Civil Service career. The Fulton idea that preference in recruitment should be given to people with 'relevant' qualifications was soon put down by the ancient universities. Even young administrators felt frustrated by the system. Fulton found that the generalist style — which it rudely called 'amateur' and thereby ensured deadly opposition from the establishment — had done enormous damage to Britain's ability to cope in the modern world and to adapt to social and technical change. The consultancy group concluded that what was needed was a new breed of managers, numerate, trained in technique and experienced in working within the unique constraints of the public service.

Sir Kenneth considers the generalist administrator (essentially untouched by Fulton or anything since) to be an inevitable result of the 'parliamentary ambience' of the British Civil Service. That is true only if you see the service from the viewpoint of the mandarin and focus only on the exciting political turbulence at the top of departments. If you stand back and look at the whole, you see the much greater executive activities of government: the collection of revenues, the payment of benefits, the maintenance of defence, finding people jobs, training, sustaining law and order, regulating commerce and industry, promoting industrial and scientific development — huge tasks which carry on in much the same way year after year. These tasks need a highly skilled management about which the administrators know almost nothing.

There has developed, in consequence, a fatal gap between 'policy', defined as serving the minister, and 'management', running the machine. This is why where these two functions meet — in planning and system development — departments are very weak.

Fulton was never implemented because the mandarins decided it would not be and the late Lord Armstrong, as a new-broom head of the Civil Service, was, contrary to expectation, never persuaded of the value of the reforms. Departments made sure that the Civil Service Department never had the power of the Treasury over them and that the Civil Service College never got the support it needed to turn it into a source of new ideas on the management of government.

John Garrett was a consultant to the Fulton Committee and Labour MP for Norwich South, 1974–83.

[from *The Guardian*, 12 September 1983]

A minister's knowledge of the subject covered by his department may be slight. He cannot hope to match the administrative expertise of his officials or their experience of negotiations with groups that have contact with and make demands of the department. What time he has to devote to the department and decision-making is influenced and largely shaped by his officials. His diary is largely controlled by his private secretary; the material that is put before him is largely controlled by the permanent secretary. He will usually lack the time and alternative sources of informed research with which to question let alone dispute the options and the advice laid before him. (One permanent secretary once told Harold Macmillan apparently that it would be 'unconstitutional' for the minister to seek advice from anyone but his permanent secretary.) A minister is denied access to the papers of his predecessors. Upon taking office, he is supplied with a briefing document prepared by his officials. This, coupled with the foregoing, ensures that civil servants can largely determine the content of the minister's political agenda. As Lord Armstrong, former head of the Civil Service, once conceded: 'The biggest and most pervasive influence is in setting the framework within which questions of policy are raised. It would have been enormously difficult for any minister to change the framework, and to that extent we had great power.'

For a minister who does reach a decision at variance with the strongly-held views of his department, there are various ways which his officials may seek to obtain its reversal. One way is to wait for a change in ministers. The new minister may prove more amenable to the advice offered him and work within the framework of the brief supplied to him. Briefs may thus be used to refight lost battles. Another way is to brief officials in other departments to ensure that their ministers are primed to oppose the minister's decision. There is close contact between senior civil servants in Whitehall, both officially and unofficially. For every committee of ministers there is an equivalent committee of officials. Senior civil servants are usually members of the same Whitehall clubs. A Cabinet minister may arrive at Cabinet to find that other ministers, briefed by their officials, are hostile to his proposal. A third way is to leak something to the press as a means of undermining a minister's credibility or policy. In 1975, for instance, an accounting officer minute sent by Sir Peter Carey to his minister, Tony Benn, was leaked. The aim was to suggest that Mr Benn's support for industrial co-operatives was somehow improper.

It is thus not difficult to see how officials may determine the framework within which a minister decides matters and influence the decisions which he reaches. In this, they are aided by the anonymity which, as we have seen, is a corollary of the convention of ministerial responsibility. This anonymity is reinforced by the provisions of the Official Secrets Act which encompasses most official documents. If officials do wield undue influence over a minister, it cannot easily be detected by outsiders. Officials are shielded by anonymity and their documents protected from outside scrutiny.

To these various factors have been added three developments of recent years which, it has been argued, have further strengthened the position of civil servants in relation to their ministers. One, probably the most important, is British membership of the European Communities. This has had the effect of increasing substantially the burden of ministers' work. Major policy questions now have to be considered in the context of Europe and this entails regular visits to Brussels and consultations with one's continental colleagues. Furthermore, the harmonisation of a whole range of national policies made necessary by EEC membership has meant that there has to be much preparatory discussion between British civil servants and their European counterparts, both in Brussels and in the capitals of the other member states. A busy minister, arriving for a meeting of the Council of Ministers, is briefed, sometimes at the last minute, by his officials: it is obviously difficult for him to challenge their advice.

[from *The Constitution in Flux* by Philip Norton (Martin Robertson, 1982)]

Questions

1   Illustrate from C1 what Garrett means by the 'parliamentary ambience' of the British Civil Service. (C2)

2   Explain, giving reasons, why senior civil servants can be an important influence in determining departmental policies. (C1–3: see also C4, C5, C8)

3   Describe the weaknesses of the Fulton Report outlined in Garrett's article. (C2)

4   How do top civil servants regard their role? (C2)

5   Why has the Civil Service tended to favour the 'generalist' rather than the 'specialist' for senior posts? (C2)

6   Mention ways in which senior civil servants maintain contacts formally and informally. (C3)

7   Justify Norton's contention that civil servants can largely determine the content of the minister's political agenda. (C3)

Class Discussion

1   To what extent were the Fulton Committee recommendations implemented? (C2)
2   Which particular civil servants help ministers with information for Question Time and for policy decisions?

Extension Work

1   At what level, grade or section of the Civil Service would the following enter after their studies: (a) a person with four 'O' Levels; (b) a person with good grades in three 'A' levels; (c) a person with a second-class honours degree?
2   What were the functions of the Civil Service Department? Why, and when, was it abolished? (C2)
3   Outline the measures taken by Thatcher after 1979 to improve the overall efficiency and cost-effectiveness of the Civil Service.
4   Compare and contrast the various interpretations of minister–Civil Service relationships given in C1–3.

C4–C5   *Criticisms of the executive*

C4

The political establishment

The possibility of change lies in the hands of a small club: Britain's political establishment. I define this as the top 3000 civil servants and, for the Conservatives, an average of 300 to 400 Members of Parliament. The commentators, who try to interpret their thoughts and actions, are guests rather than members.

As in all ancient clubs, familiarity with rules and customs is important. What the members achieve matters less than how they behave. Good behaviour brings approval. For example, the club instinct will be to evaluate a lecture like this in terms of manners rather than argument. Among the political members, there is often a proprietorial feeling towards the country as a whole, almost as if it were an estate of which they were the benevolent owners. Thus one can still read, in quite recent books of memoirs, phrases like, 'Charles had always

wanted the Foreign Office', as though it were a 21st birthday present.

Not surprisingly, in a club whose prestige has sunk over the past 30 years, fear is a powerful influence on the thinking of many of its members: fear of exclusion; fear of looking foolish; of breaking the rules; of setting a precedent; fear of anything which diminishes the importance of their present expertise. An example of this institutional timidity is the officials' fear of having their advice rejected by ministers. When advice is accepted, you score a mark. If it is rejected, you lose face. So the official either seeks to get his way by guile, or he tailors his advice to suit his minister.

I believe that fear is the reason why *most* top officials are reluctant — whatever they say to the contrary — to allow outsiders into Whitehall, unless they are in very small numbers, with very limited powers and, if possible, of mild disposition. It is significant that scientists in government — probably the only officials who have been consciously trained to think at all — should be excluded from the top policy jobs. This is part of an important pigeon-holing convention, whereby only the generalist is eligible for everything. This rule was, I assume, devised by generalists. A similar fear shows itself in Westminster. Mr Edmund Dell, a senior ex-member of the club, has spoken of 'the jealousy and inflexibility of the Commons which, contrary to the practice of many other parliamentary assemblies, will not allow a "stranger" to address it'. It is clubland indeed.

Whitehall and Westminster still enjoy a powerful mystique. Senior industrialists feel awed and flattered when invited into the corridors of power. They comment on the officials' command of language, their clarity of exposition. They never realise that these mandarins are not thinking aloud. They are rehearsing, probably for the hundredth time, departmental wisdom which may not have been questioned since they were young men. Their visitors are listening to actors, not thinkers. Thinking is less elegant work.

Despite our growing concern about the effectiveness of government, we still want to believe that at least the quality of Whitehall thinking is high. Even here, I am not so sure. There is great accumulated knowledge — at times, it seems, almost too much. But I believe that the internal dynamics of Westminster, Whitehall and Fleet Street have made second-rate thinking the establishment norm.

Mediocre thinking provides a useful defence for politicians against the stress of radicalism. It is most important that we learn to be on our guard against it. A few examples:

'We tried that in 1974 and it didn't work.'

'We must be careful not to make the best the enemy of the good.'

'You know, governments can really do very little', a favourite with Conservatives who are not sure what to do next, though they are quite sure they want to form the next government.

And, of course: 'But where are all these people going to come from?', the classic objection to bringing more outsiders into Whitehall. Note that this difficulty is raised *before* considering whether or not the matter is important. In combination, such platitudes allow the establishment to stick to sloppy thinking about second order issues.

The process of intellectual deterioration has, I think, gone something like this. For reasons I will examine in a moment, the *general* calibre of ministers is normally low. Their irrelevant experience, coupled with the impossible burdens of office, have contributed to 30 years of policy failure. The Civil Service has been left with the job of damage limitation, of making ministers look better than they really are. In the process, like someone who only plays tennis with an inferior opponent, the quality of Whitehall's own game has declined. This has produced a general intellectual slackness in the political establishment. It is mirrored in Fleet Street, which is content to evaluate Westminster and Whitehall in Establishment terms, delighting in the leaks, games, intrigues, the coded messages, never asking whether the whole apparatus can really do the job. The thinking in this small world is now, I believe, shallow, conformist and lacking in rigour. With confidence and competence so much lower than they should be, it is not surprising that Whitehall fiercely defends its tradition of secrecy. The Official Secrets Act and the Thirty Year Rule, by hiding peacetime fiascos as though they were military disasters, protect ministers and officials from embarrassment. They also ensure that there is no learning curve.

It is important to anticipate correctly the response of club members to a critique of this kind. Any career institution — a large company, a trade union, a political party, the Civil Service — demands of its members an unquestioning (and thus potentially unhealthy) loyalty. There will therefore be a natural tendency to close ranks against criticism. There will also be a genuine and decent sense of mutual loyalty between people who have to work together on difficult and exhausting problems.

Thus we hear ministers insisting that 'We have the finest Civil Service in the world'. But what does such a statement actually mean? By what criteria do they judge the effectiveness of the Civil Service? Do their own careers give them any useful models for comparison? The truth is that, for most politicians, the Civil Service is the only large organisation of which they have any experience, and it looks pretty impressive to the untutored eye. It will have taught them most of what they know. Ministers therefore feel obliged to defend their officials against what they wrongly interpret as personal attacks. No doubt retired permanent secretaries stand ready to do the same for their erstwhile masters, should the need arise. None of this need worry us, provided we do not allow it to obscure the real issue — competence.

The politicians

Once we start to judge the Civil Service by criteria that mean anything, then it is time to judge the politicians likewise. I think that every discussion I have ever listened to, among civil servants or businessmen, about this country's problems, has come back, in the end, to the quality, competence and workload of ministers. For they are the only people who can reform government itself.

This is why the most important characteristic of the politician is his lack of innovative experience, by which I mean the conception of new ways of thinking; of making new things happen; of creating organisations for new purposes (rather than simply inheriting those that already exist). This is not surprising, because most of them become MPs too young to have had such experience in a position of primary responsibility. If he is also a Conservative, with the Party's traditional concern for continuity, a Member may not even recognise discontinuity, and the consequent need to innovate, when he sees them. But the innate conservatism of almost all MPs may at least help them to accept their peculiar working conditions and lifestyle.

For the British politician's job is certainly peculiar. He works very long hours, spending far more time in the debating chamber than his counterpart in other democracies. He receives no formal training. His administrative support is negligible. Even a member of the Shadow Cabinet works in an office not much larger than a public convenience, with a single secretary paid from party funds, and research facilities to match.

Although post-war government has been a growth industry, there is no growth in an MP's career prospects. The size of the Cabinet is fixed. The number of constituencies is almost fixed. If he is frustrated, he cannot leave and set up on his own. To a surprising extent, therefore, one man's success may depend on another's

failure. It is a zero-sum world.

If he becomes a minister, he suddenly takes on enormous responsibilities, for which he may well lack both experience and training. Being a *professional* politician turns out to mean being an *amateur* minister, who must move from one colossal and unfamiliar brief to another as he climbs, step by step, towards the summit. Inevitably, some of these briefs will not even hold any intrinsic interest for him, except as career stepping stones. Because the system is closed, one promotion may trigger a reshuffle, which must take account of debts and deals accumulated with many people over their careers. Portfolios are thus changed too often. The crippling workload will frequently impair health and marriage, for the minister must do it all — Cabinet and its committees, the department, public appearances, attendance in the House — on top of his existing work as a constituency MP. Under the doctrine of collective responsibility, a Cabinet Minister is also expected to read and understand papers about his colleagues' work as well as his own. [. . .]

The essential changes

I do not believe that these antique conventions, culture and machinery, which failed us between 1950 and 1980, will somehow succeed between 1980 and 2000. Since the price of failure will be high, we should think hard before shrugging our shoulders and hoping for the best. My analysis is intended to persuade you of the need for changes in four areas. First, the Prime Minister should no longer be restricted to the small pool of career politicians in Westminster in forming a government. Secondly, Whitehall must be organised for strategy and innovation, as well as for day-to-day political survival. Thirdly, it must be possible to bring adequate numbers of high quality outsiders into the Civil Service. Fourthly, the workload on ministers must be reduced.

None of these four proposals is particularly novel. Nor are they options, from which we can select the least 'controversial', on traditional Whitehall lines. They form a minimum package necessary if government is to develop the competence needed to match its responsibilities. They should form part of a larger agenda, which should similarly be examined as a whole, not as a menu from which we can pick and choose.

That larger agenda might include such items as the financing of political parties; the doctrine of collective responsibility (which has been powerfully criticised by Mr Edmund Dell, on the basis of personal experience); and, of course, the vexed question of electoral reform.

[from 'Conservatism is not enough' by Sir John Hoskyns (*Political Quarterly*, Vol. 55, No. 1, January – March 1984)]

The master servants

'Tis mad idolatry
To make the service greater than the god.

Shakespeare, *Troilus and Cressida*

The British political system embraces three 'Cabinets' — the real one that meets at 10 Downing Street every Thursday when Parliament is sitting, and sometimes on Tuesdays as well; the 'Shadow' one, which meets every Wednesday evening in the Leader of the Opposition's rooms at the House of Commons and hopefully understudies for the day when it will take the stage; and the one that very few people outside Whitehall know anything about, that composed of the permanent secretaries of the Civil Service. This committee of heads of departments, the highest grade of civil servants, meets each week to discuss the business which will come before Cabinet and whether — and if so, how — ministers will be advised on that business.

If the Whitehall machine has a collective 'line' on policy, and it often does, it is at these meetings that it will emerge. A busy minister who requires to know the basic arguments on a particular question which might not fall within his responsibility — the Secretary of State for Defence, say, may want to take part in a discussion about invalid cars for the disabled — may well be briefed by a permanent secretary who has already had a pre-Cabinet discussion about it with *his* colleagues. In which case the briefing will favour the conclusion which the responsible department — in the instance I have cited, Health and Social Security — would like the Cabinet to reach.

The function of the permanent secretaries' meeting is similar to that of the Pathfinder aircrews during the 1939–45 war: to illuminate the target for the main force which is to follow. There have been occasions, however, when they have demonstrated an anxiety to camouflage the target rather than to expose it.

Together with the Steering Committee on Economic Policy and a group known as the 'depsecs', the permanent secretaries' meeting is at the heart of the network of official committees which formulate the advice and guidance the Cabinet receives from the civil service.

The SCEP is composed largely of senior Treasury officials, a representative of the Bank of England and a few others. Their decisions — and they are more like decisions than recommendations — are crucial to the economic success of the country and therefore to the political success of the Government. Their secretiveness is of the 'destroy before reading' variety and they keep very much to themselves.

Chairman of the 'depsecs' — the deputy secretaries of the Cabinet Office, plus the Prime Minister's principal private secretary — is the Secretary of the Cabinet, a post held for most of Edward Heath's premiership, the whole of Harold Wilson's third and fourth administrations and into Jim Callaghan's first administration by Sir John Hunt. In terms of power, he made the Secretary of the Cabinet the most significant figure in the civil service; more than the Head of the Civil Service himself and certainly more so than the head of the Treasury, who lost ground.

The growing strength of the Cabinet Office under Sir John caused tension to develop between it and the Treasury, which is not accustomed to having its ascendancy questioned. But when the leaders of the six most important western industrialised states met near Paris in November 1975, it had been Sir John Hunt who had attended the preparatory meetings on Britain's behalf and not a Treasury man. The Cabinet Office may yet fulfil the function which Harold Wilson conceived for the Department of Economic Affairs in 1964: to be an alternative source of power to the Treasury. The danger then would be that the Cabinet Office would become too powerful. There were signs of that in the 1974–6 period. The Office not only co-ordinated policy at the highest level, which is its function, but also showed strong desires to originate it.

[from *The Politics of Power* by Joe Haines (Jonathan Cape, 1977)]

Questions

1 Explain the meaning of the following: (a) 'political establishment'; (b) 'generalist'; (c) 'Fleet Street'; (d) 'Whitehall'; (e) 'zero-sum world'. (C4)

2 Give examples to justify the observation of Hoskyns concerning the 'impossible burdens of office' for a minister. (C4)

3 How does Hoskyns explain the fact that a minister often has little time to get to know a department and to understand its problems? (C4)

4 Summarise Hoskyns' main criticisms concerning senior civil servants and ministers. (C4)

5 How does Hoskyns suggest that most ministers have had limited practical experience outside the world of politics? (C4)

6 Describe briefly Britain's three so-called Cabinets. (C6)

7 Discuss the importance and influence on ministers of official committees. (C5)

Class Discussion

1 Do ministers really have 'irrelevant experience' for the tasks they undertake? Cite actual cases. (C4)

2 How realistic are the reform proposals of Hoskyns in C4, notably as regards the selection of the Prime Minister? In what ways could the workload on ministers be reduced?

3 Why do senior civil servants develop a 'collective "line"' of thinking on certain policies? (C5)

Extension Work

1 Give details of Part II of the Official Secrets Act and the Thirty Year Rule. To what extent do they impede the development of open government?

2 List the economic functions of the Treasury.

3 What is the origin of the term 'portfolio' as applied to ministers and departments?

C6 – C8　　　　　　　*Open government: three views*

C6

Ministers and civil servants

In theory civil servants are the non-partisan advisers to ministers; they are servants of the State rather than mere servants of transient governments. If Civil Service advice is to be heeded by ministers then its credibility, in the form of neutrality, is believed by officials to be of crucial importance. Hence, the defenders of Whitehall secrecy maintain that confidential advice is essential to ensure that civil servants do not become too closely identified with the policies of any particular minister or Cabinet. Another argument in favour of closed Whitehall deliberation is that more 'rational' policies will be made behind closed doors. Freed from public scrutiny, and pressure, 'wise men cogitating quietly on the nation's problems, will produce "right" answers'[1]. By this argument secret government becomes synonymous with good government.

Secrecy and neutrality are thus at the core of the normative system in Whitehall. A value system, moreover, which supposedly supports 'good' government. But in an era of rapid economic decline, mass unemployment and recurring policy failure, British government does not appear to be all that 'good'. Reasons for such failure are many and varied but many politicians and commentators are convinced that 'closed' government exacerbates policy failure. Those holding this view, especially those not in government, identify the ability of civil servants to foreclose ministerial choice through the manipulation of information as a means whereby consideration of radical options can be excluded. Their basic case for greater openness is that by making public Civil Service advice, and so setting this advice within the context of a more comprehensive range of alternatives, the capacity of officials to manipulate ministers would be lessened.

Yet politicians in government, including Labour Party members, have consistently frustrated the cause of open government. The 1979–83 Conservative government was no exception to this rule (see *Yearbook, 1982*). Nonetheless, in January 1983, the Government did commission a review of the degree of openness which had followed in the wake of the Croham directive (a Whitehall statement made in 1977 to the effect that factual background papers to policy decisions should be made generally available). This limited review was but a pin-prick in the cloak of Whitehall secrecy.

Indeed, rather than undermine the political advantages to be gained from secrecy, in particular the ability to deflect ill-intentioned partisan criticism, the Conservative Government sought to secure 'better' advice from its official advisers; 'better' in the sense of being attuned and committed to Mrs Thatcher's ideological predilections. To this end rapid promotion has been secured for those officials seen to be in the image of Mrs Thatcher. In 1982 it became clear that the PM was exercising her powers as the head of the Civil Service personally to select senior officials. By convention past PMs have simply followed official advice on who should be included on the shortlist for vacant permanent secretary and deputy secretary posts. [. . .]

The PM's expressed confidence in her new appointees stimulated speculation that such praise would merely taint these officials in the eye of a future Labour government. Mr John Silkin, as Shadow Leader of the House of Commons, did nothing to quell such speculation. Instead, in a statement of policy representing the views of Labour's frontbench issued in Novem-

ber 1982, he openly stated that 'creatures of Mrs Thatcher's ideology would have to fall with the fall of that ideology'. Although not threatening a witchhunt of permanent secretaries, Silkin did emphasise that recently appointed officials would have to satisfy a 'test of impartiality'. (A similar test would also be extended to other Thatcher appointees — including Robin Leigh-Pemberton, the new Governor of the Bank of England[2].) The irony of these statements is that for long enough leading Labour MPs have advocated the need for a stronger 'political' input into Whitehall. Their preferred solution, however, would be the appointment of more political advisers and the creation of ministerial *cabinets* outside the Civil Service career hierarchy. [. . .]

Select Committees and information

'The ability to obtain information is basic to Select Committee operations', proclaimed the Liaison Committee in its report on the general operation of the new departmental Select Committee system. In general the Liaison Committee (which is comprised of the chairmen of Select Committees) concluded that 'all the Committees have, to varying degrees, been able to establish a right to be kept informed by their departments'. Supporters of these Committees take this flow of information to be one of their principal benefits. Yet as noted in *Yearbook, 1982* and confirmed by the Liaison Committee, the power of Committees to extract information from Whitehall departments is limited in a number of ways.

One limitation is the convention of ministerial responsibility itself. This convention, in theory, forges a clear chain of responsibility both within the departments of State and between Whitehall and Westminster. Hence, civil servants are responsible to ministers for their actions and in turn ministers, both individually and collectively, are accountable to Parliament. But at the heart of this convention is a contradiction; that ministerial responsibility to Parliament rests upon internal secrecy in Whitehall[3]. As noted earlier, 'advice to ministers' is deemed by this convention to be confidential, and on this basis information about this advice has been denied to Committees. One convoluted example of this denial came in 1982 when Sir Keith Joseph upheld the right of a Chief Inspector of Schools (Miss Sheila Brown) to refuse to provide the names of local authorities criticised in a HMI report. The grounds for refusal were first, that the information provided by the local authorities to the inspectorate was confidential, and second, that advice from HMIs to the minister was also secret.

But a more general limitation upon the ability of Select Committees to obtain information was revealed in the Education and Arts Committee's investigation into the release of public documents and the extension of classification of official papers beyond the normal period of 30 years. In April 1983, Sir Robert Armstrong (Secretary to the Cabinet) refused to appear before the Committee to answer questions on the criteria for the classification of secret documents. In a letter, dated 21 February 1983, the Leader of the House of Commons had pointed out to the Chairman of the Committee that the terms of reference of Select Committees did not extend to 'the practice or administration of the Cabinet Office', and hence it would be inappropriate for the Cabinet Secretary or any member of his staff to give evidence. The Committee did, however, manage to press Mr Biffen into allowing two junior officials from the Cabinet Office to appear before it to answer questions on routine aspects on non-intelligence record keeping. On the issue of parliamentary investigation of the intelligence services the Government was altogether more resolute. In March 1983 the Home Secretary pronounced that it 'would not be appropriate for MPs to investigate the organisation of the security services'[4]. This view was shared by the Conservative majority on the Home Affairs Committee which blocked Alfred Dubs' (Labour, Battersea South) call for the Committee to investigate the operations of MI5 and MI6.

[1] Peter Kellner and Lord Crowther-Hunt, *The Civil Servants*, Macdonald 1980.
[2] *Observer*, 9 January 1983.
[3] David Judge, 'Select Committees and Ministerial Responsibility', *Teaching Politics*, Vol. 12, No. 2, 1983.
[4] *Guardian*, 18 March 1983.

[from *Modern Studies Association Yearbook, 1983*]

C7

Frankly, they'll only ever tell us as much as they want to

by Andrew Alexander

FOR those who enjoy that sort of thing, the row in the Labour Party over the Government's hesitant amendment of the Official Secrets Act is rich with irony.

Mr Rees, Home Secretary, regrets the Government cannot fulfil its 1975 pledge about a new Act; and regrets too, that he can only promise limited change to the present Act — and not even in this session.

But he is, he insists, keenly in favour of more open government.

Very well, then, would he publish the background documents to this decision, in keeping with his own protestation and in keeping with Mr Callaghan's promise last year that the Government would publish more background material?

Mr Rees's passion for openness promptly evaporated like spit on a hot stove. He doesn't think there are any such documents, he says, only judgements.

Now this really is pretty disingenuous. Seven top civil servants, headed by the Secretary to the Cabinet, have been meeting as a special committee on this topic for two years.

Are we seriously asked to believe that (contrary to all the traditions of the Whitehall paperchase) they have worked without notes, minutes, submissions or memoranda?

Invasion of privacy

Did these great men carry all the information and the arguments in their heads for two years? What polymaths they must be!

But next time, adds an anxious Mr Rees, when the civil servants study the American and Swedish Information Acts — why, then, it may well be possible to collect and publish the background notes. Ah, next time . . . next time . . .

Nor does the irony stop there. In response to MPs who were worried about government departments giving secrets about British Nationals to foreign governments, Mr Rees made indignant noises at the very idea.

Yet this year's Finance Bill, for which he voted, empowers the Government to pass on information about a person's tax and income to other Common Market governments.

In other words, the minister responsible for individual privacy has not even found out that another government department is invading personal privacy in a most unprecedented way. For, normally, the Inland Revenue is not even allowed to pass information to other government departments.

It would be easy to draw the conclusion from the first item that Mr Rees is simply hypocritical. But that would not really be fair. The trouble lies in the naive assumption that open government is possible, let alone desirable.

Indeed, open government is a virtual contradiction in terms. Only schoolboys imagine that when ministers meet they discuss policy in serenely objective terms. On the contrary, those in government do almost everything with an eye to staying in government.

That, whether you like it or not, is the real world.

In deciding whether to take such and such a decision, ministers talk about matters like the proximity of an election, the danger of upsetting the unions or employers, the need to soothe foreign exchange markets, the need to dish the Opposition, and so on.

The various Civil Service papers they have in front of them, which may describe the technical options, only make sense in conjunction with the political deliberations.

Waste of paper

Mr Benn's Industry Department has taken to publishing documents about fuel policy. They are a great waste of paper. If you really want to know what Mr Benn will do, you must look at the political power of the mineworkers, the Minister's personal ambitions, the Cabinet's view about power strikes, and so on.

None of these, under any administration, is going to be written down for current publication.

An ultimate illustration of the absurdity of open government was provided by President Carter (well, it would be wouldn't it?).

In the interests of the 'open government' which he had promised, he let the TV cameras into a Cabinet meeting.

What then took place, of course, was anything but a Cabinet meeting. Everything that mattered or was difficult was postponed for more private moments.

That is just the sort of thing which would happen if the publication of current internal government papers became automatic official policy.

Too much information

Civil servants would write with an eye to publication; and they would minute each other's memoranda with extreme caution, using the telephone to tell each other which remarks should be taken seriously.

Above all, ministers — who are not exactly inexperienced in the matter of propaganda — would write all documents with a careful eye on publication, excising the controversial items and inserting anything that was considered vote winning.

Documents from Number 11 to Number 10 Downing Street would be accompanied by covering notes which might read something like this:

Dear Jim,

Enclosed is the economic plan and forecast you called for. I have kept in mind that it may be published. So I should explain.

1. The rate of inflation used is the most optimistic one. For your own calculations, add 50 per cent.

2. You can skip the long bits about the cure for unemployment. They are there to keep the lads quiet.

3. The passage about the long-term strength of sterling has been inserted, as you suggested, to cheer up the City and Harold Lever.

4. For the real balance of payments outlook, give me a ring.

Edna sends her regards.

Denis.

If you think I am kidding then you should read the Crossman Diaries to see how politicians are liable to doctor things when they are to be published —not least, in the Crossman case, immigration statistics.

In the fashionable call for more open government — and it is a fashion, just as 'participation' was once all the rage — one should not overlook the danger of an excess of so-called information. It is as bad to be choked as starved.

Now that Mr Benn is publishing all that information about fuel policy, do you really feel more involved or informed? No, because you probably do not have the time or inclination to read all the documents.

Mr Rees himself would seem to exemplify the problem in his ignorance of that clause in the Finance Bill. A reasonable conclusion is, quite simply, that Mr Rees has so much information pouring in and out of the Home Office that he cannot keep up with it.

But if the flow of information is already too much for a conscientious minister, then it is certainly daunting for a private individual.

If these comments appear partisan, they are not intended to be. For, alas, open government is a bipartisan policy.

In 1969 Mr Heath promised to

'throw open the window' in Whitehall in office. Of course, he did no such thing. The trouble is that open government is one of those fool's gold catch phrases (again like 'participation' and 'devolution'): it glitters, it is attractive so long as unexamined.

And if one side declares itself in favour of open government, the other side responds not by asking what it means but by claiming that it thought of it first.

And that is how much of the idiocy in current British politics starts.

[from the *Daily Mail*, 21 July 1978]

C8

Who are the masters now?

Anthony Shrimsley

In any normal year anything between two and a dozen or more government ministers are likely to be sacked.

The reasons will vary from incompetence to a failure to toe the government line, or the simple aversion of the Prime Minister of the day to the face of the politician concerned.

When did you last hear of a top civil servant receiving the same treatment?

The question is of increasing importance as yet another Premier struggles both to reduce the size of the Civil Service and to persuade that service to put government policies into effect.

For even as ministers try to run the country, as they were elected to do, it becomes daily more apparent that the Civil Service, which is supposed to carry out their orders, is as big an obstacle to success as either the unions or the parliamentary Opposition at Westminster.

To put it bluntly, there are too many senior people in Whitehall who regard it as their role to tailor the policy of the government of the day to the policy of their department.

They see it as their job not simply to serve ministers with advice and action but to 'train' their masters into right and proper paths. [. . .]

In following this course of action they are protected by a valid but now much abused convention that the Civil Service is non-political and totally objective.

The mandarins are also protected from the consequence of their policies by being virtually immune from dismissal and heavily insulated against the economic hardships which they help inflict on the rest of the population.

Indeed the Civil Service, now more than ever, has its own departmental policies which it attempts with considerable success to impose upon ministers.

It also tends to operate not as a service but as an industrial pressure group seeking constantly to protect the power of its leaders and the job opportunities within its ranks.

I am moved to these seemingly harsh strictures by two events.

The first is the publication of guidance approved by the head of the Home Civil Service, Sir Ian Bancroft, to senior civil servants likely to be summoned to give evidence to the 12 new Commons Select Committees which will examine the work of government departments.

The second is a shallow but nonetheless informative book* by ex-MP Brian Sedgemore who has been both a civil servant himself and a highly political aide to the former Energy Secretary Tony Benn.

Sir Ian's view is that the Civil Service should be 'as helpful as possible' to the Commons committees, withholding only information which would inhibit good government or national security.

The definition, however, turns out to be a catch-all for anything the civil servants wish kept from MPs.

It rules out information on exchanges between departments on policy issues, advice to ministers, facts about the way decisions were taken and — most laughable of all — questions 'in the field of political controversy.'

In other words, Sir Ian Bancroft regards it as the duty of civil servants to withhold from the House of Commons precisely the kind of information which would enable MPs to make the committees effective.

There is even a hint that, because MPs would protest at being refused information which is available to a Whitehall committee on which outside experts are involved, the existence of such committees should be kept as quiet as possible. [. . .]

The arrogance of this advice is breathtaking. It suggests a Civil Service now almost totally suffused with the idea that the government of Britain is a professional closed shop in which ministers may have to be temporarily tolerated but Parliament is just an interfering nuisance.

If Sir Ian Bancroft really thinks that this is the way the Civil Service ought to operate he should be summoned before Lord Soames, who is alleged to be the Cabinet Minister responsible for the Civil Service, and be ordered to withdraw the advice.

Mr Sedgemore argues that there is a 'Secret Constitution' in which a small number of senior ministers, headed by the Prime Minister, carve up power with the civil servants, top industrialists, trade unionists and scientists. These, he says, 'make up the Establishment'. He then produces many interesting examples, mostly from his time as parliamentary private secretary to Tony Benn, of Civil Service secrecy and deviousness and the manipulation of ministerial policy.

What is really needed is a Civil Service which gives ministers advice as well as loyalty but regards its first duty as the implementation of government policies even at the expense of its own self-interest.

Once upon a time, we had just that.

[from *NOW!*, 30 May 1980]

* *The Secret Constitution* (Hodder and Stoughton)

Questions

1   What is the basic case mentioned in C6 for greater openness in government?

2   What reason is suggested for the appointment of 'more political advisers'? (C6)

3   Explain how 'the convention of ministerial responsibility' can frustrate the work of the parliamentary Select Committees. (C6)

4   What arguments are put forward in C6 for suggesting that closed or secret government is synonymous with good government?

5   Briefly explain the purpose of the Croham directive. (C6)

6   Why does Alexander think that 'open government is not really feasible or desirable'? (C7)

Class Discussion

1   For what reasons might leaks of government information occur? Mention some of the leaks which have taken place since 1980. (See B4)

2   Could it be argued that Alexander has presented a one-sided view of the case for open government and less secrecy in politics?

3　'[The mandarins] are protected by a valid but now much abused convention that the Civil Service is non-political and totally objective'. (C8) In a political sense can conventions be distinguished from doctrines or principles? Explain why the Civil Service should be non-political and objective, and also how the convention has been abused.

4　Comment on whether, in the interests of good or open government, Sir Ian Bancroft is right or not to issue guidance of this sort to senior civil servants. (C8)

5　How likely is it that a 'secret constitution' exists as depicted by Sedgemore? (C8)

Extension Work

1　Under what circumstances are democratic governments justified in withholding information from the press and public?

2　List the traditional merits claimed for the Civil Service. Do they still apply today?

3　How would you define 'open' and 'closed' government?

4　Argue a case both for and against a Freedom of Information Act, broadly based on legislation introduced already in Sweden and the United States.

Section
D

Parliament and MPs

Introduction

D1 and D3 focus on the role and importance of the House of Commons. *The Economist* (D3) employs a racy journalistic style in its particularly provocative and critical analysis of the Commons; compare its views in A2 of British government in general. Barker's 'Commons Sketch' (D2) provides a brief glimpse into both the workings and happenings of the House, and the lighter side of politics. D1 and D3 refer to Edward du Cann's remark in 1977 that the House of Commons had lost effective control of public expenditure. This matter of public funds is one of continuing concern. In July 1984, the Public Accounts Committee severely criticised ministers and officials under Conservative and Labour governments for having squandered, or at best ineptly managed, some £70 million of taxpayers' money invested in the De Lorean Motor Company in Northern Ireland.

The author of *Westminster Man*, from which D4 provides a short extract, became Labour MP for Grimsby in April 1977. He failed in 1983 with his Quadrennial Parliaments Bill to introduce fixed-term Parliaments for four years, an attempt to take away a Prime Minister's power to decide when to hold a general election.

Usually a particularly lively moment during Question Time is the period reserved for the Prime Minister on Tuesdays and Thursdays, when he or she replies to general questions which do not fall under the responsibility of specific ministers. D5 provides an extract from a Prime Minister's Diary Question. D6 and D7 focus on the work and problems of MPs, and D8 gives some of the reasons why there are so few female MPs (nineteen in the 1979 parliament and twenty-three in 1983).

D9A and D9B provide statistical information concerning the composition of the House of Commons, in terms of the backgrounds and occupations of MPs. Increasingly, they come from managerial or professional occupations and are university graduates (some 433 out of a total of 635 in 1979). Class divisions between parties were far more noticeable before the Second World War, when most Labour MPs came from the working class, and aristocrats, big landowners and Etonians formed an important section of the Conservative Party's MPs. Before 1945 Heath and Thatcher would have had only a slim chance of becoming Conservative MPs, let alone leaders of the party, because of their modest backgrounds. Today three-quarters of Conservative Members still come from the public schools and Oxbridge, while Labour Members usually come from State schools and redbrick universities. In general MPs tend to be drawn today from the middle classes, and especially from among lawyers, company directors, teachers and trade union officials, occupations which fit in with a political career. These groups form a large part of the 10–15 per cent of the population that participates actively in politics.

D10 and D11 provide two contrasting opinions on the value of a second House. In 1982 Benn suggested the abolition of the House of Lords by the creation of 1000 Labour 'kamikaze' peers, whose job it would be to vote the House of Lords out of existence. D11, however, suggests that since the 1983 election the Lords has gained in popularity and importance.

THE CASE FOR A STRONGER PARLIAMENT

IMPROVING THE EFFECTIVENESS OF THE
LEGISLATURE

RICHARD HORNBY

Traditional roles of Parliament

TRADITIONALLY the main roles of Parliament have been fourfold: to give or withhold supply of funds requested by the government; to approve, amend or reject legislation; to act as a forum of public debate, whereby the electorate can be kept informed and the government can be questioned and criticised; and lastly, to provide the recruiting ground from which ministers are chosen. In all these four areas there are well-substantiated doubts about the current ability of Parliament to function efficiently.

During the post-war years the scale of government activity has immensely increased and government expenditure has grown in proportion. As a result the task of scrutinising this expenditure has become larger and more complex. What have not grown to the same extent are the parliamentary time, resources and expertise needed to carry out this task. True, the Public Accounts Committee works efficiently, the Expenditure Committee has a larger role and more staff, albeit still too small, than in the past, and the government's budgets and Finance Bills receive a substantial amount of time in the chamber of the House of Commons. Even so, there is a lack of adequate information on which Parliament can form a considered view, and when information is forthcoming it is frequently too late to enable policy to be influenced or the government checked in its stride. The current chairman of the Public Accounts Committee has stated his view that the House of Commons has lost its control of public expenditure, and it is widely agreed both amongst MPs of all parties and outside Parliament that the government and Civil Service can get away with murder.

The same problems arise in the field of legislation. Until recent months, when the loss of its overall majority in the House of Commons diminished the government's appetite for controversial new measures, the quantity of legislation has steadily grown, and the machinery for examining it has creaked under the strain. The procedure whereby bills are normally referred after Second Reading to a standing committee is not, as at present operated, a satisfactory one. The aim of the government is invariably to get its legislation through the Committee stage with the minimum of amendment and the minimum of delay. The aim of the Opposition, more often than not, is to frustrate the passage of bills for as long as possible, either because they dislike their content or because they see other obnoxious measures in the pipeline, whose progress can be impeded by the denial of time to the government. This battle for time does nothing to improve the quality of debate in Committee. On the government side backbenchers are frequently reminded by their party Whips, one of whom is always a member of the Committee, that silence is golden and speeches waste valuable time. On the Opposition side the reverse is the case, and the more speeches the merrier is usually the order of the day. Furthermore, if by some mischance the government is defeated in Committee, there remains the opportunity to reverse that decision at Report stage in the chamber of the House of Commons. In these circumstances, and bearing in mind that the composition of standing committees is related to the strength of parties in the whole House and that individual selections within parties can be influenced by the Whips Office, it is scarcely surprising to read in Professor J.A.G. Griffith's *Parliamentary Scrutiny of Government Bills* that in three sessions of Parliament 906 out of 907 government amendments moved in standing committee were accepted while only 171 out of 3520 other amendments became law.

Keeping the public informed

As a forum of public enquiry and debate Parliament still serves an important and central purpose. The very fact that all legislation and government policy statements have to be presented to Parliament makes this so; so too does the right of the Opposition to decide what should be the subject of debate on a limited number of days, together with the opportunities available to individual members at Question Time and through short Adjournment debates at the end of each day. But these opportunities by themselves are not enough. The difficulty of obtaining detailed information about the implications of government policy makes it hard for questions to be pursued in any depth. The best that can usually be done is to alert the press gallery and through them the public that the government's case is not necessarily the whole story, nor the right course to follow. But at the end of the debate, whatever doubts have been expressed, the odds are that party discipline in the government ranks will hold firm, and the public will have received one more impression that party warfare rather than scrutiny of policy is the main preoccupation of Parliament; an impression which may well have been further emphasised by the tenor and content of the front bench speeches and the behaviour of the rival 'supporters' clubs' behind them.

A further reason for the decline of Parliament as the national forum of debate is the growth of television coupled with Parliament's own continuing refusal to be televised. At the root of the refusal of the House of Commons has lain the fear that bringing in the cameras would change Parliament's performance and influence for the worse. The objectors fear, for instance, that television would encourage MPs to address the outside audience rather than their fellow members, that it would encourage theatricality and that it would, by the inevitably selective nature of the programmes, give a distorted and incomplete picture of the work of Parliament. Some would further argue that through television Parliament would be given an importance which it no longer deserves when real power and influence on the decisions of ministers has slipped away in other corridors of power in Whitehall, the trade union movement or even the mass media itself.

If there was general satisfaction with the role that Parliament is currently playing, it would be tempting to accept these objections. In fact, there is not. Parliament is already felt to be too remote from the public and too little heeded by the government. An important step towards the restoration of its influence as the go-between for people and government would be to place its own workings, warts and all, back in the mainstream of the communications industry, as it once did by admitting the press, as it is about to do by permitting sound broadcasting, and as it should go on to do by being televised.

[from *The Round Table*, No. 269, January 1978]

Richard Crossman: "Tony, you really shouldn't get so drunk when you're going into the House".
Anthony Crosland: "How else is one to endure being here?"
(Quoted by Susan Crosland in Tony Crosland*)*

REQUEST STOP FOR HASTY BUS BILL

By GODFREY BARKER

KINGS govern by popular assemblies only when they cannot do without them, raged Charles James Fox at George III.

Fox never knew Mr Nicholas Ridley, the Transport Secretary. Nick and George have a lot in common, he would agree.

As an autocrat, though, George's hallmark was haughtiness. Mr Ridley's is irony and elegiac shambles.

With Mrs Thatcher out of the country, chaos (as normal) broke out in the Commons.

Mr Ridley blew up a first class constitutional crisis about the arrogance of the Executive. MPs of all parties accused him of trampling on the cherished backbench privileges which, since 1689, have stood between you, me and the dark night of Fascism.

Village Hampdens rose in clouds of protest. Mr Enoch Powell, playing Hampden in person, gave it all dignity. It lasted three hours.

Gasping for cash

The day began with Mr Ridley facing his usual choice between the disastrous and the unpalatable. On form, he opted for disaster.

London Transport, it emerged, will be broke by the end of February. Mr Ridley has a Bill to hand to rush it £50m. Its Second Reading went through on Tuesday night amid high farce about the 77 bus, Mornington Crescent and the Deputy Speaker nodding off.

LT, therefore, is gasping for cash. There are only 28 days in February. Today is the 21st. This Bill has still to go through the Lords as well.

Mr Ridley, with an eye on the Hackney bus garage paypackets running dry, had already persuaded the Opposition to the unusual course of storming the Bill through Committee, Report and Third Reading today. That was lucky. Yesterday he decided to go a bit too far.

His opportunity arose when, by 'a spectacular cock-up' (Mr Dennis Skinner) in the Environment Department, Commons business for the day fell suddenly vacant.

The Transport Secretary, unlike angels, rushed in. He moved his desperately urgent Bus Transfusion Bill a day forward. Over, now, to Mr Brian Sedgemore, the lugubrious Labour lefty for Hackney.

'I left the House at 3.30 a.m.', he intoned gloomily.

'I was drained of nervous energy and physical stamina, Mr Speaker. I was like a nervous rag. I got up at 5.30 a.m. to read Hansard on this Bill so I could put down amendments.

As ever the telephone rang. Then I had to do my box. Then the papers. Then the phone again.'

Sedgemore began to groan. 'I haven't had a second since to study amendments or put anything down on the Committee stage of a controversial Bill I hadn't even seen.' He went ashen. 'It's too much, Mr Speaker — even for a man of my capacity.

'It's the sort of thing', he reeled and staggered, 'that makes an MP *snap!*'

The Speaker suggested graciously that he and Sedgemore take a cup of tea together. The MP for Hackney begged a rock cake.

What emerged, as MPs wept for their stricken lot, was that a serious constitutional principle was under threat.

Bills have stages separated by intervals which allow for consultation outside the Commons, for reflection and for placing reasoned amendments by backbenchers.

Deeply embarrassed

If a Bill finishes at 3 a.m. and the Treasury bench rams it on to its next stage at 3.30 p.m., the interval is telescoped into farce.

Mr Powell allowed that in national emergency, the House had rushed through legislation in this way. But Mr Ridley's problems were not of national urgency.

Mr Ridley and a deeply embarrassed Mr John Biffen, Leader of the House, tried to smoothe, flatter and appease.

In the end Mr Biffen as good as said he loathed the measure but that Mr Ridley had a gun at his head. The placemen passed it 256–180.

'History teaches that men and women behave wisely only after they have exhausted all other options' (Abba Eban).

[from the *Daily Telegraph*, 27 February 1985]

Questions

1 List the four traditional roles of Parliament, as understood by Hornby. (D1)

2 Explain why Hornby doubts that Parliament can now perform these functions efficiently. (D1)

3 What details do D1 and D2 give concerning the procedure for passing Bills in the House of Commons?

4 Why does Hornby state that Parliament cannot fully perform its role as a forum of public debate? (D1)

5 What can you gather from D1 and D2 is the role and importance of the Opposition in the House of Commons? (See also D3.)

Class Discussion

1 Present a case both for and against the introduction of television broadcasting into the House of Commons.

2 How apt is the quotation from Abba Eban as a comment on part of the proceedings in the Commons on 26 February 1985? (D2)

Extension Work

1 Suggest at least one important reason why monarchs before the age when the supremacy of democracy was accepted needed to govern for at least part of the time with the support of a popular assembly or parliament. (D2)

2 Explain what Barker means by the following: (a) 'cherished backbench privileges'; (b) 'village Hampdens'; (c) 'placemen'. (D2)

3 Mention an important Bill which was rushed through Parliament in one half-day at the outbreak of the Second World War.

D3–D5   *Defects and shifts of power in the parliamentary system*

D3

Blowing up a tyranny

A century ago Britain's system of government was the envy of two-thirds of the world, and the overlord of much of the other one-third. Today the Mother of Parliaments is kitchen maid to two alternating party political tyrannies, neither of which is ever elected by, or represents, a majority of the British people.

Guy Fawkes was discovered 372 years ago before he could blow king and parliament up. Today he would be right to try again — to renew a democracy this time rather than a religion. [. . .]

Within the limits of British poverty, any British Prime Minister with a working majority in the House of Commons has unfettered executive power beyond an American president's dreams. He, his Cabinet and other ministerial colleagues all sit as Members of Parliament. The government — any government — with some 320 or more members on its side nominates about 85 of these MPs as ministers and another 25 as unpaid parliamentary private secretaries. The opposition produces its own list of Shadow ministers and the aim of all ambitious MPs is to join the executive.

All MPs vote with their party because to do otherwise excites disfavour, because of constituency party pressure and because they went to Parliament not primarily as local men — most of them are carpetbaggers — but to maintain their party in power. This almost absolute power in the hands of government is exercised through paid 'Whips' whose job it is to drive all members of their party, regardless of conscience or preference, through the 'division lobbies' on the government's side. Cattle were never so driven.

If anyone disobeys (beginning to be a slightly less infrequent event), the Whip can be withdrawn — which can mean that the seat in Parliament is also withdrawn at the next election. There is virtually no 'House of Commons feeling'; that is, no sense of being a corporate body, not just a partisan one, with interests that may be opposed to the government of the day. [. . .]

Because it has this almost automatic majority, the government has gained virtually total control of the house. There is not in Britain's Parliament any method for defending the citizen against the power of the executive sitting in its midst. (And outside it the ombudsman is not a strong reed.) A great test of the freedom and power of any legislature is whether it can control its own timetable and whether it can extract information from the executive. In the case of the House of Commons, in each instance, the answer is 'No'. Nowadays the standing orders of the House are put through by the government's majority.

This was not always so. The deterioration set in during the last decades of the nineteenth century, culminating in the series of standing orders introduced by Arthur Balfour. These rules became known as 'Balfour's Railway Timetable' because under them the government decided on almost all the business put before the House: it could determine how long each stage of the debate would take and when the votes would be put. Thus, at any moment, it was possible to look up the government's timetable and know just how far each legislative train had got along the line leading to enactment.

Palmerston had to tell

So it is with the eliciting of information. In the earlier parts of the last century, before governments had control of an assured majority, the House could and did extract information about important issues of policy. Blue books were published on all aspects of foreign policy containing despatches between His or Her Majesty's Government and foreign powers up to only a few months before the date of publication: something that would be unthinkable — indeed dismissed as dangerous — now. Only as governments grew more confident did it become possible to resist those motions calling for 'the laying of all papers concerned with Near Eastern affairs in the last year' (or whatever was exercising parliament at the time). The flow of these publications declined after the 1890s and had ceased by the time of the 1914–18 war. By 1956, it was impossible for Parliament to find out what had happened in the lead up to the Suez invasion, and this refusal to publish was maintained even by subsequent Labour governments whose leaders had been bitterly critical of the episode. In contrast, 100 years before, the Commons had forced Palmerston to publish all the documents concerning the origins of the Crimean war even before the war was over. [. . .]

Question Time is often held up as an excellent method of controlling an executive. In fact, a question period was introduced and developed as a substitute for MPs' former powers to insist on debates on issues of current importance. Now Question Time has become part of the theatrical battle between the Government and the Opposition. As Richard Crossman has said, any moderately competent minister can dismiss one question and one supplementary in a manner that reveals nothing he wishes to keep to himself.

As Britain's executive has done more, as its involvement in economic life has grown and its impact on citizens' powers and freedoms has widened, the capacity of the House of Commons to investigate such activities has diminished. Students of parliamentary institutions all over the western world accept that for this kind of scrutiny, for keeping officials alert and accountable, a Parliament is as effective as its system of regular committees with a settled membership and powers of interrogation.

No power to vet

Yet the Commons is the only legislature without such a committee system, with no foreign affairs committee, no defence committee, no economic policy committee, no ways and means committee — subcommittees of the Expenditure Committee cover inadequately only some of the ground. Westminster's standing committees get to see bills only after they have received their second reading; they have no power to examine the civil servants who drafted them, no staff to carry out even the most trivial inquiries on behalf of the committee. [. . .]

One really effective committee, the Public Accounts Committee, exists only because it was founded in 1860 when Parliament was still expected to watch over the executive. It got a modest staff, that of the Comptroller and Auditor-General, and was composed of equal numbers drawn from both sides with an Opposition nominee as chairman. By contrast, the Expenditure Committee set up in 1968 has an inadequate staff and a permanent government majority, service on it being in the gift of the Whips on each side. Despite the efficacy of the Public Accounts Committee, however, even its chairman, Mr Edward du Cann, emphasised in 1977 (when, among other points, drawing attention to the £10.8m wrongly paid out in welfare benefits) that the Commons had lost effective control of public expenditure.

In practice other committees are appointed only on issues which do not directly affect ministers or which do not involve watching over the work of specific government departments. Examples are the committees on race relations, on the work of the ombudsman, on the conduct of the nationalised industries and on issues of science and technology.

[from *The Economist*, 5 November 1977]

As things have been so shall they be?

Most MPs see themselves as working a system of parliamentary democracy: ministers run departments which carry out policy, government answers to Parliament for it. Problems of scale and inertia may have made the machine more difficult to control, departments may have a will of their own. The Civil Service may be a vested interest. Yet the old interpretation is still assumed to hold in broad outlines. The Thatcher experiment of major policy changes carried through by an obviously reluctant machine helps to prove it, whatever Tony Benn might say. The real problem is not that this traditional system has disintegrated, but that other patterns have grown up alongside and that Parliament is less relevant to any of them.

The structure of British government must now be viewed not as one simple system but as several, all coexisting in the same shell. Each serves a different purpose, each is uppermost for certain functions, all are necessary if the machine is to work. Yet none is dominant and Parliament's role in any of them is confused and curtailed. Thus within the broad framework of parliamentary democracy we also have government by party. Every nation has, in different guises, except Nepal, the only no-party state. In Britain, political parties are national institutions, some say mausoleums. They connect the people to government. They work a mass democracy. The electorate chooses a job lot of Prime Minister, programme, Cabinet and a built-in majority by which the Cabinet controls the House and pushes its programme through. Looked at from another point of view, we have a pressure group democracy. The diverse interests in a modern society are articulated through groups and organisations, and government builds up an elaborate machinery of consultation and involvement to integrate them all. Each department has its clientele of interest groups: institutions, organisations, firms working in a particular area. The framework is topped off by a tripartite series of relationships which at times can resemble a corporate state as government consults the great monolithic interests of the TUC and the CBI and the three do deals, compromise, persuade, bargain. Finally, modern mass communications, and the continuous feedback process built up round them, have endowed us with a framework of plebiscitary democracy of the kind populists might find themselves at home with. Government reads the fever charts of opinion through the polls, the by-elections, and now through referenda, more used in the 1970s than for all the preceding decades of the century. It also speaks directly to the nation through television, putting ministers in the living-room, just as the people speak to it through the polls.

These four systems coexist where one worked before. None is now visibly dominant. Each modifies the others. In doing so they confuse both participants and public. The diversity has never been made clear to a nation always prone to prefer myths to reality and lacking the remorseless logic of, say, the French in differentiating the real from the sham. No one seems sure what mode is operating at what time, which horse is relevant to what course, which hat participants are wearing. Confused incomprehension characterises most public discussion, and behind the face of government is confusion, with no apparent dominant will or central nerve. We get all the disadvantages of an elective dictatorship and none of the advantages.

This confusion is particularly intense in the case of Parliament. Each of the systems cohabiting within the shell has modified and undermined its power. Government by party means that a House of Commons which in theory controls and checks the executive is in fact controlled by it. Pressure group democracy means that Parliament's role in mobilising consent and charting the limits of the acceptable is transferred to departments who know the crucial views of the interested parties better than the House and can do deals in a way it never could. They present it with proposals already market-tested and often immutable: houses of cards which cannot be changed for fear of bringing the whole down. Plebiscitary democracy gives governments a more direct access to the people than they could ever obtain through the baffle and filter of the Commons. The House's job of articulating opinion is downgraded when that opinion can express itself forcibly and directly through the polls and has almost certainly changed since the freeze frame of the attitudes of months, even years, before, which is the Commons. The polls allow opinion to be quantified and measured. Even when the House is performing its natural role as a great echo chamber, amplifying the noises bruiting abroad in the land, the resultant din is of little objective use. Individual MPs when they measure opinions tend to be like cushions bearing the impress of whoever last sat on them, individual, firm, general management committee, constituency chairman or other pressure group.

Once performing real functions, the Commons have been largely restricted to formal ones. Ministers and government formally answer to it. The party debate is formally staged there. Compromises with groups are formally ratified there, ministers formally announce their intentions, often after briefing the press and providing both advance material and advance interviews, all suitably embargoed. The consent of the community is formally given there, even if the polls show that its real attitude may be very different. The major satisfaction of running the country and participating in the great decisions has been transferred elsewhere. [. . .]

[from *Westminster Man* by Austin Mitchell (Thames Methuen, 1982)]

PRIME MINISTER

Engagements

Q1 *Mr Rogers* asked the Prime Minister if she will list her official engagements for Tuesday 10 July.

The Prime Minister (Mrs Margaret Thatcher): This morning I had meetings with ministerial colleagues and others. In addition to my duties in the House I shall be having further meetings later today. Later today I hope to have an audience of Her Majesty the Queen.

Mr Rogers: Will the Prime Minister tell the House what advice she gave, and what instructions she issued, to the chairman of the National Coal Board at the secret meeting last week?

The Prime Minister: No. No instructions were issued. Mr MacGregor came with my right hon. Friend the Secretary of State for Energy to make a report on the industry as he saw it.

[from *Hansard* vol. 62, no. 179, Tuesday 10 July 1984]

Questions

1 Why do MPs normally vote with their party? (D3)

2 Illustrate and justify the observation that any British Prime Minister generally 'has unfettered executive power beyond an American president's dreams'. (D3)

3 Explain why there is hardly any 'House of Commons feeling'. (D3)

4 Show how the powers of the House of Commons have declined in the last hundred years. (D3: see also D1.)

5 What is the 'great test of the freedom and power of any legislature', according to *The Economist*? (D3)

6 Why did Question Time originate? Why is *The Economist* critical of this method of controlling the executive? (D3)

7 What can you deduce from the questions asked of the Prime Minister concerning her engagements to be the purpose of a Prime Minister's Diary Question? (D5)

8 Where in the text is indirect reference made to the 'guillotine' and the 'kangaroo'? (D3)

9 What prompted the remark of du Cann in 1977 that the Commons had lost effective control of public expenditure? (D3: see also D1.)

10 Explain the terms 'parliamentary democracy', 'pressure group democracy', 'plebiscitary democracy' and 'mass democracy' as employed by Mitchell. (D4)

Extension Work

1 Explain what is meant by the following: (a) 'carpetbaggers'; (b) 'partisan minority legislation'; (c) 'unparliamentary government'; (d) 'alternating party political tyrannies'. (D3)

2 How has the Select Committee system of the Commons been improved since 1977? (D3)

3 What is the role of a Chief Whip and the Whips' Office? (D1)

4 When did the tripartite series of relationships between government, the TUC and CBI originate? (D2)

5 Name the Secretary of State for Energy in July 1984. With what particular crisis was he dealing? (D5)

Constituency Man

Borough constituencies, with all human life in one boundary, marginals, and middle-class retirement or commuter seats, where people have the leisure, education and sense of self-importance to write, generate the most mail. Tory rurals produce the least. Yet any seat with no town hall to take the burden of complaints focuses everything on the MP, as well as creating the problem of greater distances, a particular problem in the larger Labour seats like Joe Ashton's Bassetlaw, with seventy parish councils, or John Home Robertson's Berwick and East Lothian with four towns, eight hereditary peers, and only one set of traffic lights. Neither can compare in area with Joe Grimond's Orkneys, or Nationalist seats like the Western Isles, yet such rural seats offer one big advantage: the population is rooted, not constantly turning over. To help a constituent with a housing problem in London or Manchester often moves him over the very artificial constituency boundaries to express his gratitude elsewhere. Mobile populations build up no loyalty.

Constituency work is becoming the opium of the parliamentarian. It absorbs, satisfies and distracts from the real job. Alan Clark's patrician view is that it is all a matter of duty:

> It's a burden. It undoubtedly adds heavily to your workload. But it's very rewarding. Every MP should get twenty or thirty notches in his gun every year for people who he's helped . . . it certainly consumes time but it's just part of the democratic system . . . and I wouldn't discard it because I think that the contact you get with your constituents and the familiarity that you get, particularly for someone like myself who has had an absolutely privileged existence from birth are all vital . . . Because I'm an MP I'm constantly brought into contact with really hideous individual problems and I do my best to solve them. I think it's good for MPs to be acquainted with this kind of thing.

While Julian Critchley can adopt a more sardonic approach, looking out from Aldershot at the efforts of others:

> A lot depends on the kind of constituency. If you're lucky enough to have a safe seat in an area of nil unemployment, therefore of great local prosperity, and if, in the Conservative Party, your seat is safe, it's therefore very largely a middle-class seat, and most people can afford lawyers or solicitors if they get into trouble.

So you are left with only a relatively small amount of constituency surgery work to do. Now if, on the other hand, you're a Labour MP or, indeed, if you're a Conservative or Labour MP in a marginal seat in which there is a lot of unemployment, then quite clearly all the pressures are very much greater.

The MP is the local ombudsman. Problems come to him because they are increasing and he is there. Some MPs take pains to help, others seem largely untraceable. Most are all too available. In a sample of twenty MPs telephoned at random, only one could not be contacted, and the most distant date for an appointment was a fortnight away. Most seemed embarrassingly eager for customers. This may not last because the work is growing steadily. It comes in three ways. Most MPs have surgeries, some once a month, most once a fortnight, a few weekly. Some mining MPs do not bother; the old-fashioned ones used to argue that 'they always know where my back door is', but such a view is now rare. Some Tory MPs leave such mundane business to their party agents; but nearly everyone else feels it vital because, as Jo Richardson points out, surgery provides the personal touch:

> When I go to my advice bureau a lot of people come along and they start out by saying, 'I don't really know where to start my story.' I say, 'Start wherever you want and tell me and we'll see what happens.' And in the end it turns out it's about something I can't possibly help them with, perhaps a housing problem, because I'm not on the local authority, or perhaps a legal problem, perhaps a marital problem. I always feel very pleased when they get up, as they frequently do at the end, and say, 'Thanks very much, at least you listened.' . . . I think people feel better if they're able to go and talk sometimes to a stranger about their personal problems.

A 1967 survey showed that under 10 per cent of MPs did not hold regular surgeries. That proportion must now be even lower.

Surgeries are usually held in one place, but can also be alternated round the larger constituencies, or even, in the case of John Butcher's converted taxi surgery, transferred to a confessional on wheels, parked in designated places.

Then comes the steady flow to the MP's house in the constituency or to his party office. It also comes through the agent. Nearly half of our sample — mostly Tory — had a full-time agent, a quarter had one part-time; while a further sixth had a full-time secretary in the constituency and a third part-time. Finally, the unstoppable mail pours in. A 1960s study of Members' mail showed 13 per cent receiving less than twenty-five letters a week from their constituency, two-fifths from twenty-five to fifty, and the rest more, a hundred or more in the case of a tenth. The figures have certainly gone up since then.

[from *Westminster Man* by Austin Mitchell (Thames Methuen, 1982)]

Stresses and strains of an MP's life

By MARY KENNY

LATE HOURS and long-distance commuting make life tough at the top. So does the limelight: an MP who steps out of line soon finds himself the subject of public scrutiny. The result is that parliamentarians and their families may experience more than ordinary stress and strain. Yet the Commons has resisted moves to introduce more congenial working hours and to provide family apartments for Members from the far-flung constituencies. A special report on the pressures facing MPs and the ways in which those pressures have changed in recent years.

Many attempts have been made to call attention to the irrationality of the parliamentary day, and to demand reform. In the 1970s Mrs Lisanne Radice, the wife of the Labour MP for Chester-le-Street, started the Campaign for More Effective Parliamentary Hours, and found much support, especially from the spouses of Parliamentarians. 'The system', she says, 'was devised for 19th-century gentlemen, not for professional people today. We have longer, and odder, parliamentary hours than any other democracy in the world. It has a terrible effect on family life and it almost precludes women from becoming MPs — certainly it seriously discourages women with children.'

Mrs Radice's suggestion for reform included a more normal working day, starting at around 10.30 a.m. and winding up at about 7.30 to 8 p.m. She also suggested that Parliament ought to buy or build a block of mansion flats so that — as on a university campus — MPs could choose to bring their families to London and raise them in a community. But while Mrs Radice's campaign elicited sympathy, the will to change the parliamentary schedule radically was not forthcoming. Too many MPs had other jobs to be able to begin their parliamentary day in the morning, and there were no funds available for building or buying blocks of flats. Besides, MPs already get an allowance for staying in London four nights a week.

[from the *Sunday Telegraph*, 24 May 1981]

PARLIAMENTARY RECESS

"Well — if you knows of a better 'ole . . . !"

[from the *Sunday Telegraph*, 1 August 1965]

ARE WOMEN BECOMING THE POWER IN POLITICS?

IF POLITICAL POWER IS MEASURED BY REPRESENTATION IN THE HOUSE, THEN WOMEN'S SHARE IS UNDENIABLY SMALL. BUT IF POWER RESTS WITH THOSE WHO EFFECT IMPROVEMENT IN OUR EVERYDAY LIVES, THE REAL FORCE IS ESSENTIALLY FEMALE. ANGELA NEUSTATTER LOOKS BEYOND PARLIAMENT TO THE NEW DECISION MAKERS.

Women always knew, of course, that politics were too serious to be left to men. And for the past two decades we've proved it by campaigning passionately across a whole range of issues that, as women, we believed were particularly important. We've brought to movements as disparate as CND or the Natural Birth Lobby an anger, a commitment and an energy impossible to ignore.

And yet, when it comes to representing that contribution in Parliament, the picture is quite different. Out of 1899 candidates who stood at the last election, only a forlorn 23 women emerged to take their seats in the House of Commons, a figure that has remained static since the war. Compare our dismal 3.5 per cent of women members with enlightened Denmark's 23.5 per cent and even chauvinistic Italy's 8.3 per cent, and clearly the gender gap is not so much a gap as a yawning chasm.

And yet, under the constitutional surface, there is a vein of female concern that is transforming political life at an all-important — if more subtle — level. There are, of course, plenty of reasons why we are at last realising the full extent of our political impact. Better educational opportunities have brought us closer to the technicalities of many complex debates, and even the most watered down vestiges of feminism have encouraged us to explore topics which had previously seemed irrele-

vant. It would be inconceivable now for any bright young woman not to hold opinions: political ignorance is no longer considered a pretty affectation, but the sign of a sluggish mind.

The result is that 'politics' have ceased to be the domain of an elite at Westminster, and have instead become part of the wider debate about society as a whole. Indeed, most basic of all is the point that women make up well over half the electorate; and in America, they are now beginning to take advantage of their sheer numerical power to swing elections in their favour. When President Reagan speaks of the women's vote, he is talking of a factor that could make or break his campaign.

Thus, as we begin to put muscle power into issues from the so-called women's concerns — such as abortion and the birth movement — to town planning, housing and ecology, the need to concentrate solely on pushing a few more token women into Parliament seems less intense an issue than it did 10 years ago. On the other hand, the 300 Group, the all-party pressure group which aims to get 300 women into Parliament, points to the encouraging fact that 264 women stood for Parliament last June — double the previous figure.

But Elizabeth Vallance, author of *Women in the House*, feels that until the system is radically overhauled, this power will never be converted into a greater number of female MPs. 'A first-past-the-post system will always count against women. If a party can only put up one candidate in each constituency, that candidate will always tend towards the election-winning norm: white, middle class, male.

Proportional representation, on the other hand, would open the way for many more women. Since under this system the parties put up a "slate" of candidates, rather than just one for each constituency, the inclusion of a woman to give a well balanced team would be, as the European examples suggest, an enormous vote catcher'.

Certainly the SDP has lived up to its reputation as the shining new hope for women, in theory at least: a mandatory two women were included on every candidate shortlist. But such positive discrimination was only possible for a party which had had no time to build up a grass roots administration. After all, the only way to get selected as a Conservative or Labour candidate is to produce a solid pedigree of five years' political commitment at council or union level. With no such experience open to SDP candidates, intellect and energy became the qualifying factors. The result was an encouragement to bright young women who may previously have been too busy with their careers and family life to have actively participated in politics, or else thought it wasn't worth the battle.

Opinion, though, is divided as to whether positive discrimination does really benefit the people for whom it was designed. The immensely experienced former Labour MP Joan Lestor, for instance, thunders against it. 'I think it's tantamount to saying we can't make it on our own merits.'

Anti-women chauvinism at selection level seems to be a stale red herring, the consensus being that the worst prejudice a woman can expect to encounter in political life comes from herself. A lack of self-confidence has destroyed more careers than any heavy-handed selection committee. Virgina Bottomley, a Conservative candidate at the last election, puts it best: 'All through their lives, women wait to be asked to do things — to dance, to get married, to stand for public office. They're not used to pushing themselves on other people; it's something I'm still learning to do.'

[from *Options*, September 1983]

Occupations of MPs elected in 1979

Occupation	Conservative	Labour	Liberal	Other	Total
	%	%			%
Professions	28.0 (95)	37.3 (100)	5	7	32.6 (207)
Business	58.1 (197)	7.1 (19)	4	8	35.8 (228)
Workers	0.6 (2)	32.5 (87)	—	1	14.2 (90)
Miscellaneous	13.3 (45)	23.1 (62)	2	—	17.2 (109)
Not known	—	—	—	1	0.1 (1)
Total	100.0 (339)	100.0 (268)	11	17	100.0 (635)

[from *The Commons today* ed. S.A. Walkland and Michael Ryle (Fontana, 1981)]

Age, sex and occupation of MPs, May 1979

	Labour	Conservative	Liberal	Other	Total
Age groups:					
Under 40	55	84	3	4	146
41–60	170	217	6	10	403
Over 60	43	38	2	3	86
Total	268	339	11	17	635
of which: men	257	331	11	17	616
women	11	8	0	0	19
Occupations:					
Barristers, solicitors	31	70	0	2	103
Journalists, publishers and public relations officers	19	38	1	1	59
Doctors, surgeons	5	3	0	0	8
Teachers, lecturers	53	14	3	4	74
Farmers, landowners	2	25	2	1	30
*Company directors, managers and other business positions	62	193	4	3	262
Engineers	30	8	1	0	39
Trade union officials	27	1	0	0	28
Other non-manual workers	13	23	0	4	40
Manual workers	32	0	0	2	34

*Some MPs have two or three professions and are included more than once.

[from *Social Trends 1980*]

Questions

1 Why does Neustatter state that 'politics' is now 'part of the wider debate about society as a whole'? (D8)

2 Explain the purpose of the 300 Group. (D8)

3 What evidence does Mitchell give for suggesting that the MP is the local ombudsman? (D6)

4 Why does the constituency work of an MP depend on the nature and size of his or her constituency? (D6)

5 List some issues of particular interest to women. Why have many issues become 'politicised' or 'political issues'? (D8)

6 For what reasons might an MP suffer more stress than the average working person? (D6, D7)

7 What do the statistics in D9 indicate concerning the continuing if diminishing class basis of British politics?

Class Discussion

1 Is the 'election-winning norm' always 'white, middle class, male'? (D8)

2 Why does the House of Commons contain so few women MPs (about 3.5 per cent)?

3 Comment on the likely number or proportion of Conservative and Labour MPs who would have put professions, business or workers as their occupation in 1918 and in 1945.

4 Suggest reasons why 'private means' was also considered an important occupational classification for Conservative MPs in the period 1900–10.

5 Compare and contrast the presentation of information and statistics in D9A and D9B.

Extension Work

1 What arguments have been made for and against the House of Commons starting formal proceedings in the morning and finishing in the late afternoon?

2 Explain in detail Kenny's comment 'We have longer, and odder, parliamentary hours than any other democracy in the world'. Why does Parliament work long hours, occasionally late into the night?

3 List the main factors selection committees consider when choosing parliamentary candidates.

4 To what extent is the atmosphere or working routine of the Commons unsuitable for married male MPs or women?

5 Why are some MPs 'parliament-orientated' while others are 'constituency-orientated'?

6 Describe the role of a party agent. (See also E2.)

D10

THE ABOLITION OF THE SECOND CHAMBER

The simplest course of action would seem to be the outright abolition of the House of Lords, leaving the House of Commons as a single chamber legislature. However, if this course of action is advocated it would involve certain problems. The existing House of Commons is already overburdened with work. On many occasions important legislation has been delayed because of lack of parliamentary time, and there is insufficient time to consider delegated legislation, EEC regulations, etc. While the House of Lords is at this moment adding to the Commons' difficulties, it could well be argued that the removal of the second chamber would be bound to exacerbate the problem. Furthermore, it could be said that to have just one chamber government would put more power in the hands of the executive, backed up by a Whipped majority in the Commons. This argument would undoubtedly be widely expressed in the press and elsewhere, and the public might be receptive to such an argument.

On the other hand, there is a strong case for arguing that the House of Lords has shown itself not to be especially valuable as a revising chamber, and that a second chamber is not really necessary for the tidying up and revising functions which could be adequately dealt with by a single chamber. For instance, the number of Commons' Bills amended in any way by the Lords is less than half. In 1964–70 there were 226 such Bills and only 98 were amended. Also the time spent by the Lords on many Commons' Bills is small. In 1968–9 and 1970–1, some 47 Bills were considered in Committee, on Report and on Third Reading. Of these, the Lords spent less than one hour on 18 Bills and less than four hours on 36 Bills. So on only 11 Bills did the Lords spend much time, and some of those were highly controversial and the debates were little concerned with genuine improving amendments. In 1964–70, the Lords in Committee moved 2553 amendments and of these the Commons accepted all but 125. Clearly the overwhelming mass of amendments are 'tidying-up' amendments for which a second chamber is unncessary, as the operation can be done in other ways.

Furthermore, a second chamber is not necessarily the most appropriate way of dealing with an overburdened House of Commons. This might be better dealt with by reforms to the House of Commons itself, both in its procedure and in the form of better assistance to MPs to carry out their functions. The need for greater scrutiny of the executive could also be met by introducing procedures for a more open system of government with much more pre-legislative consultation than is at present the case. While the majority of parliamentary democracies are bicameral, a number of countries, including in recent years Sweden and New Zealand, have abolished their second chambers. We believe that, given the necessary changes in Commons procedure and governmental processes, this would be the most appropriate course for the United Kingdom. [. . .]

[from *The machinery of government and the House of Lords* (Labour Party: statement by the National Executive Committee, 1977)]

D11

Thank the Lord for the Lords!

by ROBIN OAKLEY

JEREMY THORPE sneered at the House of Lords as material proof that there is life after death. Gilbert and Sullivan suggested 'the House of Peers throughout the years did nothing in particular, and did it very well.'

Now all that has changed. The House of Lords has begun to count for something. The Government has been deeply embarrassed by its defeat on the Bill paving the way to scrapping the GLC.

Ministers are in a fearful flutter. And the Labour Party, which has pledged to abolish the Upper House, has suddenly discovered a remarkable attachment to its opinions. Even the left wing Ken Livingstone starts praising their democratic virtues.

What hypocrisy! Had it been a Labour government whose Bill had been massacred by a Lords' amendment, the earth would be moving in constitutional crises.

The crushing 140-plus majority which Mrs Thatcher won in the Commons last June has been the best thing that ever happened to the Lords. A disgruntled Downing Street admits that their Lordships have acquired a new relevance. Liberal leader Mr David Steel says that the Thatcher Government 'has turned the House of Lords into the conscience of the nation'.

Already, in this Parliament, they have defeated nearly 20 Government measures.

The Lords stopped the Governmental plans for charity housing to be sold to sitting tenants. They insisted on safeguards over telephone tapping which the Government had tried to escape. Where the Tory Government lost the courage of its own convictions over postal ballots for the election of trades union officers, the Lords stiffened the Bill.

Now, when the Government has tried to push through scrambled and ill-considered legislation on the GLC and Metropolitan authorities, after inserting it in the election manifesto as a feeble substitute for past pledges to reform rates, the House of Lords has dealt the scheme a lusty blow.

There is an instinct in the country that London needs some kind of overall authority. There is an instinct that scrapping elections and replacing el- ected Labour councillors with nominated Tories, if only for an interim period, is not quite playing the game.

That instinct was voiced in the Commons on the Tory benches as well as the Opposition. But the steamroller majority saw the Government through there. Now the House of Lords is forcing a hold-up until the Government wins the people's consent for what it is doing.

Imperfect

It was a classic exercise of its true function. The House of Lords exists to delay where there are public doubts and to revise imperfect legislation.

The House of Lords is the chamber of grown-up politicians. There is no cacophony of partisan peers shouting their heads off over cheap party points at Question Time. Peers can't be threatened by their Whips or by left wing constitutency associations. They don't have to posture. Nor can they be tempted by rewards.

For the most part they've acquired those already as part of the process of arriving in the Upper House. So they can be their own men. As a result, Government Chief Whip Lord Denham admits: 'There are very few peers who haven't voted against their party from time to time'.

The Lords doesn't have guillotines. Anyone who cares passionately about a point gets the chance to raise it. There are no tight rules of procedure, merely conventions of behaviour. The reason for the lack of Commons hooliganism is, as Lord Denham puts it, 'We have the freedom and don't abuse it.'

A key factor in the Lords is the crossbencher or independent.

The Government has around 420 supporters, Labour about 140 and the Social Democrats and Liberals about 40 each. That leaves some 220 crossbenchers performing the function of a jury, listening to the arguments and weighing cases on their merits.

The sheer reasonableness and rationality is what is so refreshing about the Upper House. That is what gives it the moral authority to give governments a sharp rap across the knuckles as it did on Thursday night.

And that is why Mrs Thatcher has been foolish in not strengthening the Lords with sensible reforms and why Labour is so wrong to insist on its abolition.

[from the *Daily Mail*, 30 June 1984]

Questions

1   What is the true function of the Lords, according to Oakley? (D11)
2   Illustrate some of the differences in procedure and conduct between the Commons and the Lords mentioned in Oakley's article. (D11)
3   What arguments does the Labour NEC put forward for abolishing the Lords? (D10)

Class Discussion

1   In what ways might the Upper House be considered to have been more representative of public opinion than the Commons during the period 1979–85?

Extension Work

1   On 28 June 1984 the Lords defeated the Local Government Bill (the 'paving' Bill) which suspended the 1985 GLC elections and aimed to appoint an interim council of nominees of London boroughs. Why was there greater popular opposition to the proposals to abolish the GLC than to those to abolish the Metropolitan authorities? (D11: see also section G.)

2   What is meant by 'partisan dealignment'? In what way has it affected the Lords?

3   Why have some political commentators argued that the House of Lords should not be abolished while the House of Commons remains in its present form?

4   How do you think the Commons should be reformed to provide necessary safeguards for the public if Britain abolished the Lords?

The party system and pressure groups

Introduction

E1 publicises the aims of the Charter Movement in the Conservative Party through the medium of *Crossbow*, a magazine representing the views of members roughly in the centre or towards the left of the party. Mitchell in E2 comments on the democratic reforms in the Labour Party and warns of power being in the hands of unrepresentative activist minorities. These changes illustrate the left wing influence in the party, and represent an attempt to remedy deficiencies following criticisms made by Benn. He argued that the Parliamentary Labour Party (PLP) had over a period of time come too much under the influence of the party leader, and had refused to accept its proper subordinate position as the servant of the Party Conference.

E3 argues that a party system with a strong centre party will not work, and concludes that the two-party system still remains the best for Britain. John Cole seems to forget that the alternative to a centre party rule is not necessarily a rump of the left and right together, but could be a government formed of either right wing or left wing elements.

One major argument advanced by supporters of a two-party system is that it promotes stable politics, in contrast to multi-party systems where governments are frequently overthrown. E4, however, suggests that the experience of Britain's largely two-party system since 1964 is that the frequent change of policies is itself a cause of instability. This point is also made by Roy Jenkins, former deputy leader of the Labour Party, in his Dimbleby Lecture (E5, commented upon in E6), where he gives his own reasons as to why the mould of British politics should be broken by the creation of a multi-party system. The leading social democrats in the Labour Party, disillusioned with present trends, only went ahead with forming a new party when they became finally convinced after the Wembley Conference (January 1981) that they could no longer resist the growing influence of the Labour left. Reference is made to the origins of the Social Democratic Party in E2 and E7. In the latter David Owen explains why a four-party system is preferable for the time being to a three-party system.

E7 provides an insight into the methods and techniques used by a temporary pressure group concerned about conservation of the environment in Bristol, and popular participation in procedures relating to land development. E8 provides other details as to how groups try to achieve their aims, while E9 highlights certain aspects of industrial relations, the British economy and trade union history since the 1960s.

☐ **E1** ☐

Is this a private party or can anyone join?

Peter Sinclair, Convener of the 'Set the Party Free' Charter Movement, and a former Chairman of Greater London Young Conservatives, calls for greater democracy in the Conservative Party organisation.

'I would as soon take advice from my valet as from a Conservative annual conference' (Balfour, quoted by Robert Mackenzie, *British Political Parties*).

Is the structure and organisation of the Conservative Party as undemocratic as its critics would have us believe? Even if it is, does it really matter? And if it does matter, is there anything which ordinary members of the party can do about it?

These questions are being asked more and more widely following the recent decision of the central Party machine that the Central Council, currently the only forum for the indirect expression of grass-roots opinion on organisational matters, should be stripped of its powers. No wonder the impression is created of frightened, faceless bureaucrats desperately determined to keep the decision-making processes of the Tory Party organisation even more firmly locked behind closed doors. How much substance is there behind the impression?

Democratic principles

To help us determine just how democratic is the Conservative Party organisation, it may be salutary to consider the three normally accepted tests of democratic principle:

1 One man, one vote
2 The rule of majority opinion
3 A participating voice in decision-making;

and to apply them to some of the main areas of concern to party members.

By these tests, the Tory Party outside Parliament appears to be very unaccountable indeed. The original causes of this situation are historical. When Disraeli moved the passage of the second great Reform Act in 1867, he took care to state that democracy was a form of government with which neither he nor the Conservative Party had any sympathy. However, he was somewhat apprehensive of the fact that the Act doubled the size of the electorate (from one million to two million — men, of course!). His concern led him the same year to found the National Union of Conservative Associations with the primary aim of wooing the newly enfranchised lower class urban voters, who 'could hardly be relied upon automatically to recognise their identity of interest with the Conservative Party' (Robert Mackenzie). The second leg of the tripod (Parliamentary Party, National Union and Central Office) was in place. Theoretically the National Union might have exercised some kind of democratic authority. Its total impotence in practice is demonstrated by the fact that of the major central bodies in the organisation neither the Advisory Committee on Policy nor the Central Board of Finance nor the Standing Advisory Committee on Candidates report to it.

The Party's Civil Service

The third leg, Conservative Central Office, the 'Civil Service' of the Party, was formed (also by Disraeli) in 1870. Central Office, far from being accountable to the Party as the Civil Service is (at least in theory) to Parliament, was and is purely the private office of the Leader of the Party, who personally appoints the officers of the Party organisation who control it. There is no element of democracy in the running of the Party organisation for the simple reason that the Party was never intended to be democratic. As two American political scientists put it in 1949, 'essentially the system is one of autocracy tempered by advice and information', or, in Robert Mackenzie's words, 'it would be difficult to envisage a more tightknit system of oligarchical control of the affairs of a political party'.

More than a century after the foundation of the Party organisation, its membership still by and large acquiesces in its autocratic structure, and woe betide them if they don't.

Early calls for reform

As early as 1901 a *Times* leader commented: 'It would seem that, in the view of the experts in the curiously technical art of party management, it is deemed inexpedient to encourage the slightest indications of criticism or dissent'. Eighty years on, that most certainly remains true. But from time to time there are complaints. At the Party Conference of 1929, a Tory MP charged that 'the chairman of the Party, responsible to no one but the leader, has more power vested in him than a Tammany Hall boss'.

In 1969, Greater London Young Conservatives published 'Set the Party free', perhaps the most powerful indictment of the Party organisation ever written. The Conservative Party, it said, 'must be in some aspects one of the least democratic organisations in Britain outside the Freemasons (with which secret society it appears in structure and even personnel to have some affinity)'. 'Set the Party free', strengthened by a foreword by the late Rt. Hon. Iain Macleod MP (who also suggested the title), led directly to the setting up of the Chelmer Committee to investigate ways, if any, in which the Party organisation, outside Parliament, might be made more democratic. By 1975, its recommendations had been quietly buried and the Party leadership went its way regardless. As Robert Mackenzie wrote, the Conservative Party has 'devised a system of consultation with its mass membership which ensures that the latter will not be so exasperated with its impotence as to refuse to fulfil its function as a vote-getting agency'. (*British Political Parties*, (1964)).

		One man, one vote	Rule by majority	Opportunity to participate
a	Election of chairman	No	No	No
b	Election of other Party officers	No	No	No
c	Accountability of Conservative Central Office	No	No	No
d	The spending of the Party's money	No	No	No
e	The drawing up of the Approved List of Candidates	No	No	No
f	The organisation of the Party Conference	No	No	No
g	The selection of Party Conference motions for debate	Yes*	Yes*	Yes*

* Applied in 1981 to only two balloted motions out of 17, and only 172 motions out of 1162 (less than 15%) were included in the ballot.

The need for change

If the Tory Party organisation is so fundamentally undemocratic, does it really matter? Surely, it is argued, the main objective is that the Party hierarchy should be able to provide strong and effective leadership in order to gain and retain power at Westminster? I believe that not only does it matter, but that the extent in this decade that the Tory Party democratises its internal organisation may well determine its ability to survive as one of the two main political forces in Britain. Three reasons support this conclusion.

1 The trend in our society towards greater participation and involvement for individual citizens in the running of their own lives is becoming stronger. It can be seen in the changing relationship between employee and employer, between consumer and nationalised industry, between ratepayer and local authority, between union member and union leadership, even between investors and their building society. An autocratic Conservative Party organisation, locked rigidly in its 19th century past, presents an increasingly anachronistic picture — and one which even the most traditional Tory members show signs of resenting (witness the results of a poll conducted at the 1981 Party Conference into ways of electing the Party chairman).

2 The spectacle of a thoroughly undemocratic Party organisation clashes uncomfortably with Conservative policy initiatives in other areas. How to reconcile it with the encouragement of parental choice in education? How can the Party as presently structured credibly argue that the unions should set their equally undemocratic houses in order?

3 The threat from the SDP paints the writing clearly on the wall. There can be little doubt that its appeal to those disillusioned with the excesses of the two-party system rests very largely on its claim that the SDP will be a party run by its members for its members. The laws of competition (which all good Tories naturally support) dictate that this strong selling point must be matched sooner or later if the Tory Party is to stay in business.

The Charter's tenets

So the need for democratic reform of the Conservative Party may increasingly be seen as vital to its future. What can be done to hasten the dawn of enlightenment? In June 1981 the authors of 'Set the Party free' launched nationally the 'Charter to set the Party free', a ten-point programme to achieve the democratic reform for which they had been crusading since the mid-1960s.

The Charter's main tenets are that:

1 The chairman and other officers of the Party organisation must be elected and not appointed.

2 Central Office must be made directly accountable to the constituency associations meeting in Central Council.

3 The spending of the Party's money, the organisation of the Party Conference and the procedures for the creation and maintenance of the approved list of candidates must be brought under the democratic control of the constituency associations meeting in Central Council.

4 Every paid-up party member should have a direct vote in the choice of his or her parliamentary or local government candidate.

5 The Central Council should become the main governing body of the Party organisation outside Parliament.

This last point may be one of the reasons that the Party bosses are trying to emasculate the Central Council. The aim of the 'Chartists' is to gain so many signatures for the Charter that eventually a majority on every decision-making body in the Party will be supporters of the Charter. That way democratic change could quickly be achieved.

[from *Crossbow*, Summer 1982]

Gentleman, I am a free citizen. I can think what I like … I have a right not to think anything at all.
(Max Frisch)

A college education: electing Labour's leader

Austin Mitchell

IN 1981, the British Labour Party abandoned the system of electing leaders by ballot of the Parliamentary Labour Party (PLP), which had prevailed since the party started. Instead it opted for an 'electoral college' involving unions, party members and Members of Parliament, a complex and cumbersome new machinery for electing its leadership, variously described as a 'creaking structure of compromises', an 'activists' charter' and a 'wider democracy'. Theoretically attractive and certainly fairer, the real test of the new system is how it works. Yet two trials in the space of two years have generated totally different results.

A 1981 election exacerbated disunity and brought discredit to the party. That of 1983 welded Labour together and set it back on a path to power it appeared to have deserted.

Clearly a system of election sold to the party as a decisive new beginning, a machinery of regeneration, was nothing of the sort. Like so much else in our arthritic party machine, it merely amplifies trends without changing them: good when things go well, magnifying disaster when they do not. Machinery cannot solve basic party problems; only a general will to win can do that. Yet when that will emerges, machinery can strengthen and confirm it.

Dissension in the ranks

The wider franchise for leadership elections was part of a package of 'democratisation' including mandatory reselection of MPs, rank and file control of policy and manifesto, and a more responsive leadership. All were part of the reaction to Labour's embittering experience of governing without majority from 1974 to 1979 in the face of Britain's worst economic crisis since the war. To the leadership, that government was a triumph over adversity. To the rank and file it was a betrayal of hope. Disappointment generated a clamour for control over a leadership and a Parliamentary Labour Party seen not as a vanguard of socialism but more as the brakes in its guard's van.

Labour's preoccupation in the past has always been how to get power in a conservative electorate. The advocates of the New Model Party took power for granted and concentrated on using it for socialism. Constitutional changes were the method, ensuring that the 'betrayals' of 1974–9 could never occur again, if only, critics averred, because they made it unlikely that Labour would ever govern again.

The 1980 party conference agreed in principle to elect the leader by an electoral college of unions, PLP and constituencies. The decision was premature, foisted on the conference in an un-Citrine-like move by a National Executive committed to the idea but unable to get agreement on the method. Conference duly went on to reject the means, thus requiring a special conference, held at Wembley in January 1981, to decide the framework.

In the intervening months, the National Executive resolved on a college of one-third MPs, one-third unions and one-third constituency parties. The Parliamentary Party, doubtful about the whole idea, opted for 50 per cent for itself, a formula also supported by the Engineering Union. The proto-Social Democrats, then coming into embryonic form as a protest group, backed a one-man-one-vote formula, restricting participation to party members. All were overruled.

The activist selectorate

Cleverly manipulated by the left, conference staggered into accepting a motion no one had seriously considered: 40 per cent for the unions and 30 per cent each for the constituency parties and the PLP.

Michael Foot, in the first test of his leadership, gave none. The next day the Social Democrats issued the Limehouse Declaration, the precursor to their formal breakaway as a separate political party two months later. Labour's downhill slide had begun.

Proponents of the reform saw it as bringing Labour into line with other social democratic parties. In fact, where the others usually make a distinction between party leader and Leader of the Parliamentary Party, Labour had no such distinction and now proposed to elect its leader by a cumbersome structure which was unique.

The original argument for widening the franchise had been to democratise. Instead, a machinery concentrating power in the hands of oligarchies — activists in constituencies and unions — emerged, creating the real possibility that a candidate popular with the public and Labour voters might not be chosen by the selectorate. Such distortions are inevitable in a party dominated by unions which are naturally attracted to picking the piper and tune, as well as paying him. Yet in practice, unions have no way of taking party political decisions. Few of them kept records of those members paying the political levy.

[from *The Parliamentarian*, Vol. LXV, No. 2, April 1984]

Questions

1 What caused Disraeli to found the National Union of Conservative Associations? (E1)

2 Outline the role of the Conservative Central Office. (E1)

3 Why was the Chelmer Committee created? (E1)

4 Illustrate in what ways the Conservative Party organisation is autocratic. (E1)

5 Why do some Conservatives support the internal democratisation of the party structure? (E1)

6 In what ways do the 'Chartists' suggest reforming the party? (E1)

7 Give one immediate cause of the creation of the Social Democratic Party. (E2: see also E6.)

8 How does the Labour Party now elect its leader and deputy leader? (E2, E3). What used to be the procedure?

9 Outline the three major constitutional changes made in Labour Party organisation in 1981. (E2, E3)

Class Discussion

1 Has Sinclair adequately summed up the three basic tests of a democracy? (E1)

2 Explain and elaborate the following comment: 'Such distortions are inevitable in a party dominated by unions which are naturally attracted to picking the piper and tune, as well as paying him.' (E2) How would you distinguish between 'activists' and rank and file members? (E2)

3 Which of the following methods would you choose for selecting a party leader: (a) election by the party's MPs; (b) electoral college; (c) election by paid-up party membership; (d) another alternative?

4 Discuss the various groups or persons to whom a political party may be answerable or accountable.

Extension Work

1 Outline the organisational structure and centres of power in the Conservative party.

2 The Bow Group is responsible for the publication of *Crossbow*. Give other examples of ginger groups.

3 Explain why the leader of the Conservative Party has more personal power than the leader of the Labour Party.

4 How does the Conservative Party choose its leader now? What was the method used in the past?

5 In what way are there elements of democracy within the Conservative Party organisation?

6 Give examples of the so-called 'betrayals' of 1974–9. (E2)

7 Where does the real locus of power in the Labour Party lie?

8 Compare the influence and importance of the annual conferences within the two main parties.

9 Explain what is meant by the following: (a) 'proto-Social Democrats'; (b) 'activist selectorate'; (c) 'oligarchies'; (d) 'picking the piper and tune'; (e) 'political levy'; (f) 'Limehouse Declaration'. (E2)

E3–E4　　　　　　　　　　　　　　　　　*Adversary politics*

E3

The safety-valve of democracy
John Cole

An Opposition capable of taking over government is the safety-valve of democracy. There is sense in the doggerel couplet:

When in danger or in doubt,
Turn the sitting Member out.

For what if Mrs Thatcher's Government, beset by world recession, finds no way out? If inflation remains high, redundancies accelerate, and unemployment soars beyond two million? If the inner cities are seething with discontent by 1982 or 1983? And if the Labour Opposition, or any of the new groupings, looks incapable of taking power? Would 'street politics' and an erosion of social order not look more dangerously possible than it has done in Britain before?

Similarly, a logical difficulty of the Centre Party theory — again, seen from an observer's standpoint — is that it would not provide a viable alternative to itself. Politicians don't have to worry about that, but the rest of us should. The Centrist theory asks us to assume that a government of all the talents from Jim Prior through Roy Jenkins and David Steel to Shirley Williams would deliver the goods. But what if it didn't? The rumps of the Left and Right which such a government would leave in Opposition have their own ideas, but Sir Keith Joseph and Tony Benn could scarcely form a coalition.

If you assume, as I do, that the alternation of governments is the supreme merit of British democracy, then even if personally you favour neo-Keynesianism, interventionism, demand management, Welfare-State-with-an-incomes-policy (again as I do), you ought to beware of simplistic arguments for realignment. Unless you can see how we get from where we are to a new two-party system that better reflects Britain's mood.

If this argument sounds complacent, I admit to growing irritation with pat denunciations of 'adversary politics'. The opposite to adversary politics is what exists in the Soviet Union or Brazil, where adversaries are not a problem. Even in Britain, the era of Butskellism, which I found a congenial climate in which the political pendulum could swing, was denounced at the time as the era of 'stop-go'. Now they look back on it as the Golden Age.

Troubled

Why do businessmen, beset by Ayatollahs and oil sheikhs, expect Britain to remain a pool of tranquillity in a turbulent ocean?

What we need is adversary politics which works better. Our system has remained stable over a troubled half-century because Britain has parties of the 'haves' and 'have-nots'. This allows voters who are reasonably content with things as they are to vote Conservative, and those who want change to vote Labour.

[from *The Observer*, 6 July 1980]

E4

How the class system is preserved at the polls

Vernon Bogdanor

BRITAIN IS unique amongst European democracies in two respects. It is the only country still using the first-past-the-post method of election; and it is alone in offering to the successful party in a general election an almost complete monopoly of power and patronage, unhindered by written constitution or powerful second chamber. The first-past-the-post method of election, together with the dominant role of trade unions and companies in the provision of party finance, underwrites the two-party system which the SDP-Liberal alliance seeks to challenge.

Government in Britain, then, is pre-eminently party government. [...] it is worth reopening the question of how far the party system assists in the fulfilment of popular aspirations.

It is not difficult to show that the two-party system has in fact been a prime cause of Britain's economic decline. For it has both militated against industrial progress and hindered the achievement of national unity. The British electoral system is popularly supposed to encourage the alternation of two parties in office, thus providing for stable and effective government. Yet, paradoxically, the four changes of government between 1964 and 1979 have produced not stability, but, on the contrary, instability of a most damaging kind.

This is most clearly apparent in economic and industrial policy. Between 1959 and 1979, every government came into office rejecting an incomes policy, but found itself compelled to introduce one in the middle of its term of office. The present administration, like Mr Heath's in 1970, restored free collective bargaining, but by 1980 was producing guidelines for wage increases in the public sector.

Similar U-turns have been made in policies concerned with government assistance to industry. Labour in 1966 established the Industrial Reorganisation Corporation, abolished by the Conservatives in 1971, but resurrected in 1972 as an agency in the Department of Trade and Industry. In 1975 Labour established the National Enterprise Board as the channel for government assistance, but the NEB found its powers curtailed by the incoming Conservative government after only four years. Most damaging of all has been the experience of the steel industry which, in the words of Lord Caldecote, 'has been a political shuttlecock for a quarter of a century'.

It is hardly surprising that the CBI, which has pleaded in vain for a more consistent approach to industrial policy, decided at its 1978 conference that Britain's economic problems could not be solved without electoral reform. For the policy differences between the parties on matters concerned with industrial aid have not in practice been wide; the cumbersome changes in machinery have been dictated not by the needs of industry, but by the interests of the rhetoric of market economy and public control so beloved of the party faithful. The result has been a series of abrupt policy jerks rather than the steady progress characteristic of those countries where the policital system assists industrial development.

Defenders of the first-past-the-post system frequently claim that it leads to broad-based representative government. Yet, over the past ten years, the two major parties have been so pushed back into safe seats in their regions of strength — Labour in the larger cities, the North and Scotland, the Conservatives in rural areas and the South of England — that it has become difficult to regard either as qualified to speak for the electorate as a whole.

Moreover, because the regional distribution of party support largely coincides with the class distribution of the population, the electoral system positively encourages the parties to present issues in class terms.

Yet the two major parties, each claiming to believe in a one nation philosophy, unite in rejecting electoral reform. There is a Benn/Thatcher consensus in support of the first-past-the-post system. Labour's rejection of reform can only imply tacit acceptance of the view that socialism could not win the support of a majority of the voters in Britain; while the Conservatives, who have the most to lose from the instabilities and radical upheavals associated with the present system, break faith with the conservative interest in the country in their stubborn attachment to it.

The first-past-the-post electoral system serves the narrowly defined interests of the two major parties. Whether it also serves the nation should be for the electorate to judge. As John Stuart Mill declared when he advocated proportional representation in the Commons in 1867, 'The constitution does not exist for the benefit of parties, but of citizens.'

[from *The Guardian*]

Questions

1   Why does Cole support the two-party system? (E3)

2   Explain why Cole thinks the Centre Party theory will not work. (E3)

3   What does Cole see as the opposite of adversary politics? (E3)

4   Why is Bogdanor critical of the present party system in Britain? (E4)

5   What reasons does Bogdanor give to justify his comment that the method of voting preserves the class system? (E4)

Class Discussion

1   How far, if at all, would you accept Bogdanor's view that the two-party system has 'been a prime cause of Britain's economic decline'? (E4)

Extension Work

1   Explain the following: (a) 'neo-Keynesianism'; (b) 'demand management'; (c) 'era of "stop-go"'; (d) 'street politics'. (E4)

2   Illustrate Lord Caldecote's comment that the steel industry 'has been a political shuttlecock for a quarter of a century.' (E4)

3   Explain, with full details, what the following mean: (a) 'rhetoric of market economy and public control so beloved of the party faithful'; (b) 'the regional distribution of party support largely coincides with the class distribution of the population'; (c) 'one nation philosophy'. (E4)

E5

Home thoughts from abroad

Roy Jenkins

The British political system in broadly its present form is just about 100 years old. Over this span of a century Britain has changed enormously, perhaps even more than most other western countries.

Externally, it was the richest and most powerful country in the world, commanding an empire unparalleled in human history. Now it lies twentieth, and falling, in the tables of national wealth per head. And the empire has gone with the speed of soft snow under a warm, damp westerly wind. [. . .]

As that national performance has become increasingly disappointing, so there has developed an increasing tendency to criticise the political framework within which it has flagged, and the somewhat ossified form which this 100-year-old model has now assumed.

This brings me to why I chose to put that as its approximate age. 1868 marked the end of a confused period of mid-19th-century politics and the election of the first Gladstone Government. Hitherto, governments had mostly emerged from shifting combinations in the House of Commons, with royal preference playing a significant role. Although this was not immediately apparent, a new pattern then began to emerge.

Henceforth the general election was the key factor, and governments assumed a much sharper party shape. The House of Commons, as a selector of governments, faded into the background. It long retained its position as a gladiatorial arena in which individual reputations were made or lost, but that was different from making governments. [. . .]

Thus British government became essentially party government. Despite the significance I have attached to the 1868 date, the system did not spring fully grown from the sea. It took many decades to evolve into its full rigidity. Many MPs occupied semi-independent po-

sitions. The great majority were, of course, financially independent — they had to be, with no parliamentary salaries until 1911; they did not depend greatly upon national machines or even national policies for their votes; quite a lot were consistently returned unopposed; and a good many were without political ambition, beyond that of being a member of the House of Commons. The power of the party Whips was therefore very limited. The House of Commons might not have much power to make or break governments, but it was nobody's poodle.

The position persisted broadly until the 1920s. The major factor of change then was the rise of the Labour Party. The degree of independence which had softened the corners of the party system was an independence largely based on class. Once a working-class party arose — although there were always strong middle-class elements in the Labour Party — most of the factors I have just described obviously ceased to apply. Furthermore, the Labour party had a strong strand of 'democratic centralism' in its theory — although probably more in its theory than in its practice. It believed in discipline, in the importance of the party conference, in the idea of the mandate — of a government being elected to carry out a detailed and specific programme which it had announced in advance.

Between the wars politics were unbalanced. The Labour Party had achieved a remarkable feat in breaking through the defences of the system to replace the Liberal Party. But it had done so at the price of two decades of Conservative dominance. After 1945 the balance was restored. In the 21 years from 1918 to 1939 there were only three years when the Conservatives were not in office. In the 34 years since 1945 each major party has had 17 of government. The postwar period should therefore have been the apotheosis of the two-party system. Superficially it has worked with smoothness and with perfect fairness. But has it? [. . .]

We may or may not have too much legislation, but we certainly have too much short-lived legislation, measures put on the statute book by one party in the almost certain knowledge that they will be reversed by the other. This could be avoided if governments, before embarking on a major controversial bill, would ask themselves one simple question: is it likely to last? If it is, do it, and do it with conviction. If not, please spare us too many queasy rides on the ideological big dipper. [. . .]

One major disadvantage of excessive political partisanship is that it fosters precisely the sort of industrial mood which is rapidly turning Britain into a manufacturing desert. If on the House of Commons floor it is always the fault of the other side, how can politicians preach convincingly against the prevalence of such a mood on the shop-floor?

This, some people will say with horror, is an unashamed plea for the strengthening of the political centre. Why not? The vocations of politicians ought to be to represent, to channel, to lead the aspirations of the electorate. These aspirations, not on every issue but in essential direction, pull far more towards the centre than towards the extremes. [. . .]

A great argument has been joined about democracy within the Labour Party. It is an important subject, with political and constitutional implications extending well beyond the domestic affairs of one party. But to some considerable extent the basis for it appears to me to be misconceived. The questions are wrongly posed. It is desirable neither to stand rigidly upon the status quo nor to hand over still greater power to an unrepresentative party machine whose pretensions on policy become greater as its effectiveness in maintaining a powerful organisation in the country — the real job of a party machine — becomes less.

This applies to most of the issues in dispute. Should it be made easier to get rid of sitting MPs? No one should argue that an MP, however ineffective his performance, is entitled to a plush-covered seat for life. But equally, there is no real democracy or respect for representative parliamentary government in suggesting that tiny groups of perhaps 20 or 30 activists should have power

of political life or death over a member who has been elected by 20 000 or 30 000 constituents, and whose fault is not lack of personal effectiveness but the advocacy of political views which are probably much closer to those of the 20 000 or 30 000 than to those of the 'people's court' of the 20 or 30. 'Who can tell for certain?', it may be rejoined. Indeed. Then let it be put to the test. Let there be the full right for an MP to be challenged. But let it be done before those to whom he ought to be responsible — the mass of his electorate. Either give the MP reasonable security to get on with his job, or, if a major dispute arises with his local party, let a properly organised and officially conducted *primary election* be held.[. . .]

What has all this to do with our sluggish economic performance? Our great failure, for decades now, has been lack of adaptability. Sometimes this rigidity is a source of strength. It was very good not to be too adaptable in 1940. But, overall, it is a source of weakness. Some societies — France in the second half of the Third Republic, pre-revolutionary Russia, the Austro-Hungarian Empire — have been still less adaptable than our own. But they hardly provide grounds for comfort. Compared with post-war Germany, post-war Japan, Fifth Republic France (industrially at least), the United States for virtually the whole of its history — compared, for that matter, with early Victorian Britain — modern Britain has been sluggish, uninventive and resistant to voluntary change, not merely economically but socially and politically as well. We cannot successfuly survive unless we can make our society more adaptable; and an unadaptable political system works heavily against this. Politicians cannot cling defensively to their present somewhat ossified party and political system while convincingly advocating the acceptance of change everywhere else in industry and society. 'Everybody change but us', is never a good slogan.

The paradox is that we need more change accompanied by more stability of direction. It is a paradox but not a contradiction. Too often we have superficial and quickly reversed political change without much purpose or underlying effect. This is not the only paradox. We need the innovating stimulus of the free market economy without either the unacceptable brutality of its untrammelled distribution of rewards or its indifference to unemployment. [. . .]

After 1951, there was a decline in the active membership of the parties; there was a decline in the participation in elections; and there was a decline within that reduced participation in the share of the votes going to the big parties. In 1951, 83 per cent of the electorate voted, and no fewer than 97 per cent of those who went to the polls voted for one or other of the two big parties. In the second 1974 election only 73 per cent of the electorate voted and only three-quarters of those voted Labour or Conservative. To put it another way: the Labour Party in 1951 polled 40 per cent of the total electorate, including those who stayed at home, and it just lost. In October 1974 it polled 28 per cent of the electorate and it just won. Even in 1979, with some recovery in the total vote and a substantial victory, the Conservatives polled only 33 per cent of the electorate.

Another sign of disillusion was the growing habit for governments to lose support almost as soon as they had been elected. The Labour Government of 1945 lost not a single by-election in its six years of office. The Conservative Government of 1951 actually gained one by-election and lost none. Thereafter the pattern changed. Every subsequent government sustained swingeing by-election defeats. The Conservatives quite often lost to the Liberals, the Labour Party mainly to the Conservatives or to a nationalist candidate. But from 1958 to 1978 the safest seats were liable to topple.

This represented no settled view on the part of the electorate. The seats often returned to their previous allegiance at the subsequent general election. But for most of its period of office every government, on the evidence of by-elections and public opinion polls alike, looked unpopular and bereft. This was inevitably damaging to its authority and consistency of purpose.

There has also been a weakening of the position of the House of Commons. It has recently declined as a forum of national debate, or even as a gladiatorial arena in which political reputations are made or destroyed, on top of its long-lost government-making capacity.

[from *The Listener*, 29 November 1979]

"Well, no one can say we're not a real party now — we've got a leadership crisis, policy disagreements, we're slipping in the polls and we've had a full-scale rebellion!"

[from the *Daily Telegraph*, 10 February 1982]

Can Mr Jenkins' Centre hold?

Briefly, he blames much of Britain's economic failure since 1956 (the year of Suez) on political ossification; and he hopes for salvation through a re-drawing of Party lines, isolating the Marxist Left of the Labour Party, and creating a new Radical Centre as an alternative to Mrs Thatcher's brand of dogmatic Conservatism.

Where the argument is weak is in what Mr Jenkins calls the 'content of politics' (as distinct from the insti-tutions, about which he says most). His prescription is not greatly differ-ent from what used to be called But-skellism or middle ground politics, as interpreted in recent years by Heath, Wilson and Callaghan, particularly in the period of the Lib-Lab pact.

It has not produced success. It is now widely accepted that Britain be-gan to run into trouble during the Macmillan years. Mr Jenkins dem-onstrates this himself: during the first 13 years of the EEC, income per head in the Six rose by 72 per cent, and by 35 per cent in Britain. From being al-most the richest country in Europe, we became one of the poorest. ('You never had it so good'!). The tragedy of Britain's mistimed entry into Europe — catching the bus when it had stopped moving economically — can scarcely be blamed on the present Par-ty system.

On PR and party realignment also, Mr Jenkins's arguments have many attractions, especially to those in search of a new magic ingredient to transform our politics. But PR is not a panacea. It does not, in itself, solve problems. To extend a marrriage analogy Mr Jenkins uses into the di-vorce courts, has the present system irretrievably broken down? The ver-dict must be 'not proven' or 'not yet'.

The declining support for the two principal parties since the stirring days of 1950 and 1951, and the massive under-representation of the Liberal vote, are both worrying features of the political scene, and Mr Jenkins is right to examine them. But his argument may be circular here. Is not the drop in support for both major parties, and the rise of the Liberals, itself a mark of our general economic failure (Mr Jen-kins's starting-point) rather than a mark of the popularity or relevance of Liberal policies (which have been imaginative, but distinctly erratic, over the years). The fact is that neither Mrs Thatcher, Mr Callaghan, Mr Benn nor Mr Jenkins himself offers an economic policy which carries total conviction. Nor does Mr Steel.

The principal argument against PR is one that the lecture touched on, but did not fully examine: that the choice between policies would be re-moved from the voters and handed over to the Party leaders. The risk is that the system would seem to offer more choice, by breaking down the adversary system, but that in practice the choices would be made secretly in smoke-filled rooms.

One does not need to be a slave to manifesto politics to think that a clear choice between programmes — even if they differ only in their handling of the mixed economy and the taxation system, as Mr Jenkins clearly does from Mrs Thatcher — is a worthwhile part of democracy. Labour, as Mr Jen-kins says, is itself a coalition, and Sir Harold Wilson, Mr Callaghan and Mr Jenkins himself made their com-promises with the Left. Mr Callaghan made them with David Steel during the Lib-Lab pact. Compromises can be good or bad. Surely under PR, even a government led from the Radi-cal Centre would probably have to shop around for its majority. Is it in-conceivable, if the House of Com-mons contained no single-party ma-jority, that a firm or two would have to be nationalised to buy the parliamen-tary support of a Bennite rump?

That is not an edifying prospect. Like any other system, PR can pro-duce benign or malign results. It oper-ated in the Weimar Republic as well as in the Federal Republic today. It has produced Herr Ertl and an ossi-fied CAP, as well as Chancellor Schmidt. It has left civil war divisions in the Irish Republic ossified for the subsequent 60 years, yet it has loos-ened politics a little, and to the good, since it was reintroduced in Ulster.

[from *The Observer* (editorial), 25 November 1979]

Divided we stand for coalition

David Owen

We should not forget that before the formation of the Social Democratic Party, considerable thought was given to whether Britain would be better governed by having four parties — Labour, Social Democrat, Liberal and Conservative. The alternative would have been from the outset to establish a single third party, either by those of us in Parliament joining the Liberals, or openly to present the creation of the Social Democratic Party as the first step towards a merger with the Liberals and formation of an Alliance Party.

The first step strategy came up early in the formation of the SDP with the suggestion of allowing joint membership, but that was rejected. The expressed belief in the Limehouse Declaration was that there was a definable philosophy of Social Democracy that was unrepresented by any party in British politics and that it would provide the electoral basis for a totally new party. That belief was very soon justified by the fact that nearly 60 per cent of the members who joined the Party in the first year of its foundation had never belonged to any other political party. A new political constituency in the country had been identified and mobilised.

Four parties enable a coalition government to be formed consisting wholly or predominantly of Social Democrats and Liberals, and our Alliance is all the time establishing the two parties in the eyes of the electorate

as the natural coalition partners. We are in effect accustoming the electorate to the new politics of proportional representation. An argument against a three-party solution recognised, particularly in view of the reaction of many Liberal voters to the Lib-Lab Pact of 1977–8, that it would mean the third party choosing either one of the traditional left or right parties as its coalition partner.

It was clear that if an Alliance Party was formed, that an Alliance-Labour or Alliance-Conservative coalition would annoy and offend different sections of its support. There would always be a constant danger of an Alliance Party's identity being squeezed to the left or to the right by Labour or the Conservatives, whichever Party was not a partner in the coalition.

This is greatly reduced in a three-party coalition, Social Democrat-Liberal-Labour, or Liberal-Social Democrat-Conservative.

Both Labour and Conservatives would welcome a single Alliance Party; the two class-based parties know well that it is far easier to narrow an Alliance Party down into a small centrist band of opinion, but far harder to do this if we keep a two party Alliance.

Electoral reform gives the diversity of opinion, representation and expression which is an essential element in ensuring that the Alliance provides a stable but radical government. Coalition politics means open negotiations between parties rather than,

as in the past, closed argument within parties. Coalition government ensures that the role of Prime Minister is that of the chairman of the Cabinet. Some of the best prime ministers have been those who saw their office in this way. Clement Attlee demonstrated convincingly that this style of leadership could produce radical government.

The authoritarian style leader or leaderene that marked the 1964–7 years of Harold Wilson and the Prime Ministership of Margaret Thatcher have been singularly bad periods of government. In a coalition, there is another party leader who has to be squared and who has an independent power base that has to be accommodated. Coalition government or government by inter-party agreement has occurred for 30 years during this century, and only eight of these years were wartime. They were not noted for being weak governments. The 1977–8 period of the rather limited Labour-Liberal Pact was one of the better periods of government in the last 20 years. At least in combination it could claim 58 per cent rather than 39 per cent of the votes cast in October 1974.

The last nine months of the Labour Government without the Liberal influence showed Labour the servant of the unions, unwilling to stand up for the national interest in the infamous winter of discontent.

[from *The Guardian*, 4 July 1983]

Questions

1   When did MPs first receive payment for their work? (E5)

2   What importance does Jenkins attach to the year 1868? On what grounds does he suggest that party government did not fully evolve until the 1920s? (E5)

3   In terms of party government Jenkins suggests that there is something significant about the period 1945–79. What is this? (E5)

4   Instead of mandatory reselection procedures for MPs, what alternative does Jenkins suggest to resolve disputes?

5   What reasons does Jenkins give for the decline in the powers of the House of Commons over the past eighty years? (E5)

6   Indicate how Jenkins argues the case for strengthening the political centre. (E5)

7   'Externally, it was the richest and most powerful country in the world . . . Now it lies twentieth, and falling, in the tables of national wealth per head.' (E5) What reasons does Jenkins give to explain this economic decline of Britain since about 1879?

8   What case does Owen present to justify the following: (a) coalition government; (b) a four-party system? (E7)

Class Discussion

1   Explain what Jenkins means by the following, and illustrate with examples: (a) 'a short-lived legislation? (b) 'manufacturing desert'; (c) 'national machines'; (d) 'democratic centralism'. (E5)

2   How far would you agree with *The Observer*'s comment on the present party system that 'The verdict must be "not proven" or "not yet" '? (E6)

3   How valid do you think *The Observer*'s main objections to PR are? (See also F6.)

Extension Work

1   Mention four reasons for the decline in support for the two main political parties since 1951. Has there been a reversal of this trend in 1979 and 1983?

2   Explain the following phrases: (a) 'adversary system' (b) 'secretly in smoke-filled rooms'; (c) 'Butskellism'; (d) 'slave to manifesto politics'. (E6)

3   Explain in full detail what is meant by the phrase 'catching the bus when it had stopped moving economically'. (E6)

4   What prompted the formation of the Lib-Lab Pact in 1977? (E5, E6)

5   When, and why, did David Owen replace Roy Jenkins as SDP leader? Give details of Owen's previous political career.

6 Why has the Alliance been unable to 'break the mould of British politics' as its chief supporters hoped it would?

7 Why has the period 1956–7 been considered significant regarding Britain's foreign policy and relations with the rest of western Europe?

E8–E10   *Pressure groups and their tactics*

E8

Carry your own case

Dennis Hart

The pressure group can turn private grievance into a public cause. If passions are sustained, argument marshalled and protest properly organised, the bulkiest barricades of remote bureaucratic indifference may crumble.

The oldest and most successful pressure groups are the permanent associations of producers (the British Medical Association, for example, or the Confederation of British Industry or the Trade Union Congress), which have so managed to convince us of their importance that it is now probably a convention of the Constitution that the Government should consult them before introducing legislation that might affect their interests.

Consumers began to organise in the same way but much later, and a considerable increase in the number of consumer groups is expected in the 1970s, of which a significant number will surely be groups formed by or to protect the poor (consumers consume services, including Government services, as well as goods): already we have the Claimants Union, which represents the interests of those who receive social welfare benefits, and organisations such as Shelter or the Child

Poverty Action Group are essentially the same sort of thing.

But those of which accounts follow exemplify consumer groups of rather a different and perhaps more important sort, the group that springs up only in response to a specific official ineptitude or injustice, fights its battle, and dies. It has become the watchdog from which no bureaucrat can feel safe. It is the twentieth century's contribution to government by the people, evidence that men more or less free do not yet find it easy to sink into the placidness that unattractive political minds mistakenly suppose to represent the triumph of law and order.

The success of such a group seldom depends on a multitude of dedicated crusaders or on a marvellously skilful organisation or on an abundance of money or (thank God) on bought professional skills: what counts is the tenacity and passion of a few. For honest outrage or simple conviction, intelligently channelled, can be more than a match for a bureaucrat, as we shall see.

'Do you remember the name of Sir Albert Richardson?' Mr Gordon

Priest, lecturer in architecture at Bristol University, is driving me towards a remarkable place in England that I have never seen. 'He said Clifton was the most beautiful suburb in the world. Sir John Summerson has spoken of it as the Venice of the North. Betjeman is always eulogising it. It is an 18th and 19th century suburb of Bristol, one of the great town-planning and architectural achievements of English culture, overlooking the Avon Gorge.

'Bristol has been slow in designating Conservation Areas.' Under the Civic Amenities Act, 1967, a local authority may proclaim areas within its jurisdiction to be places of such special architectural or historic interest that their character and appearance are to be preserved or enhanced. 'I think to date there are actually two, although others, including Clifton, are about to be announced. But Clifton should have been one of the first in the country.

If Clifton *had* been a Conservation Area the situation might never have arisen.

As it was, Bristol Corporation gave outline planning permission to the owners of a Clifton hotel called the Grand Spa' — for a time in the 18th century Clifton challenged Bath as England's leading spa — 'to build a 126-bedroom hotel eight storeys high in the Avon Gorge within a stone's throw of Brunel's suspension bridge, which Kenneth Clark in his book *Civilisation* calls the most beautiful in the world.' [. . .]

Actually what happened was that the Development of Tourism Act came into force providing for grants of £1000 a bedroom to be made for a newly-built hotel if application for planning permission and a substantial start on the site were made before 1 April, 1971. If the company built a 126-bedroom hotel and fulfilled these conditions it would be given a present of £126 000. The company therefore made its planning application, the Royal Fine Art Commission gave the project its blessing subject to some readily-made modifications in the design, and Bristol gave outline planning permission within 23 days. Even so, it was already the end of January 1971.

Bristol has a number of amenity societies, including the Civic Society, in which Mr Priest serves on the committee, and the Clifton and Hotwells Improvement Society (Georgian/ Regency Hotwells is a suburb below Clifton), of which he is a member. It was the secretary of the Clifton and Hotwells Society, Mrs Jennifer Gill, an archaeologist married to a university physicist, who uncovered the situation when she made a routine inspection of the planning register.

'It's hard to remember exactly how it happened.' Mr Priest consults his diary for the period and finds it blank. 'I think Jennifer and I called a meeting in her house or perhaps it was here in mine' — we are now seated in Mr Priest's ground-floor architect's-functional sittingroom-cum-kitchen

having tea with his wife and daughter — 'of members of both societies, to see what we could do as a combined group. It must have been around mid-January, 1971.

About 20 turned up at the meeting, including Berthold Lubetkin, the very distinguished architect responsible for, for example, the Penguin House at the London Zoo and the High Point flats in Highgate, who now lives in Bristol. Also Edward Carter, who wrote *The Future of London* and was administrative head of the Architectural Association's School of Architecture. I think I took the chair. The main thing we discussed was publicity to encourage people to write to their MPs and to the Minister of the Environment and to local councillors, but unfortunately the postal strike was on.'

The only thing to do was send a courier at regular intervals to London and also make use, for delivery purposes, of anyone who happened to be going there anyway. The group, (called STAG — Save The Avon Gorge) advertised on posters and in the local press that letters to the Minister delivered to any of a series of local addresses would reach him. Letters by the hundred arrived, and every third day for about three weeks around 200 were carried from Bristol to Whitehall.

Obtaining the support of the eminent was regarded as another urgent matter.

'People were suggesting names. Betjeman, for example. I wrote to him and got a letter back saying that we simply must stop it but that *he* couldn't take part, so I wrote back and said, "You must". And he did. And he gave magnificent evidence. And that was the one day the media chaps caught on to, the one day the television cameras were there.'

Evidence of what and to whom?

'I'm talking about the public inquiry. An astonishingly large number of people opposed the scheme. Not even the recent City Docks battle in Bristol, or the argument about the future of the *SS Great Britain*, or the Docks roundabout proposal, created anything like the same response. We had also approached local MPs: Robert Cooke, Wedgwood Benn, Arthur Palmer, Martin McLaren. Palmer was the most active. He came and talked to us, and he asked questions in the House. So did Cooke.

Money had come in as the result of a not-very-efficiently organised appeal, between £600 and £700 in all, most of it collected by door-to-door canvassing. The largest donation was £25, but the bulk came in cheques for 30 shillings. At this end of Clifton you cross the boundaries between middle class and workers. Old ladies and gentlemen, pensioners, used to press small sums into my wife's hand when she'd be out shopping'.

'It was very touching', Mrs Priest observes.

'Our solicitor, Craig Begg, of Lawrence and Company of Bristol', Mr Priest resumes, 'represented us at the inquiry on a "firm's expenses only" sort of arrangement, and our counsel, a man named Paul Chadd who mainly does crime but is interested in conservation, gave his services free.'

The Minister ordered the inquiry on 4 March, 1971. It opened on 17 May, was conducted by Mr S. W. Midwinter, a Department of the Environment planning inspector, and lasted nine days. Objectors included the National Trust, the Georgian Group, and Long Ashton's Rural and Parish Councils (which, although in charge of the other side of the gorge and so about to be forever faced with what one of the councillors called a glass and concrete monstrosity, were not consulted by Bristol and learned of the proposal only from newspapers). [. . .]

'I always thought we *ought* to win, but by the time the inquiry started I was trying not to think of it. By the end of the second day I'd decided that Mr Midwinter, whom at first I'd thought rather prissy, was very much on top of the thing. We were all cheered by the intelligence shown in his questions. And all the way through the quality of our witnesses and of our legal chaps seemed to me consistently higher than those of the other side. And some Corporation officials seemed really rather silly men, not very good at standing up to intelligently posed, closely argued questioning.'

Meanwhile on 4 March, which is the day the Minister ordered the inquiry, the *Western Daily Press* had carried an enervating leader — 'Within a short time the hotel will be accepted and all objections forgotten'. On the following day its leader was even worse: 'The *Western Daily Press* believes this hotel should be built and that it will enhance the area' — and, I suppose, it encouraged the hotel company. In any case, the company was determined not to be done out of its £126 000. On 18 March, the Minister having called in the papers in the case and ordered the public inquiry and no final planning permission having been given, the company started work on the site; it had 13 days in which to do substantial work before the statutory time limit expired. Whether or not what the company did on the site *was* for the purposes of the Act substantial turned out to be academic, for on 14 October 1971, the minister accepted Mr Midwinter's report and rejected the company's plans.

[from the *Telegraph Magazine*, 3 November 1972]

| E9 |

The Politics of Persuasion

Who's wining and dining whom in Westminster? And why? There's more to political lobbying than meets the eye. Carolyn Faulder reports.

Political lobbying is a growth industry in this country. Although staid and low-key by comparison with the brash antics that go on in Washington — that city of lobbyists — more is happening in the gloomy corridors of Westminster and Whitehall, and in the plush palaces of the EEC, than we ordinary citizens and voters realise. Who are these new professionals? Whose interests do they represent? And should we feel concern or relief that newcomers are breaching the barricades of political power?

Since before the war, there have always been one or two lone operators working on behalf of private clients, but organised lobbying on a significant scale really started in the mid-Sixties. Lobbying, says the dictionary, means influencing members of the legislature, i.e. Parliament, and soliciting their votes. Ironically, considering the shady connotations attached to the activity, it was thoroughly worthy organisations like Shelter and the Child Poverty Action Group which first seized upon lobbying as a way of winning friends and bending sympathetic ears in high places. Driven by despair at the inaction of Harold Wilson's government over social reform, they turned themselves from charities into overtly political pressure groups.

Des Wilson, at a mere 42 acknowledged granddaddy of political campaigners, distinguishes firmly between what he calls the 'corridors of power lobbyists', the people who represent commercial and industrial interests and 'probably make a lot of money at it', and campaigners like himself who take on causes of public concern which can't be won behind the scenes but do require massive support. Currently chairman of CLEAR, the Campaign for Lead-Free Air (which achieved its objective of getting effective government legislation ahead of target), as well as being a director of

Shelter and Friends of the Earth, he is now devoting his considerable energy and experience to the 1984 Campaign for Freedom of Information. 'It's something which has been dear to my heart for years. It's going to be very big and it's going to be my last throw. You've got to stop before the point comes when the campaigns exist for you instead of you for them.' Small comfort for those still licking their wounds from engaging with him, and bad news for those who desperately need someone with his charisma and expertise to set their cause alight. [. . .]

They can't afford to miss a trick
The background work that goes into presenting a client's case requires many skills and qualities. A lot of the work is technical and highly specialist and requires a good deal of painstaking research. [. . .]

One lobby against another
'One of the main justifications for starting a pressure group is to fight other pressure groups', says Des Wilson. His point is neatly illustrated by 32-year-old Judith Hampson [. . .] Chief Animal Experimentation Research Officer for the RSPCA. Unlike most lobbyists, who get a regular charge of adrenalin from their political

activities, she is frankly uninterested in the wheeler-dealing aspects. 'So much of politics is rhetoric and I hate the charade of dressing for the part — wearing a business suit and flashing a briefcase — but of course I do it when it's necessary.' She regards her political lobbying as just one aspect, albeit very important, of what has become her life's work to make people understand 'that the way we treat animals is a central human activity, not a side issue. I can't imagine a world of ethical vegetarians ill-treating other people.' [. . .]

From the moment MPs arrive in the House, the lobbyists track them as carefully as big game hunters on safari. Their constituency and other interests are noted, their debating skills carefully observed and their particular affiliations recorded. Once targeted, they need handling with tact and discretion — and here women may score, because they are more inclined to use a softly-softly approach. None of the women lobbyists I spoke to would actually admit to using feminine guiles deliberately, though they suggested 'there are others who might'. Similarly, they were all at pains to deny the wining-and-dining image, agreeing that it was a regrettable practice. 'Very old-fashioned', said Jenny Jeger. 'We don't believe in buying MPs.'

[from *Good Housekeeping*, March 1984]

E10

The British disease
Peter Jenkins

Governments and Trade Unions: The British Experience 1964–79 by Denis Barnes and Eileen Reid. Heinemann
The 'trade union problem' has dominated British politics for the last two decades. It has been the downfall of three governments — Wilson's in 1970, Heath's in 1974 and Callaghan's in 1979. During that time, full employment and free collective bargaining became at last incompatible, and the former was in effect aban-

doned in 1968. As the union problem grew more acute, the relative decline of the British economy accelerated — although which was chiefly responsible for the other is less obvious. Successive governments attempted to intervene in collective bargaining with incomes policies, or to regulate the industrial relations system at law, but at the end of two decades both strategies were in disrepute. The problem seemed more intractable than ever.

During those decades Britain became more famous for its trade unions than for anything else. Strikes, demarcation disputes and tea breaks replaced cricket and the changing of the Guard as the popular stereotypes of the British way of life. As the crisis deepened, we became the butt of the kind of mocking contempt we had reserved for the French during their Fourth Republic. Typical of the verdicts passed on Britain's slow industrial death was the Brookings Institution's 'bloody-mindedness syndrome'. The 'union problem' had become a cultural deformity.

For some of this time the British, or at least some of them, imagined themselves to be blazing a trail for advanced industrial society. George Brown's incomes policy and National Plan and, later, the Social Contract were claimed as major socio-economic innovations — British firsts. The Manchu Empire had suffered similar ethnocentric delusions and had published maps which showed it to lie at the centre of the world; the British, for their part, did not seem wholly to grasp that in other countries things were ordered differently. 'Keep the law out of industrial relations', said the conventional British wisdom, but nearly everywhere else industrial relations were conducted within a legal framework. 'Wages don't cause inflation' was another superstition, promulgated by trade union leaders and monetarists alike. Trade unionism — British-style — was taken for granted like the weather: something about which there was nothing to be done except complain. Accused of drinking champagne at breakfast, Noël Coward asked: 'Doesn't everybody?' Accused of committing a form of national suicide, the British in the Sixties and Seventies merely raised their eyebrows, as if this was the way of the industrialised world. Wasn't everybody? [. . .]

Sir Denis takes up the story in more detailed form from 1964 onwards. With the election of a Labour Government came the first attempt to re-create the kind of partnership with the unions which had served the Attlee Government so well: but as economic difficulties grew, voluntary co-operation degenerated (in 1966) into the first attempt to impose a statutory pay policy. Then, after the debacle of 'In Place of Strife' and the 1970 election, we had the Selsdon experiment and the first attempt since 1912 to alter fundamentally the position of the unions in law; the famous U-turn of 1972 (following a humiliating defeat by the miners) led to the Chequers talks — another essay in statutory incomes policy — and the eventual fall of the Heath Government (again at the hands of the miners).

Three themes run through this narrative account. One is the increasing drama which surrounded the question of pay policy. Another is the politicisation of the industrial relations system itself. The third is the weakening authority of government, not least as the consequence of chronic economic difficulties. Incomes policy brought the government into direct conflicts with unions over wages: as strikes against the government's policies became more frequent and serious, 'it became politically impossible for ministers to ignore the issue of trade union power'; as trade union power was called into question, so the lines between industrial and political activities became more and more blurred. The government was greatly enfeebled by the devaluation of 1967 and the failure of its economic policies. By 1970 both the attempt to regulate collective bargaining with incomes policy and to curb trade union powers by law had been abandoned.

The problems inherited by the Heath Government were considerably worse than those which had faced Labour in 1964. Sir Denis is reserved about his own role in those years but, if we read between the lines, it is plain that he was most sceptical of the attempt to open a new chapter of pay policy in 1972 and, later, opposed to the course of confrontation on which the Government set itself with Phase Three, and held to in spite of the transformation of the international economic situation by OPEC in 1973. The ambitious character of the elaborate incomes policy which was being put together in Whitehall (one may suspect that the late Lord Armstrong is the chief target of Sir Dennis's criticism), combined with the Prime Minister's characteristic determination, was, he judges, 'politically disastrous'. It was the 'inflexibility' of this policy which was to set the Government on a collision course. Sir Denis hints strongly that he would have used the energy crisis as an excuse to take avoiding action. But it was the Armstrong view which prevailed. By January 1974 (with Sir Denis removed from the Department of Employment) it was too late. Heath was now on a hiding to nothing. The choice was between a humiliating and grossly inflationary capitulation and confrontation together with almost certain defeat. He had been misled, Sir Denis suggests, by the unions (who had never intended to come to an agreement with a Conservative government), and then trapped into a statutory pay policy.

The final sections of the book are written with a freer hand and are for that reason the best. Sir Denis still knew pretty much what was going on but, from the sidelines, feels more able to say what he thinks. He regards the Social Contract as marking an important change in the unions' attitude towards government: by extending the scope of collective bargaining, they set themselves more openly political goals. He compares the crisis over 'In Place of Strife' with the crisis of 1931, and Jack Jones's role to that of Bevin, who determined that the unions would in future keep the Labour Party under firmer control. The result this time was the Liaison Committee which gave birth to the Social Contract. In the aftermath of the Heath debacle, a return to pay policy was a most dubious political and practical proposition. Sir Denis finds it impossible to believe that ministers (Michael Foot?) seriously supposed that the unions would be capable of voluntary wage restraint. So he at least was not surprised when this 'trade union pay policy' resulted in 31 per cent wage inflation between July 1974 and July 1975.

He concedes that the 5 per cent policy which ensued — Jack Jones's policy — was 'remarkably effective in terms of wage restraint' and achieved 'the most severe cut in real wages in twenty years'. But, Sir Denis argues, 'like the standstill and the period of "severe restraint" in 1966–7, it was in a sense wasted effort'. That is, inflation soon gathered pace again. He dates the demise of the Social Contract from 1976, which was the year of the worst sterling crisis since the war. Agreement between unions and government became impossible. The partnership was broken. In 1979, 'For the first time the unions openly used their industrial power to wreck the policy of a Labour Government.'

Sir Denis peers into the future with the aid of three bleak assumptions. There will be no change in the two-party system. The relationship between each of the two parties and the trade unions will not change. The trade unions themselves will not change: that is to say, the TUC will continue to have little authority over its affiliates, unions will continue to compete for membership, and union leaders for power within the Labour Movement. On the basis of these assumptions, he predicts that the unions will continue to insist upon free collective bargaining, will demand changes in the law to assist them in this purpose, will pursue 'syndicalist objectives' — through public ownership, 'industrial democracy' and planning agreements — and will seek to increase further their political power. In the final paragraph of the book Sir Denis wonders, gloomily, about his forecasts and assumptions. 'The continuation of the existing relationship between governments and the trade union movement in a situation of continuing economic failure could have unpredictable political consequences. These may compel changes in the trade union movement itself, the party political system in which it plays a key role, the relations it has with governments and the legal framework within which it operates.' Although what he seems to have in mind is some sort of political crisis or breakdown, it is difficult to disagree with the logic of his conclusions.

Since his book went to press, there have been some signs of a check to trade union power. Membership is falling, especially in the public service unions; militant leadership has been in some cases spurned; the 'economic whip' may be having some effect. Whether the balance of power can be redressed it is too early to say. The massive unpopularity of trade unions, not least among their own members, suggests that their legal immunities and privileges are not indefinitely sustainable, and yet during the period covered by this book we have seen the trade union habit of mind and behaviour spread almost across the nation. Professional, technical and managerial groups have organised themselves and engaged in — or at least threatened — 'industrial action'; essential services have been withdrawn and humanity, occasionally, forgotten; hospital consultants have become 'militant' and the language of Dave Spart has taken on a middle-class accent. We are all trade unionists now.

[from the *London Review of Books*, 21 August–3 September 1980]

Questions

1 How does Hart distinguish between the following pairs of groups: (a) producer and consumer; (b) permanent and temporary? (E8)
2 What measures did STAG take to promote its cause or achieve its objective? (E8)
3 Suggest reasons why STAG won the campaign to prevent a hotel being built in the Avon Gorge. (E8)
4 What can you discover from E8 concerning procedures relating to appeals or campaigns against town or country development projects?
5 Why did certain organisations like Shelter change from charities into overtly political pressure groups? (E9)
6 What information does E9 provide concerning the reasons why pressure groups start?
7 For what reason did blue-chip companies start to form their own lobby in the early Seventies? (E9)
8 Illustrate with extracts from E10 what is meant by 'the British disease'.

Class Discussion

1 Why are some pressure groups more powerful and influential than others?
2 Are trade unions partially or wholly pressure groups? (E9, E10)
3 Why have successive governments since 1965 had difficulty in regulating trade union power by means of legislation? Refer to the phrase mentioned by Peter Jenkins, 'Keep the law out of industrial relations'. (E10)
4 Concerning the possible decline of trade union power, how true is the comment by Jenkins that the 'economic whip' may be having some effect? (E10)

Extension work

1 Distinguish between the following chief types of pressure groups: (a) protective (interest); (b) promotional (cause).
2 Why can house-owners be considered an implicit lobby? What special interest legislation particularly benefits this section of the community?
3 Which group is known informally as 'the Lobby', as distinct from political lobbying in general?
4 Find examples of organisations, such as the Police Federation, which have an MP as a spokesman to defend or promote their ideas in Parliament.
5 Why, and in what way, has the trade union movement been able to maintain an entrenched position within the Labour Party?
6 Explain how the 'trade union problem' (E10) contributed to the downfall of the governments of Wilson (1970), Heath (1974) and Callaghan (1979).
7 Give details on the following: (a) George Brown's National Plan; (b) the Social Contract; (c) Peter Jenkins' book *The Battle of Downing Street*; (d) the famous U-turn of 1972; (e) the Selsdon experiment; (f) the Bullock Report.

Elections, voting behaviour and political participation

Introduction

Most people's participation in politics is limited to voting in elections. F1 assesses the relative influence over time of the various factors that affect voting behaviour, and refers to growing electoral volatility of partisan dealignment, the weakening of loyalties or class allegiances to particular parties.

Since 1964 the electorate has become less polarised along class lines, and Conservative victories in 1970 and 1979 were based on increased support among skilled, semi-skilled and unskilled manual workers (labelled classes C2, D, E in F1 and F3). F3 also shows increased support for the Conservatives and the Liberals in 1979 (compared to October 1974) among the clerical and office workers (class C1) and the professional/managerial groups (class AB). The 1983 election eroded class-based voting even further, since only 47 per cent of the electorate voted as might be predicted from their social class. Ivor Crewe suggests that the important political division now occurs within the working class. He distinguishes between the old pro-Labour working class member: (typically a council tenant working in the public sector and living in Scotland or the North) and the pro-Conservative new working class member (typically an owner-occupier working in the private sector and living in the South)[1].

Disraeli once warned of a gulf between the rich and the poor in Britain. F2 suggests that the real division is now between North and South. Certainly the declining Conservative support in Scotland since 1955, their relative weakness in Wales, and the ending of the alliance with the Ulster Unionists, are factors undermining the Conservative claim to be the party of the whole UK. In 1979 89 per cent of their vote came from England.

F4 is an extract from a publication of the all-party campaign for electoral reform, of whom the political leaders are Roy Jenkins, Austin Mitchell and Sir Ian Gilmour. The Alliance's share of the vote in 1983 was 25.5 per cent, higher than any gained by the Liberals since 1923. Yet Labour won 186 more seats than the Alliance even though it gained only 700 000 more votes. The unfairness of the present system is shown in F4 and F5. (For an extreme opposing view, however, see K2.) F6 explains the single transferable vote form of proportional representation (PR), advocated by the Electoral Reform Society in preference to the present simple majority or first-past-the-post system.

Any modern system of democracy in a heavily populated or territorially large country implies representative or indirect democracy. People who are busy earning a living, studying, etc., elect councillors and MPs to administer and govern for them. Some people may get involved in election campaigns, in pressure or community groups, or through contacts with MPs and other officials about personal matters. Peter Tatchell in F7 argues a case for Labour supporters to take part in extra-parliamentary activity, another name for forms of direct action and protest activities such as demonstrations, sit-ins, boycotts and strikes. Such measures usually form a legitimate part of democracy, widening the base of popular participation. They could, however, be described as anti-constitutional or anti-parliamentary (if the purpose is to overthrow democracy and parliamentary rule by violence and terror so as to establish rule by dedicated minorities), or unconstitutional and undemocratic (if any group not representative of the electorate sought deliberately to overthrow a properly elected government). One problem is that with the present voting system few governments have the majority support of all the electorate, and this weakens its legitimacy or authority to rule in the eyes of those dissatisfied with its policies.

F8 looks at some of the activities undertaken by a branch, the basic 'grassroots' unit of the Labour Party. A danger is that a branch, like any organisation, ceases to be democratic in practice if the majority fail to participate and the activist minority, which does participate, elects leaders with views and policies that lack majority support. The fault, however, lies with the non-participants and is part of the price or risk of a democratic society.

[1] See also Crewe's 'The disturbing truth behind Labour's rout', *The Guardian*, 13 June 1983.

F1

'I was wary of another March election: British winters had a habit of remaining cold through most of March, and it seemed too much to hope that we could repeat the mild weather of March 1966. My caution, in the event, was justified: apart from a cold December, the winter barely began until February and remained cold through most of March and early April.'

That was the former Prime Minister, Harold Wilson, writing in his memoirs about why he called the 1970 general election when he did, and paying tribute to the theory that the Labour vote suffers when the weather is bad.

The idea that something as important as a general election can turn on something as trivial as the state of the weather may come as a shock, especially as there is still a popular idea of elections as times when voters act in a purely rational way: sifting impartially the issues put before them during the campaign and casting their votes as reason dictates, unaffected by such mundane concerns as whether one needs to put on an overcoat to get to the polling-station.

Popular as this idea may be, it bears almost no relation to the way voters behave in the real world.

In the real world, for example, most voters would have made up their minds long before the election is even called: the actual campaign has relatively little success in getting them to change their minds.

In the real world, too, specific 'issues' play only a small part in deciding elections. Indeed, most voters would be hard put to say what the specific issues in most elections are. What counts is the generalised image, or overall impression, which a party makes in the voter's mind.

A famous example is the 1955 survey of Bristol voters, quoted by J. Blondel, showing that, of Labour supporters, 68 per cent saw their party as being 'for the working class', while 85 per cent saw the Conservative Party as being 'for the rich, big business'.

Of course, issues play a part in forming images.

Indeed the regular opinion polls, such as those taken by Gallup, show that voters often have strong opinions on which party is best able to deal with the broad issues of politics: law and order, race, the economy, etc. But these opinions are often based on extraordinarily little detailed knowledge. For example, voters may well feel the Conservatives are better than Labour at dealing with law and order. Yet they would be hard put to list the practical measures by which the two parties mean to tackle rising crime.

So, given what Blondel calls 'the fairly narrow limits of the rational element in voting behaviour', how *do* people decide which party will get their vote? The question itself contains the first clue to an answer: this is the idea of *party*.

Elections are about choices between parties, not about choices between individual candidates. Although there is such a thing as a 'personal vote', when support is given to a candidate because of who he is rather than what he stands for, it is generally not thought to be worth much more than 1000 votes.

On the whole, voters are loyal to parties, not people. This is a truth which is quickly discovered by those occasional MPs who leave their party to strike out on their own. What usually happens is that though they may win one or two elections on a 'personal' vote following their resignation, quite soon the 'natural' primacy of party reasserts itself and they are out of office. By the same token, people who stand as independents (not tied to any one party) are almost never elected.

What lies behind this intense loyalty between party and voter?

One factor stands out above all. That factor is class. The most obvious truism of British politics is also, as it happens, the truest: the working class vote Labour and the middle class vote Conservative.

The tie between class and party may, as we shall see, be weakening. But it still seems to be stronger in Britain than in most other countries. (Alford, comparing

Britain, Canada, the US and Australia, found class had most effect on voting in Britain).

Elsewhere race or religion may have more effect. But in Britain class is still the major factor behind the 'political cleavage' — the way opinion divides.

Even in the October 1974 general election, when class voting was less obvious than usual, more than half the middle class votes were Conservative and more than half the working class votes were Labour. Less than a quarter of the votes of each class went to the party of the 'opposite' class (see Table 1).

Other cleavages do, of course, exist in Britain. In Northern Ireland, for example, the cleavage is almost wholly along religious, not class, lines: Protestants vote one way, Catholics another. Indeed the 'class' parties (Labour and Conservative) hardly bother to put up candidates there, so little chance of success do they have.

Even on the mainland, religion still has some effect on voting. In the last century there were strong links between Anglicanism and Conservatism, and between Nonconformism and Liberalism. While these links are now very much weaker, an area like Wales, traditionally Nonconformist, is still strongly anti-Conservative.

What does class mean? Here it means occupational class. Manual workers and their families are defined as working class. Non-manual workers and their families are defined as middle class.

Manual workers (i.e. those who work with their hands) tend to vote Labour. Non-manual workers (i.e. those who do white-collar jobs) tend to vote Conservative. The important word there is 'tend'. As Table 1 shows, there is a large minority in each class who vote with the 'opposite' class.

Why? Part of the answer may lie in a group of factors which seem to affect the strength of the 'natural' tie between class and party. Belonging to a trade union is one such factor. Working class voters who belong to a union are more likely to vote Labour than those who do not belong. Another such factor is the type of area in which the voter lives. Take, for example, two working class voters. One lives in a strongly working class area. The other lives in a strongly middle class area. In this situation the first voter is more likely to vote Labour than the second.

Richard Rose noted another factor: working class people who owned cars or telephones were more likely to vote Conservative than those who did not. A possible reason, he suggested, was that 'A telephone provides a means of communication outside the face-to-face boundaries of a working class community . . . A motor car provides a means of mobility outside the working class community and can bring workers into contact with a wide variety of new experiences and individuals.' But other explanations are possible.

Such factors help to explain what is usually seen as the central problem of voting behaviour in Britain: given that two-thirds of voters are working class, and given the strong tie between class and party, how can Conservative governments ever come to power?

It is a genuine problem. On the face of it, Labour holds all the cards. For example, there is a strong likelihood that children will vote for the same party as their parents. But, since working class parents tend to produce more children than middle class parents, it would seem that Labour would have an increasing advantage, taking over a larger and larger share of the electorate as time progressed.

So how *do* Conservative governments come to power?

The simple answer is that the party consistently manages to win a big slice of working class votes. As Table 1 shows, in October 1974, even though the Conservatives lost the election, they still managed to capture 24 per cent of the working class vote.

To some extent these 'working class defectors' are offset by their middle class equivalents who vote Labour (19.5 per cent in October 1974). However, as the differences in the figures shows, the middle class are less likely to 'defect' than the working class. Besides, the difference in votes (which is what elections are about) is much bigger than the differences in percentages might suggest.

Translated into votes, that 24 per cent of working class defectors was worth some 4.5 million votes to the Conservatives. The 19.5 per cent of middle class defectors was worth only about two million votes to Labour. Put another way, the Conservatives drew nearly half their total support from the working class, while Labour drew only about one-sixth of its total support from the middle class.

A study was made by E. A. Nordlinger of the 'working class Tory' ('Tory' is just another way of saying Conservative). He split the group into two: *deferentials* and *pragmatists*. ('Deference' means showing respect for supposedly superior authority. 'Pragmatism' means looking at things in a practical, matter-of-fact way.)

Nordlinger suggests that the deferentials vote Tory because they like their leaders to come from the upper classes and indeed think their own class does not produce good leaders. The pragmatists, on the other hand, vote Tory because they think that, in practice, Conservatives run the country better than Labour. (A later study by McKenzie and Silver came to much the same conclusion but describes the second group not as 'pragmatists' but as 'seculars'.)

According to Butler and Stokes there seem to be more pragmatists than deferentials in the current British electorate: 'We had in our sample a number of respondents who could be described as pure specimens of the socially deferential. But we were much more impressed by the fact that the Conservatives attracted working class support for many of the same reasons they attracted support throughout the country.'

Further help for the Conservatives comes from demographic factors such as age and sex. Women, for example, are more likely to vote Conservative than men. (According to Butler and Kavanagh's study of the October 1974 general election, 39 per cent of women's votes were Conservative compared with 32 per cent of men's.)

The reasons are not clear. They may, however, reflect the fact that women's jobs are more likely to be non-manual than men's. (The 1977 edition of *Social Trends*, the annual digest of government statistics on social policy and conditions, shows 56 per cent of women's jobs as non-manual compared with 38 per cent of men's.)

The old are more likely to vote Conservative than the young. (In October 1974, 49 per cent of the votes of the 65 + age-group were Conservative, compared with 24 per cent of the 18–24 age group.) Part of the reason is presumably that middle class people live longer than working class people. Women, too, tend to live longer than men, so the older a group of voters is, the higher the proportion is likely to be from these two groups, both tending to vote Conservative.

One theory sometimes put forward to explain the tendency of the old to vote Conservative is that of

'senescence' (literally, 'growing older'). This suggests that people naturally start on the left (the Labour side) of the political spectrum, and move right (towards the Conservatives) as they grow older.

This fits the popular idea that the young are radical and the old are Conservative. But the evidence of Butler and Stokes points to the opposite theory of 'immunisation' or 'conservation', which suggests that voters tend to stick to the party they choose when they first vote — and indeed to become more firmly attached to it the older they get.

Social mobility (the movement of people from one social group to another) is yet another factor helping the Conservatives. Those who move up the occupational ladder tend to absorb the political colour of their new surroundings. But those who move down are less likely to do so. This means a net gain for the Conservatives. At the same time the proportion of manual to non-manual jobs is changing — in the Conservatives' favour. The trend is to more jobs in offices (middle class) and fewer in factories (working class).

At least one factor — immigration — helps *both* parties. It helps Labour because, broadly speaking, immigrants vote Labour. Over the past ten years some of the biggest swings to Labour have been in areas where a lot of immigrants live.

But immigration is itself an issue in politics. Some working class voters who do not like immigrants may well switch their vote to the Conservatives. This seems most likely to happen in white constituencies next door to areas with high concentrations of blacks (for example, in areas like Bromsgrove or Lichfield on the fringes of Birmingham).

So far we have concentrated on the two main parties. After all, they still take the lion's share of the vote. But in a number of recent elections a sizeable share of the vote has been captured by 'third parties' (parties other than Labour or Conservatives).

In 1951, third parties took only 3.2 per cent of the total vote. By October 1974 their share had jumped to 25 per cent, a huge increase (Table 2). In Scotland and Wales, third parties did even better. In Scotland, where they did best of all, they took nearly 40 per cent of the total vote.

The parties which did most to eat into the Labour/Conservative dominance were the Liberals,

Table 1: Voting allegiance, October 1974

	All %	Middle class A, B, C1	Working class C2, D, E
	100	35	65
Con.	36	55.5	24
Lab.	39	19.5	53
Other	25	25	23

[derived from Butler and Kavanagh, '*The British General Election of October 1974*,' (Macmillan, 1975)]

Table 2: Third parties' share of total vote at general elections

1945	12.4
1950	10.4
1951	3.2
1955	3.9
1959	6.8
1964	12.5
1966	10.0
1970	10.5
1974 Feb.	24.9
1974 Oct.	25.0

[derived from F. W. S. Craig, *British Electoral Facts 1885–1975* (Macmillan, 1975)]

and the Scottish and Welsh Nationalists. Interestingly none was a class-based party. (As Table 1 shows, the 'other' parties won about the same share of support from the working class as they did from the middle class.) At the same time the two main parties may themselves have become less easy to differentiate on purely class lines.

All this may provide evidence that the ties between class and party have weakened to some degree. Indeed Richard Rose has suggested that the only reason those ties have been so strong in Britain is that other bases for

[from 'Society Today', *New Society*, 12 October 1978]

political cleavage have been so weak: 'In the absence of large groups of voters differing on religious, nationality or linguistic grounds, there is nothing left to divide voters but class. Class influences predominate by default.'

Many social scientists would disagree with that view. But it provides at least a potential key to future patterns of voting behaviour in Britain.

F2

Law of diminishing majorities

David McKie on the electoral swings that might throw Labour off

THE GREATEST merit claimed for the first-past-the-post election system in Britain is that, whatever its apparent unfairness, it can be relied on to give us governments with decent working majorities. But according to a new academic analysis unveiled last week, even that strength may be

seeping away; from now on, it may be more and more likely to produce hung parliaments.

This diagnosis was delivered at the Political Studies Association conference in Hull by Mr John Curtice, of Magdalen College, Oxford, and Mr Michael Steed of the Department of

Government at the University of Manchester.

The condition they discuss is largely the result of the demise of that good old psychological tool of trade, the cube law. This principle said that under the British electoral system the main parties could expect to take seats not in the ratio of the votes they won but in relation to the cube of that vote: that's to say, if the Conservatives polled 50 per cent of the vote and Labour 45 per cent they would take seats not in a 10 to 9 relationship, as equity might appear to dictate, but in the relationship 503 to 453, which is nearer 14 to 9. Thus a fairly narrow lead in terms of votes polled could be converted into a much more substantial lead in the number of seats gained, and so into a durable majority.

In the past, the working of this principle enabled you to predict pretty accurately how many seats a party would gain on a given swing. In 1959, for instance, the cube law principle said that for the swing which actually occurred, the Conservatives would have a lead over Labour of 108 seats; what they got was a lead of 107. For every 1 per cent of your swing against your main rivals, you could expect in those days to pick up 18 seats.

More recently, however, the cube law has begun to backfire and may now, according to Curtice and Steed, be off the road for good. In 1979, Mrs Thatcher got a swing in her favour of more than 5 per cent. In the mid-fifties, she could confidently have expected on this basis to have a Commons majority of about 100. In fact her majority was only 43. It may have been the biggest electoral achievement since 1945, but it still brought nothing like the prize which it once would have done.

There are all sorts of reasons for this: but the main influence, according to Curtice and Steed, is that the country no longer swings together as it used to do. Since 1959, there has been a developing divergence between the voting patterns of North and South; since 1964, there has also been a developing divergence between urban and rural voting.

You can see the point by looking at an electoral map of Britain. In the South and West, Labour, outside London, has been all but eliminated. Seats like Buckingham and Faversham, which Labour used to win in its better years, now look solidly Conservative; while in the North constituencies like Liverpool Walton, which Eric Heffer captured by a whisker from the Conservatives in 1964, and Hartlepool (Conservative from 1959 to 1964), no longer offer the Conservatives any hope at all.

There are, on this analysis, almost two Britains; a Labour Britain (overwhelmingly urban and northern) and a Conservative Britain (overwhelmingly southern and rural).

The effect of these changes has been to diminish the number of marginal seats — those where the outcome at a general election is genuinely in doubt, and on which every election must therefore turn. The number of Conservative and Labour MPs with majorities under 10 per cent, which used to be around 180 (or more than a third of them) is now, Mr Steed has calculated, reduced to less than 120 (or under a fifth). A 1 per cent swing, on 1979 standards, will bring you only about 10 seats, instead of the 18 you might have expected 20 years ago.

Not only is this awkward for the major parties: it may also have undesirable consequences for democracy. 'A Parliament consisting of two geographically distinct party blocks, each securely entrenched in its half of Britain and able to neglect with impunity the interests and aspirations of the other half' say Curtice and Steed 'cannot be healthy.'

The full analysis, which runs to 45

closely argued pages, and is, needless to say, a far more complex and sophisticated work than this simple summary might suggest, allows for the fact that trends once observed do not necessarily continue. It is just possible that marginals will begin to multiply again, especially with the constituency boundaries at present under review, though Curtice and Steed believe it is unlikely. Even so, a number of possible consequences now suggest themselves.

Some have to do with PR: acceptance of the Curtice-Steed formula not only weakens the case for first-past-the-post, but — because it envisages hung Parliaments becoming more and more the norm — makes PR look more likely. Others bear directly — and ominously for Mr Foot — on Labour's chances of regaining power at the next election.

To get a working majority next time Labour must aim to gain more than 50 Conservative seats. In the fifties they could have done that on a modest 3 per cent swing: now they must aim to surpass the 5 per cent the Conservatives got in 1979. On top of that they must contend with a boundary review which will remove the present built-in electoral bias towards Labour and perhaps replace it with a modest bias towards the Conservatives.

Not that the system will serve the Social Democrats very generously either: Curtice and Steed quote another academic exercise which shows that if its support is evenly spread across the country (as that of the Social Democrats promises to be) a party fighting under the first-past-the-post system could take 30 per cent of the vote and still not win a single seat.

[from the *Guardian Weekly*, 19 April 1981]

The Working Class Vote
– And How to Get It

John Hanvey, managing director of Opinion Research Centre, shows that the Tories owe much of their success in the general election to increasing support from the working class.

Readers who remember the publication of David Butler and Donald Stokes' *Political Change in Britain in 1969* may also remember Ian Macleod's review of the book in *The Times*. It was typically intelligent, witty, readable but very unfair — to the political scientist. In it Mr Macleod introduced the 'Macleod Chameleon theory' which basically dealt with the transportation of self-evident truths into voting behaviour.

Chameleon theory

His devotees would no doubt claim that after the 'winter of discontent' in 1978/79, the results of the May election demonstrated the Chameleon theory. In fact the results serve rather more to demonstrate some of the truisms of the Butler and Stokes arguments, mainly that the traditional class patterns of voting were breaking down and, as the introductory chapter of the book states, 'Allowances must be made for the very pro-Labour readings of many of our measures . . . our findings would be clearer . . . if this work could be extended over a period in which the balance of party strength swung sharply against Labour.' Conservative and Labour Politicians alike might profit from (re) reading it.

Much has already been written about regional variations in the 1979 elections. There is obviously a correlation with social class voting behaviour but essentially the pattern is no more than a confirmation of a trend between 1950 and 1974. Where broad comparisons are possible the balance of Labour and Conservative

seats had been changing — a Conservative concentration appearing in the area South of the Trent, mainly in borough country/suburban seats, while Labour's strength had correspondingly increased in the inner city areas and particularly in Lancashire. The changes were sharper this time but not out of line with what had been happening.

Analysis

An analysis of over 3700 questionnaires administered to a nationally representative sample of voters as they left the polling stations on May 3rd produced the following analysis of voting.

VOTING BEHAVIOUR — MAY 1979
(Source ORC/ITN Poll)

	Social class				
	All	AB	C1	C2	DE
	%	%	%	%	%
Conservative	44	61	52	39	33
Labour	38	20	30	42	52
Liberal	14	15	15	14	12
Other	4	4	3	5	3

Compare this now with the result of the 1974 October Election [*shown opposite*] (Butler and Kavanagh p.278: source, Louis Harris International).

While the two samples are not strictly comparable, the accuracy of the 'All' percentages compared to the actual results as well as the substantial nature of some of the changes suggests that these changes are real.

| | Social Class | | | | |
	All	AB	C1	C2	DE
	%	%	%	%	%
Conservative	36	63	51	26	22
Labour	39	12	24	49	57
Liberal	19	22	21	20	16
Other	5	3	4	5	5

The evidence indicates the following characteristics:

i That amongst the skilled and unskilled working classes the Conservative vote increased by a net 50% over October 1974.

ii That amongst the middle classes the Conservative share of the vote remained effectively static while it was Labour who ended up as the net beneficiaries from the reduction in the Liberal vote.

The inroads into the 'DE' vote by the Conservatives are made more interesting by the fact that the Conservative share of the vote remained static, at about 50%, amongst old age pensioners suggesting that the swing was even greater amongst the economically active part of the unskilled working class.

Sadly the census data relating to individual parliamentary Constituencies is now hopelessly out of date. It will, however, be fascinating to see the demographic characteristics of those constituencies which did or did not swing when the 1981 census data becomes available.

There certainly are a number of peculiarities in the way constituencies with different characteristics behaved.

Special factors

Firstly it would be foolish to ignore the weight of the ethnic minority vote. There are a number of constituencies which ought on any reasonable criterion to have gone Conservative but in fact remained with Labour. For instance, Leicester South and Leicester East, Battersea South, Walsall South, perhaps even Dulwich or Southall or even Birmingham Sparkbrook. In all these constituencies with a significant number of ethnic minority voters the swing to the Conservatives was much less pronounced than in the surrounding areas.

Secondly there are a number of seats in which the Conservatives did better than in the areas nearer to them. In so far as one can tell, the common characteristics of these seats were that they had a higher proportion of skilled workers and in many cases a higher proportion of those working in the motor manufacturing industry (Birmingham Northfield, Hornchurch, Dagenham and Barking).

The feature of the London Metropolitan situation has been the emigration of young skilled workers to the new towns. Here again there was a higher than average swing to the Conservatives — Harlow, Basildon, Hertford and Stevenage.

As Ivor Crewe pointed out, in his commentary in the *Times Guide to the House of Commons*, in the *marginal* constituencies with new town characteristics the Conservatives did less well than average. The final point for politicians to remember is probably also one that Ivor Crewe places special emphasis on, namely that the Liberal Party emerged from the 1979 election in a much stronger position than it had emerged in from any election since the war, following a period of Labour Government. In 1970 they had lost half of their MPs but on this occasion they lost only three of the fourteen. In addition those constituencies in which the Liberals obtained a 30 per cent share of the vote held up extremely well given that Liberal fortunes generally revive during a period of Conservative government. They are probably better placed than they have been for many years. This, however, cannot be said of either the SNP or Plaid Cymru. In both cases their representation and their share of the vote suffered substantially. Nevertheless the truth remains that, largely thanks to their substantial increased popularity amongst working class voters, the swing to the Conservatives in 1979 was greater than the swing in favour of any party since 1935.

[from *Crossbow*, Autumn 1979]

Questions

1 At elections are choices mainly made by the electorate between candidates or between parties? (F1)

2 How important is class as a factor in influencing voting behaviour? (F1, F3)

3 What other factors may also be important in determining how a person votes at elections? (F1)

4 How important was the working class vote to the Conservatives in the 1974 election? (F1) Comment on the differences between the presentation of statistical information on the 1974 October election in F1 and F3.

5 Explain why some working class members support the Conservative Party. (F1)

6 Based on past experience, what is most likely to be the party allegiance of the following: (a) women; (b) the old; (c) manual workers; (d) members of a trade union; (e) immigrants; (f) ethnic minorities? (F1)

7 Suggest reasons for the lessening influence of class in determining voting behaviour over the past twenty years. (F1)

8 Explain the principle of the cube law in elections. Why do Curtice and Steed think that it no longer applies? (F2)

9 PR might result in a hung parliament in the same way as the first-past-the-post system. What particular development to which Curtice and Steed refer strengthens the case for a PR system? (F2)

10 Suggest reasons why the term 'ethnic minority voters' (F3) is more appropriate than 'immigrants' (F1). Comment on the different observations in these two extracts concerning the influence of ethnic minorities on elections.

Class Discussion

1 Suggest reasons for the growth of the Labour vote in Scotland and the North of England since 1945.

2 Why is the bulk of Conservative support concentrated in the southern half of England?

3 Is it broadly true today that Labour win industrialised urban and inner city seats and that the Conservatives win rural and suburban seats? (F3)

4 Discuss Hanvey's point that Liberal fortunes generally revive during a period of Conservative government. (F3)

5 Discuss to what extent, if any, the 1983 election results illustrated the working of the cube law or verified the ideas of Curtice and Steed. Did it provide evidence of a Britain divided into two nations, politically speaking? (F2)

Extension work

1 Why did the SNP and Plaid Cymru vote decline in the 1979 general election? (F3) What has happened to these voters since then?

2 Explain what is meant by the following: (a) floating voters; (b) marginal constituencies; (c) growing electoral volatility.

3 Give reasons for the increase in the Conservative vote among the unskilled working class in 1974 and 1979. Was this support sustained in the 1983 election?

4 Assess the relative importance of the 'Winter of Discontent', the Labour policy on devolution and other factors you consider relevant as contributory causes of the defeat of Labour in the May 1979 election. (See also E10.)

5 How often are boundary reviews held? Explain why they can result in a bias towards a particular political party. (F2)

F4 – F6   *The case for electoral reform*

F4

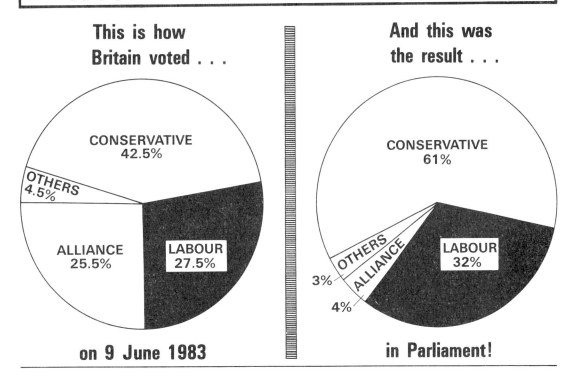

A SCANDAL THAT MUST BE STOPPED

This is how Britain voted . . .

CONSERVATIVE 42.5%
OTHERS 4.5%
ALLIANCE 25.5%
LABOUR 27.5%

on 9 June 1983

And this was the result . . .

CONSERVATIVE 61%
OTHERS 3%
ALLIANCE 4%
LABOUR 32%

in Parliament!

[from the *Campaigner* (Liberal Party Organisation on behalf of the Campaign for Fair Votes, June 1983)]

1979 Election: The Final Score

	Total vote	% of all votes	% of total electorate	Seats gained	Seats lost	Final total
Conservatives	13 697 753	43.9	33.3	61	6	339
Labour	11 509 524	36.9	28.0	11	51	268
Liberal	4 313 931	13.8	10.5	0	3	11
SNP	504 259	1.6	1.2	0	9	2
Plaid Cymru	132 544	0.4	0.3	0	1	2
Nat. Front	191 267	0.6	0.5	0	0	0
Others	971 512	2.8	2.4	2*	4	13

* 2 Democratic Unionist gains from Official Unionist

Percentage poll: 76.0 per cent   Swing to Conservative: 5.2 per cent
Total number of seats changing hands: 74
Highest swing to Conservative: 13.9   Barking
Highest swing to Labour: 4.4, Glasgow Cathcart.
Highest majority (excluding Northern Ireland): E. L. Gardner (Con.), Fylde South, 32 247
Lowest majority: R. Atkins (Con.), Preston North, 29

Regional swings:

Greater London	6.4 to Con.	North	4.5 to Con.
S and W England	6.6 to Con.	Scotland	0.1 to Lab.
Midlands	6.3 to Con.	Wales	4.8 to Con.
East Anglia	5.6 to Con.		

[from *The Guardian*, 5 May 1979]

Why Change the Way we Elect the House of Commons?

Because under the present system:

* About half of those who vote elect nobody.
In the 1979 general election, of the 31 million who voted, over 14 million failed to elect an MP —
4 million Conservative
5 million Labour
4 million Liberal
1 million others.

* Many thousands are in that position all their lives —
e.g. Conservatives in the industrial North
Labour people in most of southern England.

* The seats won by any party bear little relation to the voters' support for it.
The party forming the government in 1979 was supported by only 44 out of every 100 people who voted, but got 43 more MPs than all other parties combined. Nearly all British governments come to power with less than half the votes.

* A very few voters changing their minds can produce a very large change —
e.g. in Hertfordshire nearly as many people voted Labour in 1979 as in 1974, but Labour lost *all* its four MPs in that county, including a Cabinet Minister.

* But very many people changing their minds may have no effect —
e.g. in Harlow the Conservatives nearly doubled their 1974 vote but remained unrepresented.

* Even those on the winning side may not get an MP they really want.

X beside a candidate's name may mean anything from enthusiastic approval to reluctant acceptance. To support a party, a voter in one place may have to vote for an extreme left winger, in another place for an extreme right winger. Hence, the voters have no control over who leads a party or what policies it shall pursue.

* Differences are exaggerated, co-operation discouraged.

We have to vote as if we thought candidate X was perfect and all the others no good at all.

And one part of the country is made to appear totally opposed to another. Co. Durham appears in the House of Commons as if inhabited only by Labour people, although 43 out of every 100 voted for something else, while Berkshire has only Conservative MPs although 45 out of every 100 voted for something else.

* Even the votes cast (let alone the seats won) may not show the voters' real opinions.

Too many vote not for the candidate they most want but for the one they think has the best chance of defeating the one they want least.

* People running a business, a factory, a school etc. cannot confidently plan ahead beyond the next election.

A different party taking office is liable to reverse what the previous government did — including things the majority of voters would rather leave unchanged.

How should we change the way we elect the House of Commons?

We need to give the voters means of *saying* what they want and of *getting* what they want.

Instead of having to vote X for one candidate selected by

one party, the voter should be able to express his opinion about all candidates seeking his support — not necessarily confining himself to one party. This is easily done by numbering candidates — 1 for the candidate the voter thinks is the best, 2 for the next best and so on.

But the voter also needs assurance that the opinion he thus expresses will almost certainly affect the result of the election in the way he wishes.

That is impossible so long as we elect only one MP from each constituency, for even if we make sure that the winner is elected by a clear majority anything up to half the voters may fail to elect anyone. If we elect several MPs together, it becomes possible to ensure that voters of several different opinions all get their views fairly represented.

This is achieved by the numbering of candidates, combined with a provision that a candidate needs for election not a majority of the votes but a quota. The numbering of candidates tells the returning officer to give the vote to the candidate the voter has marked 1, but if it cannot help to elect him, to transfer it to the candidate the voter has marked 2 — and so on if necessary. Suppose that instead of dividing Berkshire into five single-member constituencies we leave it as one 5-member constituency. The result of the 1979 election was:

	Conservative	Labour	Liberal	Others	Total
Votes polled	163 474	69 529	63 816	3 283	300 102
Seats won	5	0	0	0	5

If about one fifth of the voters vote 1, 2, 3 . . . for all the candidates of a particular kind, this will cause their votes to accumulate on one of those candidates and elect him; twice as many votes will elect two and so on. So if the support for the parties were the same as in the actual election, the 69 529 Labour votes and the 63 816 Liberal votes would each elect one MP, and the 163 474 Conservative votes would elect three.

And in each case the candidate(s) elected would be whichever the voters most favoured.

This — the single transferable vote form of **PR** — thus gives proportional representation to the parties but also to anything else that many voters think important — to right and left wings, to those who like their **MP** to be a dependable toe-er of the party line and those who prefer him to be more independent, to those who want more women MPs and those who prefer men, etc. STV is a 'supervote'! Help to get it.

[from *Why change the way we elect the House of Commons?* (Electoral Reform Society, 1980)]

Questions

1 Estimate from the figures in F4 and F5 the following: (a) the total number of seats gained by the Conservatives in 1983; (b) the percentage of seats gained by the Conservatives in 1979.

2 Illustrate from the figures in F4 and F5 that although the Conservatives won a landslide victory in terms of parliamentary seats in 1983, it was not a victory based on increased popular support.

3 Why are votes not of equal value under the present system of voting? (F6) (See also A1.)

4 Explain why many people appear to be disenfranchised under the first-past-the-post system. (F6)

5 How does the STV form of PR enable the voter to express an opinion about all candidates? (F6)

Class Discussion

1 Comment on the following: (a) the nature of the regional swings during the 1979 election; (b) reasons for the Alliance's large share of the vote in the 1983 election. (F4, F5)

2 What requirements are necessary for a 'fair' as well as a 'democratic' system of voting?

Extension Work

1 Until which date did the following survive in Britain: (a) double-member constituencies; (b) university seats with the STV method of voting?

2 What arguments have been advanced against the introduction of the STV system? (See also E6.)

3 Show how the present voting system helps minority parties only if their basis of support is strongly concentrated in particular regions.

F7

Two legs good, one leg bad

Peter Tatchell answers his critics on the contentious issue of extra-parliamentary activity

As a result of the ideas expressed in *London Labour Briefing*, many members of the Parliamentary Labour Party believe that Michael Foot was right to repudiate my candidature for Bermondsey. In particular, they cite my criticism of the Party's 'obsessive legalism and parliamentarism'.

This does not, however, mean that I am against legality or Parliament, as Jeff Rooker implied in *The Times* of 7 December 1981. What I sought to emphasise is that before Labour can win elections and pass laws, it has first to create a base of political support in the electorate outside Parliament.

To establish this power base, the Party needs to concentrate less exclusively on activity inside the House of Commons and the passage of legislation. Instead, we have to expend greater efforts to rebuild our mass membership and develop a more outward-going and campaigning style of politics rooted in workplaces and local communities.

Labour has become too obsessed with the formalities and institutions of parliamentary power. We have neglected the preliminary task of persuading and organising people so that we can capture this power and use it effectively to carry through far-reaching social reforms with the active support of the electorate.

Evidence of this is Labour's declining share of the vote, culminating in the election defeat of 1979, and the failure of Labour governments to implement their manifestoes fully against the pressures of the extra-parliamentary right — the Law Lords, IMF, NATO and the multinationals.

Jeff Rooker further cited as proof of 'anti-parliamentary' views my argument in *Briefing* that extra-parliamentary protests are necessary because the Labour opposition is 'token and ineffectual' and 'debates and parliamentary divisions are fruitless cosmetic exercises given the Tories' present Commons majority'.

My line of argument attempted to highlight the desirability of a much stronger Labour opposition to slow down and obstruct the passage of Tory legislation. The PLP has to come to terms with its own relative powerlessness.

Whatever the logic and reason of our argument and the oratorical finesse of our MPs, Labour is outvoted every time. If the PLP cannot be an effective opposition, we must look outside Parliament to other forms and arenas of extra-parliamentary struggle to realise the party's goals — through trade unions taking industrial action, tenants' associations organising rent strikes, and the peace movement occupying nuclear bases.

Neil Kinnock, in the *Sunday Times* of 20 December 1981, derided my modest suggestion in *Briefing* of a 'tent city' of the homeless and jobless outside Parliament to remind the government of the human devastation caused by its monetarist policies.

He claimed that such protests 'may stimulate temporary rushes of blood, but they will never secure political power for socialism'. Why then has he lent his personal support to other 'temporary rushes of blood' such as the People's March for Jobs and last October's CND demonstration?

The idea of a 'tent city' is not a new one. In 1925, George Lansbury urged the unemployed to march on London and set up a 'tented encampment' outside the

British Empire Exhibition at Wembley. More recently, a group of women set up a peace camp at Greenham Common air force base to protest against the siting of cruise missiles.

These protests, and countless others like them, are premised on the belief that socialism cannot be achieved by Parliament and MPs alone. It also requires the conscious and organised support of the citizens outside the House of Commons — not only organised within the Labour Party, but also through the myriad pressure groups campaigning on issues such as feminism and ecology. Far from being a threat to democratic institutions, these extra-parliamentary forces supplement and strengthen the PLP and enrich the political process.

Michael Foot and Frank Field recently embarked on an historical reappraisal of the role of extra-parliamentary action in *The Observer* of 10 and 17 January 1982 and *The Times* of 9 January 1982. They accept the legitimacy of extra-parliamentary action prior to the granting of the universal franchise. The peasants' revolt, the Levellers, Chartists and suffragettes were defensible because they did not have the vote.

However, Foot and Field apparently doubt that it is possible to cite equally impressive and justifiable cases of extra-parliamentary activity since the adult suffrage was won. They go so far as to suggest that the winning of the universal franchise has made such protests unnecessary and perhaps even illegitimate.

This is a surprising view from parliamentary representatives of the Labour movement. Ever since the granting of the vote, the recent history and finest moments of our movement have included struggles not only outside Parliament but sometimes even outside the law.

In response to the threats of longer hours, wage cuts and lock-outs in the mines, the 1926 general strike bought organised labour into direct confrontation with the government.

Only a decade ago, free and independent trade unionism was preserved at the cost of workers refusing to recognise the Industrial Relations Act. The AUEW incurred huge fines and five dockers were imprisoned in Pentonville for contempt of court. Their release, and the eventual defeat of the Act, was won only through a campaign of non-compliance with the law and the threat of large-scale strikes.

Labour has never accepted that election by universal franchise gives any government automatic moral authority for its every action. When governments exceed their mandate, cease to be accountable to the electorate, or impose draconian laws, they have always been challenged by the Labour movement through extra-parliamentary action.

Bill Keys of SOGAT has called for defiance of Tebbitt's anti-union laws and said he is prepared to go to prison to defeat the new legislation. Twenty-four Scottish MPs gave their backing to the workers' occupation of the British Aluminium plant at Invergordon. Labour Parties and local authorities all over the country advocated the non-implementation of Heseltine's new strictures on town hall finance and expenditure.

There is an urgent need for such extra-parliamentary protests, both at a local and national level, to defeat the present Tory administration. But it would be presumptuous to assume that a future Labour government will not also require extra-parliamentary pressure to keep it accountable to the movement and on a firm socialist course.

Far from fearing such pressures from our supporters, every Labour MP should welcome them as a source of strength and inspiration.

[from the *New Socialist*, March/April 1982]

> *All animals are equal, but some are more equal than others.*
> *(George Orwell)*

In Your Branch

Branches are the democratic foundations of the Labour Party. They are also the main campaigning units of the party.

Branch members:

- **Campaign** in the community
- **Fight** against local hospital closures and job losses
- **Raise** funds to support the party and local community groups
- **Recruit** new members
- **Keep** in touch with council and community affairs, by talking, meeting councillors and inviting groups to talk to the branch
- **Spread** Labour's ideas, by running bookstalls and sending out local news sheets

- **Choose** Labour candidates for council elections and work to have the candidates elected
- **Send** delegates to put the branch's point of view in the constituency party
- **Make** resolutions about how they want to have things changed and . . .
- **Have fun.** Yes, that's also part of being a party member!

Meetings in the Labour Party can be lively, too. To make sure everyone has the the chance of speaking, we have to have some 'groundrules'. The chairman or chairwoman (we usually just say *chair*) is there to make sure the rules are observed and that everyone has a fair chance to join in the debate.

1 Branches elect a chair and secretary every year. Their job is to help meetings run smoothly. They organise the meetings through the *agenda* — setting out the order of topics to be discussed.

2 The 'business' side of the meeting includes reports from officers and delegates elected by the branch to the General Committee and other groups in the party.

3 Any member who wants the party to change its policy on any issues, or who wants the branch to support a local campaign, may *move a motion*. The motion, a short statement, has to be *seconded* by another member.

4 The motion is then discussed, or debated, *through the chair*. That is, members signal to the chair that they want to speak. This way, every member should be able to have their say.

5 The chair asks members to make a decision on the motion. If it is by more than half the members, it is carried, and becomes a *resolution*. If the resolution concerns party policy, it is passed to the General Committee.

6 Members are active in a lot of different ways. Some of us get together in smaller branch *working groups* to discuss community and party affairs — or to plan campaigns, social events, fund-raising or news sheets.

[from 'Welcome to the Labour Party' (Labour Party, 1983)]

Questions

1 What does Tatchell suggest is necessary before Labour can win elections? (F7)
2 Under what circumstances do the following particularly support or advocate extra-parliamentary activity: (a) Tatchell; (b) Foot? (F7)
3 What can you discover from F8 is the importance or role of the branch in the Labour Party?
4 In what way does F8 illustrate 'grassroot politics' or 'micro-politics' at the local level?

Class Discussion

1 Comment on Tatchell's reference to the Law Lords, the IMF, NATO and the multinationals as being part of the extra-parliamentary right.
2 Can one distinguish between extra-parliamentary forms of protest and anti-parliamentary activities?
3 Do you think that pupil councils should be introduced into one or more of the following types of school: (a) secondary; (b) middle; (c) primary? If so, what powers should such councils have?

Extension Work

1 Suggest ways in which ordinary people can participate in politics or political activity in addition to voting or joining a political party or various pressure groups.
2 Find out key details on the following: (a) Levellers; (b) Chartists; (c) suffragettes; (d) feminists; (e) the CND. (F7)

Local government and decentralisation

Introduction

The first of a series of laws to impose stricter financial controls on local authorities (a problem raised in documents G1–G4) was the Local Government Planning and Land Act (1980). Previously the rate support grant (a 'matching' grant) automatically increased with spending, and in theory there were no limits on how much a local authority could spend. The government felt this system did not encourage thrift and wanted to obtain tighter control over local authority spending. The block grant now replaced the needs and resources element of the RSG, and was to be based not on past spending but on a Whitehall estimate of how much was needed by local councils to provide services at a uniform national level.

G2 indicates one reason for the increased growth in the proportion of local authority income from central grants rather than from local revenue (rates or miscellaneous income), a point raised in G1. Other reasons include the growth in local government staff (from 1.9 million in 1963 to 3.1 million in 1979), the increase in real wages of local authority workers, and increased demand for social services.

G1, G2 and G4 also discuss the relations between central and local government. Strictly speaking, in law local councils have only that authority which is derived from the sovereign power in Britain's unitary state, namely Parliament. According to this 'agency' model, local authorities act as servants, implementing what they are told to. However, a tradition also exists (strongly stressed in G2) that local government should exist in its own right, that local councils should have a certain autonomy and be accountable to their electors rather than purely answerable to central government, and that the central/local government relationship should be one of partnership, as advocated by the Layfield Report.

In 1981 the government obtained powers to impose selective rate capping (rate controls) on individual high-spending councils in Scotland (referred to in G4 as the 'Scottish Act'). From 1980 the government failed partly in its policy to restrict local authority current spending (though capital spending was cut drastically), because certain high-spending councils that lost part of their grant, through penalties described in G3, increased local rates or took other measures. For example, in Birmingham a Conservative-controlled council (in power 1981–84) raised council house rents. As a result of this partial failure, the government decided to introduce legislation in late 1983 to impose general rate capping in England and Wales. (Note that the almost doubling of the average rates bill of householders during the period 1979–84 was caused partly by the reduction in the government grant. Thus the interesting question comes to mind of how far increased rates were the cause, and how far the consequence, of stringent government financial controls.)

G1 points out that a Cabinet committee under the Home Secretary, William Whitelaw, failed to find agreement on any alternative to the rates, and that the government then decided to abolish the GLC and the six metropolitan county councils. G5 and G7 suggest that the Labour party and the Alliance had also considered this possibility. The government, however, faced considerable opposition to this measure, and was accused of being politically motivated since the GLC and the metropolitans were high-spending authorities controlled by Labour since 1981. G5 puts part of the case for the abolition of the GLC. The government argued in its White Paper 'Streamlining the Cities' (1983) that doing away with these authorities would remove a source of duplication and conflict with the borough councils, that their role was not important since their functions could be undertaken by the borough councils or precepting joint boards or authorities (e.g. police, fire, public transport, probation), and that costs of administration would be considerably reduced.

The case for retaining the metropolitan counties is far weaker than the argument advanced for retaining some overall strategic regional authority for London, whether it be a new GLC with stronger powers, a smaller resurrected London County Council, or a larger regional authority. The LCC, though it covered a smaller area than the GLC (in fact, the area covered by ILEA), did control from 1889 to 1964 every major local government service.

| G1 |

LOCAL BRIEFING

Francis Wheen

Labour's campaign poster [*for the 1983 general election*] shows a man (as always) being squeezed in an enormous vice. 'Caught in the Tory trap?' the caption asks. 'Vote Labour for the local services *you need.*'

The Tory trap in question is an elaborate system of grant abatements, holdbacks, penalties and other paraphernalia attached to the Rate Support Grant. [. . .] The proportion of local councils' income coming from central grants (rather than from locally-raised revenue) has grown rapidly in recent years. In 1976, the Layfield Committee on local authorities' finance noted this trend and remarked that central government 'cannot provide local authorities with a preponderant share of their income . . . without sooner or later taking responsibility for their expenditure'. This has now come to pass, in the form of the devilish block grant, which severely penalises 'overspenders'.

Not surprisingly, Labour councillors and MPs have howled at the wickedness of a Tory government interfering with the 'local autonomy' of democratically-elected councils. It has been conveniently forgotten that the first official recommendation of such central control over local authorities came from the last *Labour* government. A Green Paper, published in 1977, proposed the creation of a block grant very like the one Michael Heseltine finally introduced. This was because 'central government needs to be able to exert more effective influence over total local authority expenditure'.

Today, the Labour Party claims to be a reformed character. In its policy document, published last month, Labour promised to abolish the present block grant, particularly its financial ceilings and penalties.

But what should be put in its place? As Layfield pointed out, local authorities are unlikely to achieve greater autonomy unless they are able to raise a much greater share of their revenue themselves. This cannot be done under the present rates system, which has become horribly distorted. Layfield's solution was a reformed rating system in tandem with a Local Income Tax. The Social Democrats also favour a Local Income Tax, while Labour is studiously non-committal.

However, Labour's lack of a clear policy is as nothing compared with Mrs Thatcher's problem. She came to power committed to abolishing the rates 'within the lifetime of a Parliament'. But in January this year a Cabinet committee, chaired by Willie Whitelaw, told her that there was no alternative to the rates, given that she will not countenance the idea of a Local Income Tax. As a palliative, it is recommended instead that she should abolish the metropolitan counties. Undaunted, she said she liked the idea of a local sales tax. Even her colleagues accepted that this tax would be unworkable (and would also upset Thatcher's sacred cow, the low inflation rate). With a general election looming, Thatcher has to have some alternative to the rates to put into her manifesto. It will be amusing and instructive to see how she wriggles out of her own version of the Tory trap.

	ENGLAND AND WALES					SCOTLAND	
Types of authority	Metro-politan counties*	Metro-politan districts*	Non-metro-politan counties	Non-metro-politan districts	Parish and community councils	Regional councils	District councils
Functions	Planning: includes structure plans, some development control. Public transport. Highways and traffic (including parking). Refuse disposal. Consumer protection. Fire service. Police.	Education. Libraries. Personal social services. Housing. Local planning and development control. Refuse collection. Health and safety.	Education. Libraries. Personal social services. Transport planning (but not operation). Planning: including structure plans, some development control. Highways and traffic (including parking). Refuse disposal. Consumer protection. Fire service. Police.	Housing. Local planning and development control. Health and safety. Local bus services (in some areas). Refuse collection (except in Wales, where it is a county function).	Provision of some amenities (e.g. village halls, playing fields). Upkeep and signposting of footpaths and bridleways. Consultation with counties and districts on planning, transport etc.	Education. Water, sewerage and drainage. Transport and highways. Strategic planning. Social work. Police. Fire service. Consumer protection. Industrial promotion.	Housing. Refuse collection and disposal. Environmen-tal health. Libraries. Leisure and recreation. Countryside. Nature reserves and tourism. Local planning.
	Shared functions: museums and art galleries; acquisition and disposal of land; airports; parks and open spaces; physical recreation and swimming pools; creation, protection, diversion and abolition of footpaths and bridleways; footway lighting.					Shared functions: There are three island councils, which combine the functions of regions and districts except for fire and police, which are shared with Highland Regional Council.	
Elections	Whole council elected every four years (last election 1981).	No election in year of county elections; in each of the other three years, one third of council is elected in rotation.	Whole council elected every four years (last election 1981).	Most are elected as 'whole coun-cils' every four years (1983 is election year for all these); the rest are elected one-third at a time, like metropolitan districts.	Whole council elected every four years: 1983 is election year (except in some non-metropolitan areas where elections are arranged to coincide with elections for one-third of district council).	Whole council elected every four years (last election 1982); island councils are elected at the same time.	Whole council elected every four years (last election 1980).
	* London is a special case, the most notable difference being that the Inner London Education Authority is responsible for education in the 13 inner London boroughs; in outer London, education is a function of the borough council. The GLC is elected in the same way, and at the same time, as other counties; London borough councils are elected whole every four years (last election 1982).						

[from the *New Statesman*, 29 April 1983]

Jenkin strikes again

A WIDELY HELD myth persists that this country has an active system of democratically accountable local government. The reality is that year by year over the past two decades the independence of local government has been steadily eroded by Westminster politicians and Whitehall civil servants. The process has accelerated significantly under this government and has been politically motivated. Mr Patrick Jenkin's announcement on Tuesday that he was docking £280 million more from the rate support grant that would have been paid to mainly Labour-controlled councils is only the last in a series of steps taken to transform nominally independent and elected bodies into puppet-agents of central government.

Education and housing are two of the main functions administered by local government. In each of them, central government has persistently intervened in one direction or another to curtail or remove the rights of directly elected politicians to carry out the policies on which they were elected. In the Labour case it was to enforce the introduction of comprehensive schools. In the Tory case it has been to put up council rents, or to enforce council house sales. Central government already has an effectively complete veto on capital spending projects by local government. Now, via the penalties being attached to the payment of the rate support grant to *individual* councils, it is also taking effective control of all current spending.

The reality, despite all the paraphernalia of local elections, council meetings, committee meetings and the mountains of paper, is that local political influence (let alone local political control) has been removed from more than nine-tenths of the activity that goes on in the name of local government. The social service departments of local authorities are simply the agents in the field of the Department of Health and Social Security. No government yet has seen fit to make policing, which

is paid for by the ratepayer, politically accountable to the ratepayers' elected representatives. Local chief executives or town clerks are now more affected by instructions contained in Circulars from the Department of the Environment than by instructions from their nominal political bosses. The whole structure has become an elaborate charade — and an inefficient and expensive one at that.

What applies to individual local councils applies even more to the further layers of the metropolitan counties and the Greater London Council. As Ken Livingstone has discovered, despite all the trappings of power and the apparent political prestige of being 'in control' at County Hall, there is in practice almost nothing that can be done independently of central government to make things different in London. In the one area where he tried — the attempt to introduce a half-way sensible transport and fares policy for the capital — the government reaction was to promise to remove control of London Transport from the GLC. When Herbert Morrison at County Hall failed to persuade the Transport Minister of the day that a sensible transport policy for the capital should include the building of a new Waterloo Bridge, at least he was able to go ahead on his own and build it on the rates.

Like other local authorities, the GLC has become little more than a powerful political sounding box, with only marginal capacity to affect the lives of the citizens of London in any direction. That, as Mr Livingstone and some of his colleagues have shown, can be a useful political activity; for persuasion, the generation of ideas and propaganda are a central part of the political process. But it is not the purpose for which the very elaborate structures of local government were established.

Needless to say, neither this nor any other government asked for a mandate for systematically removing the few remaining powers of local government. It is able to do so, however, because local government is not popular. As it is presently organised it seems largely remote from the experience of the overwhelming majority of the population, and no one likes paying rates.

If, then, viable and democratically accountable local government is to be a part of the post-Thatcher reconstruction of this country, some radical thinking needs to be done about it. The centripetal tendencies of the past have come from two sources. The first has been financial. As more and more functions have been laid on local authorities by statute, a greater and greater proportion of expenditure has been financed by central government grant, with the almost inevitable political interference that goes with it. The second is the political desire of the government of the day to see centrally determined policies administered as evenly as possible over the whole country. No reform of the functions of local government will get anywhere unless it is accepted from the start that a fundamental change of attitude is required in both respects.

In its most recent proposals for local government in Scotland, the Labour Party has at last come to accept that political devolution means nothing unless a Scottish Assembly is given some revenue-raising powers of its own. The actual effect would almost certainly be worse than nothing. For to create a political body which would obviously want to press for more spending in Scotland, which did not at the same time have any direct responsibility for how that spending was to be financed, would be a recipe for political disaster. But the same logic has also to be carried to all local government. Unless, over a significant part of its activity, a local authority can make genuine alternative choices about spending and be accountable to its local electorate for the financing of that expenditure, there is no reality to independent local government. Unless and until the rating system is reformed, that means allowing local authorities to raise what rates they decide and defending their decisions locally.

Equally, if local government is to have any real meaning, central government must accept a self-denying ordinance and allow local councils not to follow central advice. Subject to general rules of conduct, freedom must include freedom to work differently and even freedom to make what may seem from Whitehall to be mistakes. Devolution and decentralisation will remain nothing but buzz-words unless the implications of these two policy changes are thought through and accepted.

[from the *New Statesman* (editional), 8 July 1983]

G3

Not-so-little local difficulties

Paying for it

Local councils have three main sources of cash: government grants; charges, mainly council house rents; and property rates, expressed in the form of a 'rate poundage'. If your property has a 'rateable value' of £500 (a figure supposedly related to its rental value in 1973), and the rate poundage is '150p in the £', you must pay £750. Councils can also borrow, on the market or from Whitehall, but only for capital spending.

At budget time in March, 1983, Whitehall expected local authorities to spend £37.9 billion in 1983–84, financed by £19.9 billion from government, £13 billion from ratepayers, £5 billion of charges. In fact, their current spending — two-thirds of the total — may be £1 billion more.

The *grant* system is designed to prevent this. Grants come in two forms: *i* specific grants, usually a percentage of spending on a particular service such as police or transport; *ii* the (larger) rate support grant made up of

Getting and spending
Local authority finance 1983–4*, total : £37.9 bn

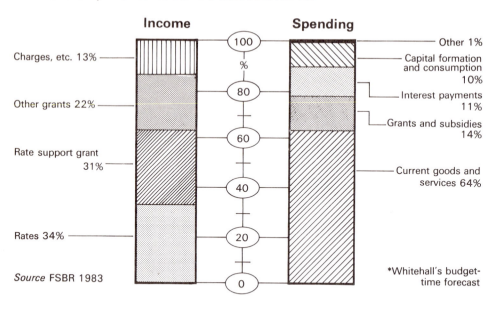

Income

Charges, etc. 13%

Other grants 22%

Rate support grant 31%

Rates 34%

Source FSBR 1983

Spending

Other 1%

Capital formation and consumption 10%

Interest payments 11%

Grants and subsidies 14%

Current goods and services 64%

*Whitehall's budget-time forecast

a 100% subsidy for 'domestic rate relief', and *b* a 'block grant'.

This is the difference between each council's current spending (after some adjustment) and the amount it could raise by charging a 'grant-related poundage' (GRP) set by Whitehall, at, say, 160p in the £. But an extra £10m spending does not bring in an extra £10m from Whitehall: the GRP is altered so that the grant rises less — and slower still, or even falls, if the total spent is more than Whitehall's computers think it should be.

On top of this comes a much tougher control. Separately, Whitehall fixes each council a spending target based on past spending, inflation and government policy. A council that overspends this target will lose some of its block grant. So ratepayers pay twice, for the extra spending and the lost grant.

The penalties are already tough: 1p in the £ for each of the first two percentage points over target, 5p for each point thereafter. In 1984–5 they will be far tougher: 2p for the first point, 4p for the next, 8p for the third, then 9p for each point.

[from *The Economist*, 19 November 1983]

The *rates* system is practical but bizarre. Rateable values bear little relation to the real-world rents at the valuation in 1973, and none at all to capital values: a house in the country can be rated at half the level of a house costing as much in London. Nor do rates take any account of capacity to pay: a money-losing corner shop must pay just like a profitable one.

There are special subsidies. All houses get 'domestic rate relief', of 18.5p in England and Wales, 3p in Scotland. In Scotland, manufacturing industry (but not warehouses, shops or offices) is spared half its rates bill. Agricultural land and buildings pay no rates at all anywhere.

Businessmen, with no vote as such, yet paying about 55 per cent of all rates, have protested fiercely, and are to get a new right to be consulted before rates are fixed. There have been many calls for reform or abolition of the rates. But a Green Paper of 1981 examined possible alternatives — local income tax, sales tax or poll tax, for instance — and backed none of them. For the time being, hopes of reform have been abandoned.

Rate capping, or knee-capping?

With council elections a week tomorrow, Robert Maclennan, MP, gives the SDP argument for decentralised local government

The Layfield Commission, reporting on rating reform, strongly backed local accountability. It recommended that the bulk of local authority expenditure should be locally financed to ensure that voters were not insulated by vast government subsidies from the consequences of their vote. A high level of services or an extravagant new town hall would be reflected in a high level of local taxation. Low taxes would mean poorer services.

The last Labour Government recoiled from the prospect of losing control over local authorities and shelved the commission's report. The Conservative Government came to power committed to rating reform but it too rejected Layfield's proposals, choosing instead sharply to increase central control.

Rates in Scotland jumped by 30 per cent then by 34 per cent in the two years following the Conservative victory in 1979. Did this show a reckless surge in expenditure by the Scottish hard left in defiance of the Government? The answer is an emphatic 'no'. Lothian Council, one of the Conservatives' favourite enemies, did indeed increase expenditure in 1980–1, but only by 2 per cent. The combination of cuts in the government grant, high interest rates and high inflation required a rate increase of 41 per cent.

Between 1979 and 1982, government grants were cut by nearly 17 per cent in real terms. Rates inevitably rose to cover the short-fall.

Once the present rate capping Bill becomes law, England and Wales will follow the Scottish precedent. There is no objective definition in the Scottish Act of the 'excessive and unreasonable' expenditure which renders an authority liable to penalties. In practice, as the *Scotsman* complained last July, excessive and unreasonable expenditure 'occurs when Mr Younger and his officials say it does'. (Humpty Dumpty, as he told Alice in Wonderland, had a similar way with words.) A major constitutional change has been engineered. But to what purpose?

The Government maintains it needs to control the level of rates in order to control inflation. The argument is absurd. Local expenditure, provided it is financed by local taxation, is not inflationary since it has little or no effect on aggregate demand and cannot affect the public-sector borrowing requirement and money supply. Borrowing is inflationary and is controlled by the centre — the rates are not.

Even if rateborne expenditure increased in real terms by as much as 30 per cent, aggregate demand would only be affected by 0.25 per cent.

Is the Government's reason for controlling the rates a belief that it may thereby increase investment? The bludgeoning of local authorities is not necessarily a practical way of achieving this.

If ratepayers collectively choose to buy more British Leyland buses than individually to buy more Japanese cars, why should the central government object?

The answer surely is simple. Since 1979 the Conservative Government's expenditure (even when the costs of unemployment benefit are excluded) has increased while local authority spending has decreased. The Government needs a scapegoat to deflect attention from its own record. [. . .]

Meanwhile real problems caused by the aberrations of the present system are being ignored. Scotland has always held regular rating reassessments, while there has been no reassessment in England and Wales since 1973. Growth industries in Scotland, contrary to regional policy, are thus taxed considerably more severely than their counterparts south of the border.

The machinery of local government needs to be redesigned. Centralisation is leading to the death of local responsibility. Soon local authorities will be no more than pressure groups or agents of central government.

The SDP is committed to the decentralisation of power. An Alliance Government would introduce the local income tax scheme proposed by the Layfield Commission. (Similar schemes work well in Scandinavia and various States in the US.) Central government subsidies would be cut to no more than was needed to equalise resources between rich and poor areas. Local services — from snowploughs to psychiatric day centres — would be locally determined at a cost acceptable to local voters.

We would rescue commercial ratepayers from being the non-voting milch-cows of local authorities. Instead, they would pay a nationally decided rate (to be used towards the Government's equalisation grant) which could be varied in accordance with regional policy.

The system would be simple and comprehensible. Control of expenditure and waste would depend on local voters, who know local conditions, and not on London bureaucrats.

[from the *Daily Telegraph*, 25 April 1984]

G5

London's Future

In the continuing debate on the future of London's local government, John Wheeler (Conservative MP, Westminster North) puts the Government's case for abolishing the Greater London Council.

Why abolish the Greater London Council? That is a question that is going to occupy the minds of Members during the months to come as the Government's proposed legislation goes through its parliamentary stages. It is, as they say in politics, a good question.

Let us get one thing clear at an early stage. Much as it will be a major disappointment to him, it really has nothing at all to do with removing Mr Ken Livingstone from the political scene. The reason is much more important and pressing than that.

What it boils down to quite simply is that the GLC has no genuinely useful role to play. It forms an expensive and unnecessary tier of local government. Those of its duties which are prescribed by Act of Parliament could be more efficiently and less expensively performed by the London borough councils. The duties that the present GLC tries to perform which are not prescribed in the Act are presumptuous, expensive and irrelevant.

The move to abolish the GLC and other metropolitan county councils is no bolt from the blue, no sudden flash of genius. It has been considered for some time, not only by the Conservative Party but by both the Labour and Alliance Parties.

At the last general election, Labour was committed to the reorganisation of local government, which would have meant the abolition of the GLC. The Alliance Party made it clear that its proposals would inevitably involve the abolition of the GLC, but not ILEA. Three minds with but a single thought.

And they had strong support from no less a person than Mr Livingstone himself. At County Hall in 1979, he declared: 'I feel in a sense a degree of regret that (the Marshall inquiry into the GLC) did not push on and say "Abolish the GLC" because I think it would have been a major saving and would have released massive resources which could have been put into far more productive use.' Well, who could argue with that?

The furore which the proposals have caused, the cries of anguish from the GLC, and the £2 000 000 of ratepayers' money being spent on anti-abolition propaganda by the GLC, all constitute the final death-rattle of an organisation still bent on self-preservation. An organisation which, incidentally, Mr Livingstone is still not too happy about. He told the Institute of Public Finance and Accountancy conference in June 1982 — less than two years ago — 'To be really effective that means we have to have unitary local government in this country, and clearly people would be better served if it was provided by the borough councils in the metropolitan areas. I have always at heart been committed to the borough council rather than to regional government.'

Mr Livingstone almost puts the case for me. It is a pity he couldn't spend £2 000 000 on supporting what he really thinks!

The myths

Be that as it may, the protests voiced by the GLC, mainly through the medium of Mr Livingstone, are many and varied and appeal largely to the emotions rather than to sound judgement. The adoption of scare tactics to frighten Londoners into believing that the GLC is an essential way of life is particularly reprehensible.

Among the worst of these is the allegation that more Londoners will die in fires if the GLC is abolished. The convoluted logic behind this Machiavellian prophecy is difficult to follow but it goes something like this — money will be short, *ergo* fire stations will be closed and fire appliances removed from fire stations. The joint board which will operate the London Fire Service will, by its very nature, be so inefficient as to be unable to operate an adequate fire service.

This arrant nonsense completely ignores the fact that the Home Secretary alone is responsible for ensuring a proper standard for the fire service. No fire station can be closed, no fire appliance can be removed without his express permission. It also ignores the fact that the men and women who will serve on the joint board will have already proved their ability to operate efficient local government services.

Another example of the oblique logic adopted by Mr Livingstone and his colleagues suggests that the removal of the GLC will lead to more bureaucracy. Of course, the opposite is true. A whole tier of local government will be removed and many of its responsibilities handed to existing local authorities. Mr Livingstone demands less centralised government on the one hand and yet complains when the government of London is decentralised and put into the hands of local communities.

One of the more alarming observations made by Mr Livingstone and the GLC anti-abolitionists is that the GLC sees itself as an alternative government, challenging that of Westminster in its objectives and functions.

They really have to be taken back to basics and reminded that in this country Parliament is sovereign and that it is from Parliament that local government, even the GLC, gets its powers.

There is also the oft repeated claim that abolition of the GLC will lead to a proliferation of the much-despised quangos. Tiresome as it may be, we have to return to basics again and remind GLC propagandists that quangos are appointed by ministers. The joint boards which will be established when the GLC goes will be local bodies composed of elected members of the borough and district councils. And there will only be one of them — to operate the fire service. Of course, Mr Livingstone knows this perfectly well; it just momentarily slips his memory.

The facts

The Government was returned to office in 1983 with a massive majority on an election manifesto which promised the abolition of the GLC. Rather than being horrified by the prospect, the voters of London returned the highest proportion of Conservative Members than at any time since the war.

It is an attractive concept to call, as the GLC does, for a 'Voice for London', but it really is illusory. The 'voice' currently has little say in housing — that is largely the responsibility of the boroughs. It never has had a say in the police. Soon it will lose its biggest service — transport. It has no say at all in the ambulance service or the vital services of sewerage and sewage disposal. But unfortunately it uses its 'voice' loud and long on matters totally divorced from local government. It is a voice that pontificates about matters of national defence and foreign affairs and supports terrorists in Northern Ireland. Is that what Londoners really want?

The GLC's statutory duties include responsibility for strategic planning, the fire service, traffic control, parks and countryside, highways, weights and measures, museums and art galleries and refuse disposal among other things. Education is, of course, a responsibility through a special committee, the ILEA, which is directly elected.

The astounding fact is that to carry out this diminished list of duties the GLC needs a revenue of over £900 000 000, a staff of some 20 000 and around 35 committees and subcommittees. It is bureaucracy gone mad.

Studying the list of activities it is easy to see that there is duplication with the work of the boroughs, and obvious danger of conflict. It can be imagined what delays are engendered, for example, in planning when applications have to pass through two tiers of local government.

Under the proposed legislation, most of the GLC's functions will be taken over by the boroughs. They are already the main providers of services in London. After abolition, town halls will become the focal point for local people on local issues and problems — accountability with simplicity.

[from *The House Magazine*, (weekly journal of the Houses of Parliament) 4 May 1984]

Questions

1   What important function is performed by metropolitan district councils but not by non-metropolitan district councils? (G1)

2   When, and for what immediate reason, did Thatcher decide to abolish the metropolitan county councils (MCCs)? Why does Wheeler suggest that this decision was 'no bolt from the blue'? (G1, G5)

3   What does the *New Statesman* editorial suggest is the essence of independent local government? (G2)

4   Outline the three main sources of revenue for local councils. (G3)

5   Name the two forms of government grant now available to local councils. Why was the 'block grant' introduced? (G1, G3)

6   How is the rate poundage calculated? (G3)

7   What arguments have been made for and against abolition or reform of the present rating system? What other options exist? Refer to the proposals of the Layfield Commission. (G1, G3, G4)

8   Why did rates in Scotland rise steeply in many local authorities between 1979 and 1981? (G4)

9   Cite examples of areas where central government has curtailed or removed local government powers in the past. (G2)

10   How has the government penalised certain local authorities which overspend? (G1, G3, G4)

11   Suggest two reasons why the *New Statesman*, according to its editorial, does not appear too concerned about the forthcoming abolition of the GLC. (G2)

12   What criticism is made in G4 of government attempts to control rates as part of its anti-inflationary policy?

13   Explain how the question of local government accountability is linked to the rating system. (G1, G2, G4)

14   What reasons does Wheeler put forward to justify the abolition of the GLC? (G5)

15   Find the sentence in G5 where indirect reference is made to the concept of delegated legislation.

Class Discussion

1 Suggest reasons why some functions in local government are 'shared functions'. (G1)

2 Why is the provision of libraries a responsibility of metropolitan districts but not a responsibility of non-metropolitan districts? (G1)

3 Is the government wise to abolish the GLC? Discuss the idea that London should have some locally elected overall strategic authority, a kind of reformed or streamlined GLC.

4 Argue the case for and against greater decentralisation and autonomy in local government.

Extension Work

1 Give a clear definition of the following: (a) quango; (b) joint board; (c) precepting authority.

2 Why did the Conservative government in 1984 rescind its decision to abolish ILEA?

3 Name the major high-spending local authorities during the period 1979–84.

4 What is rate capping and when was this system introduced? How effective has it been?

5 Why does the government plan to abolish the MCCs? Explain how the government intends to reallocate the functions of the MCCs.

6 Why did the GLC never have 'a say in the police'? (G5)

G6 – G7   *Local authorities: how they work, and the case for more independence*

G6

HOW LOCAL AUTHORITIES WORK

The committee system

Councils could not consider at their six weekly or quarterly meeting every item of business which needs their attention. They set up committees and subcommittees to deal with certain services or aspects of their work. Local authorities may appoint such committees and subcommittees as they think fit — but some committees, notably Education and Social Services, are required by statute.

Most local authorities now organise their committee systems and their structures along the corporate lines recommended by the Bains Report*. The report gives examples of suitable committee structures, but it must be borne in mind that they are for guidance only. An authority has a large measure of freedom in arranging its committee structure. It is usual to appoint subcommittees if the work of a committee is heavy and can be conveniently divided. Most authorities have a policy committee which co-ordinates the work of the authority. Its membership consists of leading members (in some cases of the majority party alone) with officers present to give expert advice. It is the local authority equivalent of a cabinet system.

* *The New Local Authorities: Management and Structure* (HMSO, 1972).

The management of local authorities

Councillors are local politicians elected to take responsibility for the provision of local services. The permanent staff of local authorities administer the services which it is the policy of the council to provide. Councillors are frequently criticised for being too concerned with details and too little concerned with policy. A study of councillors revealed that two-thirds of them believed that officers had certain techniques, including the following, for getting the decisions they wanted:

1 Writing such a large number of long reports that committee members cannot possibly find the time to read them all.

2 Writing reports which are so short that they contain inadequate information for committee members to make their own decision.

3 Writing reports which are full of technicalities and statistics.

4 Bringing in supplementary agendas in order to catch committee members unawares.

5 Introducing plans for departmental reorganisations which are supposed to cut costs but which actually increase them.

6 Introducing a few deliberate errors in the first paragraphs of a report in the hope that members will be so pleased at finding them that they let the rest go through.

7 Trying to sell ideas to the committee so that the committee believe they were theirs in the first place.

8 Withholding information or bringing it forward too late to affect decisions.

9 Presenting reports which make only one decision seem possible.

10 Rewriting but not changing a rejected plan, and submitting it after a decent interval.

11 Claiming inadequate resources to carry out a policy.

Councillors should aim to have as much control as possible over officers, subject only to the limitations of the amount of time they have available for decision-making and the importance of the issue. Councillors should also ensure that the management structure of the authority is capable of realising the policies and the levels of service they require. Most authorities have a management team consisting of all or most chief officers, or directors as they are usually called. The management team is chaired and led by the Chief Executive who probably does not have a department for which he is directly responsible.

Corporate planning

The modern structure of officers and committees enables local authorities to use modern systems of corporate planning. Corporate planning is concerned with three things:

1 Taking a comprehensive look at the local authority's area to establish what action, direct or indirect, a local authority wishes to take to promote its physical, economic and social well-being.

2 Establishing priorities for policies and programmes to meet political objectives.

3 Keeping a careful watch on the impact of what the local authority is doing and learning from experience.

Corporate planning should provide a sound basis from which to make essential political choices. The immediately obvious, short-term interests of particular departments and their committees will tend to pull against any attempt to take an overall look at policy. One of the main purposes of corporate planning is to promote policies and programmes which are not simply dictated by the vested interests in the various services but which spring from the true needs of the community.

[from 'New and potential councillors', 25th Local Government Conference (The Labour Party, 1981)]

DECENTRALISING GOVERNMENT

In addition to electoral reform, the Alliance is committed to two further constitutional reforms: decentralisation to make government more accountable to the electorate, and basic legislation to protect fundamental human rights and freedoms.

Our system of government is inefficient because it is over-centralised. Departments, ministers and Parliament are hopelessly overloaded and Parliament cannot adequately control the executive; there is great reliance on non-elected quangos, particularly at regional level — such as Regional Health Authorities and Regional Water Authorities, which together with the regional 'outposts' of central government departments now constitute an undemocratic regional tier of government; local government is too dependent on and dominated by central government — which has eroded not only its independence but also its sense of responsibility — and the Tories have made the spending of individual local authorities subject to central control. The overall result is lack of efficiency and lack of accountability, and the concentration of political power in London leads to a concentration of economic power there too, accentuating the trend to two nations — a relatively prosperous South, and a relatively deprived North. We need to disperse power in order to help spread prosperity.

In the light of these deficiencies in the structure of government, we propose:

● *to transfer substantial powers and responsibilities, currently exercised by the centre, to the nations and regions of Britain*. The demand for devolution is clearly stronger in Scotland than in Wales or in some of the English regions, and we do not believe that devolution should be imposed on nations or regions which do not wish it. But there is a strong practical case, especially in terms of regional development, for relevant public expenditure to be allocated between and within regions in line with regional needs. We therefore propose:

a *immediate action to set up a Scottish Parliament* with a full range of devolved powers, including powers to assist economic development and powers to tax, but not to run a Budget deficit;

b to enact Scottish devolution in an Act which would also provide the *framework for decentralisation to assemblies in Wales and the English regions as demand develops*;

c in the English regions, to set up *economic development agencies with substantial powers*. To make these development agencies, and other nominated regional authorities which already exist, accountable in the first instance to *regional committees of a reformed Second Chamber*;

d *in Northern Ireland* to encourage a non-sectarian approach to the problems of the province. We support the present Northern Ireland Assembly and will work towards a return to devolved power in place of direct rule from Westminster. We favour the early establishment of an Anglo-Irish consultative body at parliamentary level representing all parties at Westminster, Belfast and Dublin.

● *to revitalise local government*, restoring its independence and its accountability to the local electorate by:

a introducing proportional representation at local level to make local government representative of its electorate and responsive to current of opinion in that electorate;

b simplifying the structure of local government to make it more effective by abolishing one of the existing tiers of local government. This will be done by stages against the background of our proposals for the development of regional government. It would inevitably involve the eventual abolition of the metropolitan counties, and the GLC (but not ILEA), and would also allow for the restoration of powers to some of the former county boroughs;

c paving the way to the abolition of domestic rates and reducing local government's dependence on central grant, by introducing a local income tax. This change in

the structure of local government finance will increase the independence of local government;
d extending the right of local communities to have statutory Parish or Neighbourhood Councils.

● *to increase the accountability of Government to Parliament* by reforming the operation and procedures of the House of Commons, to make its control of the executive more effective and to reform the powers and composition of the House of Lords, which must include a significant elected element representative of the nations and regions of Britain.

This set of proposals amounts to an extensive decentralisation of power from the centre, both to the nations and regions and to local government, and to a considerable strengthening of democratic accountability at all levels of government.

[from *Working together for Britain* (SDP/Liberal Alliance Manifesto), May 1983]

Questions

1   Why do local council committees appoint sub-committees? (G6)
2   What is the equivalent in local government to a cabinet system? (G6)
3   Describe the composition of the management team of a local authority. (G6)
4   Identify one main purpose of corporate planning. (G6)
5   What constitutional reforms would the Alliance like to implement, according to the 1983 manifesto? (G7)
6   How does the Alliance propose to increase government's accountability to Parliament? (G7)
7   For what reasons does the Alliance support a regional tier of government? (G7)

Class Discussion

1   Why might Chief Executives have different objectives from those of the elected councillors? Comment on the opinions of councillors concerning their officers as reflected in this article. (G6)
2   To what extent does Britain have regional government at the moment? Do you think it should be enlarged or extended?
3   For what reasons does the Alliance: (a) want to encourage a non-sectarian approach to the problems of Ulster; (b) favour the creation of an Anglo-Irish consultative body at parliamentary level? (G7)

Extension Work

1   Apart from the policy committee, what are the main committees of a typical county council? (G6)
2   What is the role of the Chief Executive? (G6)
3   What arguments have been advanced for and against the introduction of a local income tax to replace domestic rates?
4   Why did public demand for devolution grow and then decline during the 1970s?

Section

H

The judiciary and the police

Introduction

Legislation is the chief source of law. This covers statute law (Acts of Parliament) and what is commonly known as delegated legislation (which includes orders — rules and regulations made by ministers — and by-laws made by local government and other authorities). A recent source is European Community law, mentioned here in H7; and another source which engenders controversy and public discussion from time to time is case law, made by judges interpreting statute and common law.

John Griffith is critical of the present state of case law because he feels the judiciary, for reasons he gives in H1, are predominantly right wing in attitude and, in pursuing their functions, are able to take what amount to political decisions in certain cases. Griffith states in an extract from the same article that some of the judiciary thought that the Law Lords would avoid direct political involvement in the action brought by the London borough of Bromley against the GLC:

It would have been easy for the Law Lords to have decided that, however much they deprecated the policy of the GLC, the action was one which the GLC were entitled to take and the control was one to be exercised through the ballot box, not through the courts.

The short extract from the Law Reports in H1B gives details of the Bromley case.

Magistrates' courts deal with most criminal cases in England and Wales, and conduct preliminary investigation into serious offences. Crown Courts deal with serious criminal cases. Trial is normally by jury, though a High Court judge sits alone for the most serious cases. H2 bemoans the devaluing of the importance of the jury in Britain's legal system over successive years, while H3 criticises the composition of many juries today. Fenton Bresler, in another extract from the same article as H3, wrote:

Urgent action is called for. Trial by jury is the greatest single Anglo-Saxon contribution to world jurisprudence. It becomes a mockery when jurors themselves are suspect.

H4 presents an argument for abolition of the jury system rather than mere reform. Some have argued that the verdict of the jury in the Ponting case (H5A–H5D) showed the continued value of jury trial in the legal system. H5A gives details of the historical background surrounding the leak of the 'Crown Jewels' defence documents. Clive Ponting, author of this material, felt justified in the interests of 'open' or 'good' government in passing information to Tam Dalyell, MP. During the trial the prosecution did not accuse Ponting of damaging national security, but of breaching confidentiality under Section 2 of the Official Secrets Act. After the trial Sir Robert Armstrong, Cabinet Secretary and Head of the Civil Service, reminded civil servants that their first duty was to the minister in charge of their department and that they should keep confidences. This view of 'closed' or 'secret' government relating to Civil Service behaviour can be compared with those of the documents in Section C. The Ponting case should also be compared with the Sarah Tisdall case, in which a Foreign Office clerk received a six-month sentence in March 1984 for leaking confidential memos to *The Guardian* on the arrival in 1983 of Cruise missiles.

H6 and H7 look at two different aspects of the role of the police, preservation of law and human rights. H6 stresses the need for reform, the need for stronger human rights legislation and for accountable police forces. H7, written by a former Chief Constable, comments on the development of community policing and the role of the police in protecting and enforcing individual human rights.

H1A

A law unto themselves

The power of judges is becoming increasingly political, as recent actions against trade unions and the GLC show. Professor John Griffith calls for radical reform to make the judiciary more responsive to the needs of society.

[. . .]If the law were a comprehensive code of clear principles, adjudication (once the facts were established) would be largely a mechanical exercise, one of feeding in the facts, feeding in the law, and (almost) pulling a lever, with the decision being printed out — what is sometimes called slot-machine jurisprudence. But the law is neither clear nor comprehensive and given the infinite ingenuity and inventiveness of human beings, will never be so. It follows therefore that judges interpret the law, particularly to decide whether and to what extent the general words of the relevant statute cover the case before them.

But, in Britain, judges go much further than this. When judges review the actions of public or administrative authorities, they apply tests, which they have invented, to ensure that those authorities do not act in ways which the judges consider to be unreasonable or based on irrelevant considerations or embarked on for an improper purpose. Such tests are highly subjective and enable the courts to evaluate what public authorities are doing according to the judges' own criteria of conduct. These subjective judgements are, therefore, inevitably political although the language judges tend to use is often couched in terms of the public interest.

The reason why the judges (especially those in the Court of Appeal and the House of Lords) are so important a part of the political machinery is that they may decide either that a public authority had no power to act as it did, or that it exercised a legal power in a way of

which the courts disapprove. I do not suggest that judges should have no power to restrain the activities of public authorities. But nowadays the courts have adopted a policy of intervening and of substituting their own judgement of what is desirable — and that includes what is politically desirable — over wide areas of administrative activity and for a great variety of reasons.

For more than 100 years, relations between judges and trade unions have been strained. In the nineteenth century, Acts of Parliament had to be passed to enable unions to perform their function of protecting the wages and conditions of work of their members, to enable them to withdraw their labour without being prosecuted and to involve themselves in other union activities. [. . .]

Judges in the United Kingdom cannot be politically neutral because they are placed in positions where they are required to make political choices that are sometimes presented to them, and often presented by them, as determinations of where the public interest lies.

It seems to be inevitable, for judges, as it is for other people, that their interpretation of what is in the public interest will be determined by the kind of people they are and by the position they hold in our society.

It is well known that about four out of five judges attended independent schools and Oxford or Cambridge. Out of all the statistics one may be selected: a survey covering the period 1876 to 1972 analysed the 317 judges who sat in the High Court, the Court of Appeal and the House of Lords. It found that 33 per cent had attended one of the so-called Clarendon Schools (Charterhouse, Eton, Harrow, Merchant Taylors, Rugby, St Paul's, Shrewsbury, Westminster, Winchester). In 1978, the answer to a parliamentary question listed 74 High Court judges then sitting. Of these 41 per cent had attended one of the Clarendon Schools.

Professional background is as important as education. Judges are recruited from barristers who have practised for, usually, at least 25 years. The bar is a conservative profession, in both senses of the adjective.

It is against this background that reforms of the judicial system must be considered. We know comparatively little about the administrative and other procedures which lead to the appointment of a judge to the circuit or High Court bench. The actual appointments are made by the Lord Chancellor, or, in the case of the more senior appointments (by promotion from the more junior) by the Prime Minister after consultation with the Lord Chancellor. In recent years it seems that the Prime Minister in practice accepts the recommendations of the Lord Chancellor who, himself a barrister of seniority, is appointed by the Prime Minister and is invariably a member of the Cabinet. He is, therefore, a party political appointment and is someone of considerable political significance who, in addition to his executive and judicial functions, also presides over the House of Lords when it is sitting as a part of the legislature. He may sit as a Law Lord and, if he does, sits as the most senior. [. . .]

The combination of social class, schooling, university and professional career at the bar produces the kind of person, however capable, intelligent, even individualistic, who will have a philosophy of life, an attitude of mind, and a collection of values easily recognisable as belonging to the centre-right of middle or upper-middle class society today.

There are, therefore, two separate questions (among others) to be considered when we talk about desirable reforms of the judiciary. They are: what limits should be placed on the power of judges? And what changes should be made in the methods of appointment?

[from the *New Socialist*, March/April 1982]

It is clear that the powers of judges (and this means, in effect, primarily those of the Court of Appeal and of the Law Lords) to make essentially political decisions should be greatly curtailed. We speak of the sovereignty of parliament but presently too much discretion is left to the judges to overrule the actions of public authorities pursuing political purposes. The principle should be that politicians take political decisions — not because politicians are more trustworthy but because they are vulnerable and accountable and judges are not. And because politics is their business. [. . .]

Two possible reforms in the method of appointment may be learnt from other systems or other countries. First, the power of appointment should be taken from the Lord Chancellor and Prime Minister and vested in a permanent Judicial Commission which would include non-lawyers as well as lawyers.

The variations in the membership of such a commission are so many and so obvious that they need not be itemised here but the main purpose would be to remove the Lord Chancellor from his present dominant position. I see no objections on principle to the introduction of this reform as soon as the necessary legislation is passed.

Secondly, and more radically, the judiciary could become a career service, as is common on the European continent. Law graduates, with or without some limited professional experience either as solicitors or as barristers, could compete at an open, public and anonymous examination, for entry to a Judicial College. There they would be trained as judges for, perhaps 2 1/2 years, much of which time would be spent as apprentices to working judges.

Such a system, if made universal over a number of years, would mean the creation of a heirarchy, and a structure of promotion, from the lowest to the highest ranks of the judiciary. This would inevitably involve competition for promotion and so evaluation of merit.

> *He that will not reason is a bigot; he that cannot reason is a fool; and he that dares not reason is a slave.*
> *(Sir William Drummond)*

The following is a short extract from a judge's summary of the events and factual background of the Bromley case, when the London borough of Bromley contested the legal right of the GLC to impose a supplementary rate precept to pay for reduced fares on London Transport's bus and underground services (the Fares Fair experiment).

The local elections in 1981 resulted in a narrow Labour majority on the GLC and, almost within a matter of days, without consultation and apparently without legal advice, a decision was made that the whole level of fares was to be radically changed as a matter of political policy.

In October 1981 fares were cut by 25 per cent on average and the burden on the ratepayers was doubled.

This was done on the basis of one of the statements in the election manifesto and, as was unanimously held by the Court of Appeal and the House of Lords in the Bromley case, without any regard to the powers of the GLC under the 1969 Act and arbitrarily, without any regard to the interests of ratepayers but solely in the interests of passengers.

[from *All England Law Reports*, Vol. 2, ed. Peter Hutchessson (Butterworths, 1983)]

What's happening to the ideal of twelve good men and true?

by Fenton Bresler
Mail Legal Correspondent

The whole concept of the ancient terms of Magna Carta 'trial by our peers', selected at random and bringing their own independent knowledge of life to bear on the issues before them, is now under attack as never before in our long legal history.

In life, people generally get what they deserve. If you start juggling with the age-old concept of a jury chosen at random — which is the opposite of 'jury vetting' — you are at risk of getting a jury which you deserve.[. . .]

Tradition
For consider the record:
1 Majority verdict. It was also the rule that a jury's decision had to be unanimous. The traditional and honourable view of English law was expressed in the famous old tag: 'Bet-

ter that a hundred guilty men go free than that one innocent man should be condemned unjustly.'

But the 1967 Criminal Justice Act brought into Parliament by that one time darling of the trendies Mr Roy Jenkins, and, to their shame, supported by both Labour and Tory lawyer MPs, altered all that.

Because of some 'jury nobbling' cases at the Old Bailey in the mid-sixties, when some pretty obvious London villains were acquitted under dubious circumstances, the authorities panicked and, instead of dealing through resolute police action with that purely local problem, altered the whole basis of English criminal law and enacted that henceforth the supreme question of guilt or innocence could be decided by a mere majority verdict of ten to two.

The change has undoubtedly made it easier to obtain convictions. But at what cost to principles of justice?

2 The Defence Right of Challenge. Traditionally the prosecution always had to give a reason for challenging a juror in open court if they wanted to prevent him sitting — but until 1948 the defence had an advantage. In keeping with old fashioned ideas they were entitled to challenge as many as 35 jurors 'without cause' — i.e. without giving a reason in court. It may simply have been that, on checking the jurors' particulars on the jury panel, it was seen that their occupations might make them suspect as not being truly impartial: like 'retired policemen' when dealing with a case of alleged police brutality.

In such a case defence counsel merely had to get up and utter the one vibrant word 'Challenge!' Attlee's Labour Government cut these challenges to seven, and Callaghan's Labour Government in 1977 cut them even further — down to three.

3 Cases Taken Away from Jury Trial Altogether. The old rule was, generally speaking, that if a defendant was liable, if convicted, to be jailed for more than three months he had the positive right to trial by jury.

He could demand that his case be heard by a higher court before a judge and twelve of his fellow citizens rather than in his local magistrates' court — where it has long been the view of experienced lawyers that it is generally much easier to get a conviction than persuade the Bench to grant an acquittal.

The Criminal Law Act 1977 did away with all that libertarian sort of nonsense. Again, with the benign blessing of most Tory and Labour MPs, people — presumed (it will be remembered) innocent until their guilt had been proved — were deprived of the right to jury trial in a whole range of delicate and difficult cases: from drink driving and breathalyser charges to homosexual soliciting offences and catch-all political offences.

4 Jury vetting. This is perhaps the most tawdry episode of the whole saga, with both prosecution and defence vying with each other in an attempt to rig the jury to their own best advantage — for that is what it amounts to — by vetting out of court and away from the public eye the potential jurors in their case.

Vetting

The prosecution has a head start on the defence with, as we were officially told in September, 29 cases in the past five years where the Director of Public Prosecutions has authorised police vetting of jurors in 'sensitive cases'.

The defence have so far had to be content with a somewhat limited right to employ private detectives out of legal-aid funds to investigate potential jurors in similarly 'sensitive' types of cases.

Scotland gets by quite happily without any jury vetting by anyone. Lord Emslie, the Scottish Lord Justice General, the equivalent of the English Lord Chief Justice, ruled in 1973 in the High Court of Edinburgh that there should be no vetting of potential jurors in Scottish criminal trials.

Yet in England all that we have is an assurance by Sir Michael Havers, the present Attorney-General and himself the son of a late distinguished High Court judge, that jury vetting will take place only with his direct approval — which, of course, presumes that the practice will continue.

Dangers

So what is the result of all this?

It means that the jury is devalued. It means that we are in danger of creating a climate of thought where the jury ceases to be regarded as the essential lynchpin of our system of criminal justice.

[from the *Daily Mail*, 21 December 1979]

> *Without diversity there would be no choice and without choice there is no freedom.*
> *(Prince Philip)*

The mockery that puts crooks on the jury

by Fenton Bresler
Mail Legal Correspondent

WHAT on earth is happening to the English jury?

We have a senior police chief — Metropolitan Deputy Police Commissioner Patrick Kavanagh — accusing defence lawyers of rigging juries to let their guilty clients go free.

We have a shocked jury foreman complaining to Scotland Yard and his MP about his experiences while serving at an East London Crown Court where a 'we'll go along with the majority' attitude prevailed among his fellow jurors.

We have an Old Bailey juror saying that sometimes his colleagues gave more thought to going home than properly considering the evidence.

Just a short while ago I was told of jury rigging in some London Crown Courts by another high-ranking Scotland Yard officer. 'And it's not only rigging', he said. 'Jurors are being downright "nobbled" — got at by the villains and bribed to help bring in false verdicts.'

Certainly juries are not what they were: the old days when jurors, in Lord Devlin's classic phrase were, 'predominantly male, middle aged and middle class', have gone for ever.

On August 9, 1974, the Juries Act came into effect and the old property qualification for jurors went out of the window, at the same time as the minimum age was lowered from 21 to 18. At a stroke, an estimated 22 million more people became eligible for jury service — nearly three times the previous total of only eight million.

It was an overnight revolution in the law, unremarked by the general public. In many ways, it was a just and necessary reform — but the price has been heavy.

Young jurors now go into court dressed as if they were at a disco rather than helping in the administration of justice — and the modern breed of judge says nothing.

The story is told in the Temple of a certain Crown Court in the London area, notorious for its high proportion of acquittals 'mainly because most of the jurors have done the same thing themselves'.

One case at this particular court concerned the theft of 100 £1 notes. They comprised exhibit one. When the jury retired to consider their verdict, they asked to take the exhibits with them. Only after they had all gone home, having brought in their

inevitable 'not guilty' verdict, was it spotted that five one pound notes were missing.

But the malaise goes much deeper than mere funny stories.

There was the famous occasion of Judge Alan King Hamilton's last case at the Old Bailey in December 1979 when four alleged anarchists were acquitted, after a 14-week trial, of conspiracy to rob and arms offences, and the judge told the five women and seven men on the jury that their verdicts were 'remarkably merciful' in the face of the evidence.

He ordered that jury to return to court the next morning — to hear a fifth defendant plead guilty to conspiracy and name two of the acquitted men as 'out and out' anarchists and pin-point one of them as having helped him rob a supermarket at gunpoint.

'You now know what you have done, and I pray to God that none of you will ever have occasion to regret it', said the angry judge before going off into retirement.

But can juries actually be 'rigged'? Very easily, I'm afraid. The defence can challenge, without giving any reason at all, up to three potential jurors per defendant. They have to stand down.

In cases of organised crime, such as robbery, there generally are at least four people in the dock. So that gives them an entirely new jury of 12 just for the asking!

How does the defence know whom to challenge? Clothes are usually a good giveaway. Sir Michael Havers, the present Attorney-General, once said, when Opposition spokesman on the law, that anyone wanting to avoid jury service no longer needed to think up elaborate excuses. Walking into the jury box wearing a sober suit with one of the 'heavy' newspapers under his arm would be enough.

[from the *Daily Mail*, 4 February 1982]

But the more sinister aspect of 'rigging' is that, quite literally, more and more people serving on juries now are likely to aid the accused criminal because they are themselves convicted criminals.

When the law was changed in 1974, the existing ban on jury service for anyone who has been sent to Borstal or served more than three months in jail was left more or less intact.

For decades someone who was merely fined or went to jail for less than three months was regarded as not having committed a sufficiently heinous offence to merit loss of his fundamental right to sit as a juror.

Serious offences

Fair enough! But the authorities completely overlooked the fact that ever since 1967 there has been such a thing as a *suspended* prison sentence, where the convicted person does not go to jail at all.

Furthermore since 1974 there has been a lot of pressure on courts to relieve the strain on our prisons by wherever possible fining instead of jailing, and suspending or passing a short jail sentence, if you actually have to send someone to prison.

The result is that the present ban on jury service is totally inadequate and out of date.

H4

Many are called, few are chosen
The cost of the jury system

Sidney Bunt
Youth training officer

SURELY it is time for the 12 good men and true of the jury to be led from the nation's courts of justice and into the knacker's yard.

Leaving aside the sexist bias of that traditional description of the jury, and the conundrum of what constitutes goodness and truth in 1980, the process of selecting 12 citizens who embody those qualities seems badly out of step with the times.

Its cost to the public purse is huge. At a Crown Court in London where I recently had two weeks of my time squandered, an official threw out the

figure of £5 per minute needed to maintain that particular court. Matched throughout the country, the total cost to the taxpayer is astronomical. A sizeable proportion is attributable to the presence of well over a hundred jurors-in-waiting who, at that particular court complex, are kept on tap to satisfy the voracious appetite of the system. And who can calculate the hidden social costs of plucking all those citizens from their families and work places?

There is a high-handedness that touches on the arrogant in the as-

sumption that the affairs of the courts ought to have, and legally can take, priority over the other commitments of people chosen randomly from the electoral lists. On my recent stretch I met many jurors-in-waiting whose neglected jobs were clearly of much greater social importance than serving as Crown Court fodder.

Having been called for jury service, some were then not chosen. They were assigned to cases which apparently decided not to go to judgement, or they were challenged by counsel who seemed able to assess with a rapid glance whether a juror would be prejudiced for or against a defendant. This seems both offensive and capricious.

Even when 12 citizens are finally sworn, the machinery of trial by jury is clearly heard to creak. Its effectiveness depends upon jurors being capable of understanding, even at a surface level, the rituals, procedures, assumptions, jargon and nuances of the court system. Without that understanding, the jury-room debate may be mere window-dressing, to create an illusion that the people have sat in judgement on their peers. Yet no test of anybody's ability to do this is applied. There are usually some jurors who make no contribution to the sifting and weighing of evidence, or, if they do more than acquiesce in what the front-runners urge, instantly reveal that they have not grasped the significance of much that has been said in court. Occasionally, jurors who cannot read the words of the oath, and need it read out for them to repeat, will be faced with voluminous documentary evidence.

The interaction, the unspoken negotiations and the attempts to claim status in the jury room are a rich source of material for the student of group dynamics. Even the process of establishing who is to be foreman — a crucial role if the discussion leading to a verdict is to be given cohesion and direction — may add to one's scepticism. Someone who has dominated the waiting room chit-chat may, on that basis, be judged the proper holder of this office; but he or she may have little to offer, perhaps no skill whatever in drawing out the diffident or damping down the dominant, and even less sensitivity to the non-verbal messages within the group.

A unanimous verdict is still looked for, despite the acceptability of a majority verdict in certain circumstances. A single juror who retains doubts may stand fast and detain the other 11 for longer than they had hoped; such a maverick may be abused or wooed by the others — and jury foremen, from whom the doubters might expect protection, have been known to join in.

It is over a century since W. S. Gilbert lampooned the system in *Trial by Jury*. Surely public opinion is now ready for reforms?

[from the *Sunday Times*, 14 September 1980]

Questions

1 What is 'slot-machine jurisprudence'? (H1A)

2 How does Griffith suggest that judges are likely to be conservative in attitude and middle class in origin? (H1A)

3 Explain what is meant by 'jury vetting' and the 'defence right of challenge'. (H2)

4 Why was it felt that the requirements for a unanimous jury verdict had ceased to be necessary? (H2)

5 Why is it true to say that juries are no longer 'predominantly male, middle aged and middle class'? (H3)

6 Explain how Bunt illustrates his point that the interactions in the jury room provide a 'rich source of material' on 'group dynamics'. (H4)

Class Discussion

1 How important is judge-made or case law in our legal system? (H1A)

2 Griffith argues that political decisions should be the prerogative of the politicians. Is it not inevitable that judges will sometimes be involved in making judgements interpreted as political? (H1A)

3 What arguments can be made both for retention and for abolition of the jury system?

Extension Work

1   Find evidence to support Griffith's contention that relations between judges and trade unions have been strained for more than a hundred years.

2   What powers do the Courts have to review the activities of the executive branch of government?

3   Explain what is meant by the following: (a) 'hidden social costs'; (b) 'public purse'; (c) 'non-verbal messages'; (d) 'sexist bias'. (H4)

4   The Appeal Court ruled on 10 November 1981 that the GLC's action was *ultra vires*, and issued a *writ of certiorari*, to cancel the *precept*. Explain the meaning of the terms and words in italics.

5   Explain exactly what is meant by the term 'Law Lords'.

6   Professor Griffith commented in another part of his article, not included in H1A, that the Law Lords might have decided that the GLC was entitled to take the action it did, and that control should be exercised through the ballot box and not through the courts. (See the introduction to this section.) Find out more about the Bromley case and present a case both for and against the decision made by the Law Lords.

H5A – H5D   *The Ponting case*

The Belgrano still a hazard for Government

by James Lewis

THE acquittal of the senior civil servant, Mr Clive Ponting, on a charge of breaching the Official Secrets Act sparked off a furious parliamentary row between the Prime Minister and the Opposition Leader which totally obscured the important constitutional issues underlying the case: whether ministers are entitled to cite national security as an excuse for lying to Parliament, and whether public servants owe their duty to ministers or to Parliament.

Mr Ponting was prosecuted under the odious Section 2 of the Act because he released to the Labour MP, Mr Tam Dalyell, documents from the Ministry of Defence about the sinking of the Argentinian destroyer, *General Belgrano*, during the Falklands war. The documents revealed details which ministers had refused to divulge to the tenacious Mr Dalyell in reply to his Commons questions on the grounds that the information was highly classified. Mr Ponting maintained that the information was not classified and that national security was not involved. He further perceived that the Commons Select Committee on Foreign Affairs was also about to be misled in its examination of the Falklands war, and accordingly decided to blow the whistle.

The ruling of the judge — which the jury rejected — was that 'the interests of the State', which Mr Ponting was pledged to protect, should be defined as meaning 'the policies of government ministers at any given moment'. This obviously raised serious constitutional issues about the role of the Queen and Parliament in a democratic system.

The trial raised further important questions about the course of the *Belgrano* when she was sunk; about whose finger (that of the Defence staff or the War Cabinet) was really on the trigger when torpedoes were unleashed on the destroyer; and about why Parliament had been misled in its attempts to establish the precise circumstances that led to the sinking, with the loss of 368 Argentinian lives.

In the immediate aftermath of Mr Ponting's acquittal, however, the chief concern of the Labour leader, Mr Neil Kinnock, seemed to be to discover who authorised the civil servant's prosecution, and why. In his initial refusal to accept Mrs Thatcher's assurance that she had not been personally involved he came close to calling the Prime Minister a liar. This is something parliamentarians are not supposed to do. The fact that ministers are not supposed to mislead MPs was all but forgotten, which evidently suited Defence ministers very well indeed.

Though the row will go on for a long time yet, the immediate conclusions are that a hamfisted prosecution has failed; that the 'catch-all' Section 2 of the Official Secrets Act is further discredited; that civil servants cannot be relied upon to be unquestioning lackeys; and that the *Belgrano* story is very far from sunk.

For Mr Ponting, the outcome is the sacrifice of a promising career. Though he could obviously not be dismissed the withdrawal of his security clearance would have kept him out of the mainstream of the public service. Even more importantly for him, perhaps, was the fact that continued government employment would have prevented the publication of his promised book called *The Right to Know*. So he chose to resign.

[from the *Guardian Weekly*, 24 February 1985]

H5B

Interests of the State

From Mr A. C. Geddes
Sir, The jury in the Ponting trial had to be satisfied that they were sure that Mr Ponting, in communicating the information in question to Mr Dalyell, did so to a person 'other than one to whom it is in the interest of the State to communicate it' (section 2a of the Offical Secrets Act).

The proper construction of the term 'interests of the State', which is a matter of law for the judge and not a question for the jury, was considered by the House of Lords in *Chandler v. DPP* (1964) AC763. Lord Pearce, with whom Lord Devlin agreed, stated that in the context of the Act 'the interests of the State must in my judgement mean the interests of the State according to the policies laid down for it by its recognised organs of government and authority; the policies of the State as they are, not as they ought in the opinion of the jury to be'.

The other members of the House, while not being so explicit, did not dissent from these judgements. Mr Justice McCowan would have been bound by that decision. I fail to see therefore how the judge's direction, which you misquote in your leader of February 25, was a 'disgraceful statement'.
Yours etc,
A. C. GEDDES,
Goldsmith Building,
Temple, EC4.
26 February.

From Mr Raymond Blackburn
Sir, Those who have criticised your editorials on the Ponting case have ignored the main principle at stake. This is that where there are two or more possible interpretations of words in a statute that interpretation should be adopted which is most favourable to the liberty of the subject. This rule should require the words 'the State' to mean more than 'the government of the day'.

A similar reasoning lay at the heart of Lord Atkin's great speech in *Liversidge v. Anderson* (1942) AC306. Moreover, those who believe that the rule of law should serve the cause of freedom will rejoice that Lord Denning has spoken in the same sense as you.
Yours faithfully,
RAYMOND BLACKBURN,
50 Homefield Road,
Chiswick, W4.
28 February.

[from *The Times*, 4 March 1985]

H5C

The judge in the Ponting trial has propounded an eccentric and potentially totalitarian view regarding the phrase 'the interests of the State'.

There is no support in constitutional precedent or democratic theory for his argument that this phrase means whatever 'the established organs of government and authority' choose to have it mean. For to define it thus would *ipso facto* imply that all the constitutional institutions and processes of opposition, including the constitutionally ordained position of Leader of the Opposition, were opposed to the interests of the State.

The learned judge must be reminded that the distinction between government and State is not only crucial to the survival of democracy, but is also personified in this country by the Queen. His arguments are not only false and dangerous; they would expose him to the crushing humiliation of a fail grade in O-level law.
WILF ATTENBOROUGH,
Spital Street, Lincoln.

[from the *Guardian Weekly*, 24 February 1985]

H5D

Moment of truth for the Secrets Act

by Shirley Williams

THE implications of the verdict in the Ponting case have been obscured by the row over whether or not ministers were involved in the decision to prosecute Ponting under Section 2 of the Official Secrets Act. That is a minor diversion compared to the central issue — the misleading of the House of Commons by ministers and the weakness of the safeguards in Britain against the abuse of power.

Only the jury's decision stands between us and 'elective dictatorship', of which Lord Hailsham once spoke.

Incidentally, the furore over the juror who was a Labour councillor in Islington is a dangerous irrelevance. No juror should be chosen or rejected on the grounds of his or her political beliefs.

The judge was clearly impatient with the evidence given to the court by expert witnesses. As Professor Wade, probably the most distinguished authority on administrative law in

> **What Section 2 says**
>
> Under Section 2 of the Official Secrets Act, 1911, it can be a criminal offence for any servant of the Crown to communicate 'any secret official code word, or pass word, or any sketch, plan, model, article, note, document, or information which relates to or is used in a prohibited place or anything in such a place or which has been made or obtained in contravention of this Act, or which has been entrusted in confidence to him by any person holding office under Her Majesty, or which he has obtained or to which he has had access owing to his position' whether as a servant of the Crown or an employee of a servant of the Crown.
>
> The offence applies if he communicates this information to anyone 'other than a person to whom he is authorised to communicate it, or a person to whom it is in the interests of the State his duty to communicate it'; or 'uses the information in his possession' for the benefit of any foreign power or in any other manner prejudicial to the safety or interests of the State'.
>
> It is also an offence if he retains the above information 'when he has no right to retain it or when it is contrary to his duty to retain it, or fails to comply with all directions issued by lawful authority with regard to the return or disposal thereof'; or 'fails to take reasonable care of, or so conducts himself as to endanger the safety' of the information.

Britain, gave his evidence, Mr Justice McCowan drummed his fingers and interrupted to ask defence counsel where this evidence was leading.

'It is for me', he said 'to direct the jury as to the law.' But of course, there is no law. Mr Justice McCowan's definition of the 'interests of State' as being identical to 'the policies of the government then in power' is his own, and is based on no statute.

The great political philosopher, de Tocqueville, argued that liberty is based not only on the politics of consent, but on the mores, the unwritten rules and conventions shaped by the procedures and institutions of a free society. In his classic book *Administrative Law*, Professor H. W. R. Wade makes the same point. Referring to the rule of law, he described its primary meaning as being that everything must be done according to law.

'But the rule of law', he wrote, 'demands something more, since otherwise it would be satisfied by giving the government unrestricted discretionary powers, so that everything they did was within the law . . . The secondary meaning of the rule of law, therefore, is that government should be conducted within a framework of recognised rules and principles which restrict discretionary power.' And that is what Professor Wade told the jury in the Ponting trial.

Respect for such constitutional conventions matters in Britain above all. No written constitution guarantees our democracy. No Bill of Rights underpins our freedom. Our liberties rest on the integrity of ministers, the conscience of public servants and the independence of the courts.

The Official Secrets Act was described by Mr Justice Caulfield in the Biafra case as a blunderbuss. It is a potent weapon for a government to employ, and can be used for the most partisan ends. In 1976, the then Attorney General, Sam Silkin, told the House of Commons that he would take into account the report of the Franks Commission in deciding whether to bring prosecutions under the Act.

The Franks Commission had recommended the repeal of Section 2, the section under which Clive Ponting was charged, and the introduction of legislation to ensure freedom of information. Any prosecution under the Official Secrets Act requires the assent of the Attorney General; reluctance to bring prosecution has acted as a safety-catch on the blunderbuss in the past, but the present government seems only too ready to use it to protect itself from embarrassment and to club conscientious civil servants into silence.

The greatest missed opportunity of the last decade was the 1976–79 Labour government's failure to reform the OSA. It meant to do so: Merlyn Rees, the then Home Secretary, published a White Paper setting out its intentions. But reform of the OSA fell victim to a more ambitious aim, the passing of the Freedom of Information Act.

Labour lacked sufficient common purpose in the Cabinet and a sufficient majority in the House of Commons to carry the comprehensive legislation. So the country got neither a loaf nor a half loaf. It got no reform at all. Merlyn Rees, the only political witness in the trial of Clive Ponting, put his finger on the seductive temptations of the OSA as a means of avoiding political embarrassment. On the importance of the constitutional conventions, he was blunt. 'It matters to tell the truth to Parliament', he told the jury. 'It wouldn't work otherwise.'

Accountability to Parliament is the mechanism that is supposed to control the executive in Britain. Constitutionally, Parliament is sovereign, and historically Parliament alone could authorise the levying of taxes. In practice, however, party discipline has made accountability to Parliament an unconvincing safeguard. The stick wielded by the Whips, and the carrots of preferment and patronage, mean that the executive, the government of the day, given a majority of seats, can get whatever legislation it wants through the House of Commons.

The OSA is a potent weapon for a government to employ, and it can be used for the most partisan ends. The British courts, as the GCHQ case showed, decline to challenge ministers' assertions that a decision is based on considerations of national security. The courts readily accept ministers' classification of official documents, although the appellations 'top secret' and 'secret' are often used to conceal information of no possible danger to the State. The OSA, binding on all civil servants, provides a convenient cover for ministers, and only their personal integrity inhibits its use.

The executive is now exploiting its power, breaking the fragile mechanisms of consensus and scorning the traditional practices and values on which our liberties depend. The OSA is being used, not to ensure national security, but to silence public servants.

The jury's verdict in the Ponting case has bought us time in which to underpin our assaulted democracy. That democracy can no longer rest on a gentlemanly consensus now fragmenting under the hammer blows of ideological politics. The ludicrous, and now threatening, Section 2 of the Official Secrets Act must be repealed. The European convention on human rights should be written into British law. Legislation to ensure freedom of information should be prepared urgently. There is little time left but the Ponting verdict has now given us an unprecedented opportunity.
Shirley Williams is President of the SDP

[from the *Guardian Weekly*, 24 February 1985]

[from *Marxism Today* (publication of the Communist Party of Great Britain), March 1985]

Questions

1   Why did Ponting pass Defence Ministry documents (called the 'Crown Jewels'), of which he was the author, to the Labour MP, Tam Dalyell? (H5A)

2   For what chief reason did ministers mislead the House of Commons over a period of time concerning the sinking of the *General Belgrano*? (H5A)

3   Cite passages from H5A which indicate the political nature of the trial of Ponting.

4   Could one assume that the jury thought Ponting gave the documents to a person whom it was in the interest of the State to do so? (H5B)

5   Why is the distinction between the government and the State considered important in a democracy? (H5C)

6   In the last resort, what do our liberty, freedom and democratic system depend on, according to Williams? (H5D)

7   How does Williams indicate that Section 2 of the Official Secrets Act can be used for purposes not originally intended in the Act? (H5D)

8   What reasons are given in H5D to support the view that Parliament's control of the executive has declined considerably?

9   List the various principles or problems of government and relations between various parts of the political system that the Ponting case highlights. (H5A–H5D)

Class Discussion

1   Discuss the factors that you think most likely to have led the jury to acquit Ponting in the Old Bailey trial.

2   Was Mr Justice McCowan right to define the 'interests of the State' as being the policies of the government in power?

3   Discuss the points for and against making the European Convention on Human Rights part of British law. (See also Section A.)

Extension Work

1   Why has there been so much interest in the precise circumstances that led to the sinking of the *Belgrano*, including its actual course at that time? (H5A)

2   Of what constitutional significance is the case *Liversidge v. Anderson* (1942)? (H5B)

3   Explain the meaning of the phrase 'the constitutionally ordained position of Leader of the Opposition'. (H5C)

4   What are the chief aspects of the 'rule of law'? How important is this concept as part of Britain's democracy? (H5D)

H6–H7   *The police and human rights*

H6

Law, order and justice

Labour's aim is to ensure that all sections of the community are safe on the street and at home, free from the fear that crime generates. We believe that the police should have the support of the community, have their rights safeguarded, and be fairly paid. But we also believe that it is as much in the interests of the police as of their local communities that they are properly accountable and fully subject to the law. We will ensure that, throughout the country, the police are encouraged to return to the beat and therefore be closer to the communities they serve. That is the best way of preventing and detecting crime.

We intend to protect the rights of individual suspects, while providing the police with sufficient powers to do their job effectively whilst not infringing the civil rights of individual suspects. We aim to create elected police authorities in all parts of the country, including London, with statutory responsibility for the determination of police policy within their areas. We will also:

- launch a major initiative to help victims, including extending and simplifying the present Criminal Injuries Compensation Scheme.
- give priority to crime prevention as part of our action programme for run-down estates.
- bring about better co-ordination in the technical, support and information services of the police.
- replace the present police complaints procedure with an independent system accountable to local communities, with minority police representation.
- create community police councils to provide an opportunity for open discussion between police and the community as to the quality and manner of police provision.
- introduce strict limits on searches of people in the street, searches of premises, the use of the power of arrest, and on the time a prisoner can be held in custody before being charged.
- protect the rights of those in police custody by giving revised Judges' Rules, which safeguard those under arrest or interrogation, the force of law, and, in England and Wales, take the role of prosecutor away from the police by implementing a public prosecutor system on the Procurator Fiscal model.
- repeal the Police and Criminal Evidence Bill, because it infringes the rights and freedoms of individuals.

[from *The new hope for Britain* (Labour Party Manifesto), 1983]

H7

Alderson's book a guide for European police

By DEREK LEAN

THE CONCEPT of the community 'copper' — something pioneered in Devon and Cornwall — could in future become, in a way, part of the thinking of over a million police officers throughout Europe.

Not that France or Italy, for example, is about to embrace the typical English community bobby as we know him.

But the ethos of community policing — the whole notion of a policeman's work having a vital social role to it as well as pure law enforcement — is one of the many approaches advocated in a new training manual for police which has been accepted by the 21 member nations of the Council of Europe.

Called '*Human rights and the police*', the book has been written by the former Devon and Cornwall Chief Constable, Mr John Alderson, a man who has been a champion of community policing.

This morning he and Mrs Cathune Cape, a UK member of the European Commission on Human Rights, will be launching the important publication in London.

This week I talked with Mr Alderson about the book and how he came to write it.

He said that, bearing in mind it was going towards the education of police officers in other parts of Europe, he had taken the opportunity to include and stress the traditional British police values of encouraging acts of help to the community which had nothing to do with the enforcement of laws.

These acts embodied the social role of the police. 'I took the opportunity to stress many of these things because I know European police forces do not always embody them in their traditions', he said.

'I have argued that the police have two roles. On the one hand they are officers of the law in whichever country they happen to be, but equally they are social workers in as much as they should be active in the prevention of crime and assisting members of the public in emergencies both great and small.

They should also be helping other government agencies in their work, which includes education, social workers, health and community workers of various kinds.

The police for many people are the last social service. When people do not know where to go for help of one kind or another they should be able to turn to the police.

If they are afraid of the police — which they are in some countries — they will not do it. They cannot do it because that fear acts as a barrier between police and public', he said.

Mr Alderson agreed that these were the basic principles of community policing — something this country was trying to develop further following the Scarman report on inner city riots.

I asked him if it was taking it too far to say that the ideals of community policing he brought to Devon and Cornwall were being advocated as part of observing human rights throughout police work.

'I do not think you are taking it too far', he said. 'One should not have to wait for laws to be passed to protect every human right and dignity.

A good police officer and a good police force will instinctively understand what is fair and what is right and proper to protect in individual dignity and safety, which is really what human rights boil down to.

And the concept of community policing as we developed it in Devon and Cornwall leads you straight into this philosophy of looking after, protecting, individuals, particularly the young, old, and weak', he said.

In his book Mr Alderson stresses that there is no conflict between the maintenance and enforcement of law on the one hand and the preservation of human rights on the other.

'On the contrary', he writes, 'the trainee should fully understand that the ultimate basis of true order in a democracy is founded on upholding the rule of law.'

Even so, it is a book that does not shirk the difficulties that are bound to

arise for police in the narrow ground where law enforcement and crime prevention overlap with the individual's right to enjoy freedom of action and thought.

For instance, if violence erupts on picket lines, to what extent is police action likely to interfere with an individual's right to express his opinions?

Or again, if a senior officer suggests that a prisoner is hooded, deprived of sleep, food or drink, or subjected to continuous noise, as a means of lowering resistance to interrogation, does this constitute a denial of his basic human rights or is it a legitimate method of achieving co-operation?

These, and many more, are the sort of issues Mr Alderson raises. He seeks to answer them by reference to case law such as is provided by the judgements of the European Court of Human Rights or the Commission on Human Rights — a charter drawn up in 1950, and much of which was based on British law.

For those who have to train Europe's policemen, Mr Alderson says they should first of all study the meaning and implications of the rule of law and stress them from the beginning.

'The rule basically', he writes, 'is that nobody is above the law, least of all the police who were appointed to preserve it.

There will be occasions when the criminal actions of a person or persons are so gross as to be repugnant to decent people and this will require great strength of will if improper police behaviour is to be avoided.

It is not for the police but for the courts to exact the penalty for the crime.'

Mr Alderson told me that it was in 1981, while he was still the peninsula's Chief Constable, that the Education Committee for Human Rights of the Council for Europe invited him to write a training textbook on human rights and the police for the 21 countries that make up the Council.

It was a pilot project and the first text of its kind sponsored by the Council.

'To that extent it is quite unique because it is an international training manual and it is the first, to my knowledge, that has ever been accepted by 21 countries all with different legal systems, different criminal laws and criminal procedures, but all subscribing to the European Convention on Human Rights.

So it was that kind of exercise which seemed to me at the time quite a formidable task', he said.

'I had written a book called *Policing Freedom* and I think they must have got hold of that somehow. I had referred to the role of the police in protecting human rights. It might be that is why they asked me to do it', said Mr Alderson.

The work involved a tremendous amount of research, including study of the Articles of the European Convention on Human Rights and the many decisions made by the European Court of Human Rights.

It also demanded visiting Strasbourg for consultations with lawyers and members of the Directorate of Human Rights.

Now it has been agreed as a training manual, and although it is not mandatory on any government, it is bound to have considerable influence, having been accepted by the countries' ministers.

'It is likely that policemen in all these countries will receive the same training in human rights as each other although obviously their training in their own laws and procedures will still remain different', he said.

To make sure that there is action and not just words to *Human Rights and the Police* (published by Her Majesty's Stationery Office Books), a conference is to be held in Strasbourg in two years' time to monitor progress.

[from *The Western Morning News*, 28 February 1985]

Questions

1   Illustrate how the Labour Party, in this extract from its 1983 manifesto, stresses democratic procedures and the importance of human rights. (H6)

2   Explain the nature of community policing. How is it linked with the Scarman report? (H7)

3   How does Alderson relate the role of the police with that of preservation of human rights and liberties? (H7)

4   Explain why and in what manner Alderson refers to the following: (a) 'rule of law'; (b) 'case law'. (H7)

Class Discussion

1   Should the victim's rights become an integral part of human rights legislation? Ought the criminal to make redress to the victim?

2   Distinguish, with examples, between law enforcement and crime prevention.

3   How has the role of the police changed over the last twenty years? Give your own ideas on ways the police can more effectively carry out their tasks relating to law and order.

Extension Work

1 Did the Conservative government make amendments to the Police and Criminal Evidence Bill to ensure that it did not infringe rights and freedoms? Why has the Labour Party accused the government of violating human rights with its police legislation since 1979? (H6)

2 What developments, if any, have taken place since 1980 relating to the following: (a) a public prosecutor system; (b) community policing; (c) reform of police complaints procedure; (d) increased protection of people in police custody?

3 What powers do the police now have to question, detail or arrest citizens?

4 Give examples to illustrate the point made in H7 of how the police encourage 'acts of help to the community which have nothing to do with the enforcement of laws'.

5 Describe the functions and composition of police authorities. Why are they not 'properly accountable', as the Labour manifesto indicates? (H6)

Section J

Political issues and public opinion

Introduction

Political considerations, the desire of a party to gain or to retain office or power, or the influence of party ideologies and attitudes, often lie at the back of measures taken, policies adopted and party statements made, even if the optimist hopes that certain problems can be treated in an objective, non-partisan manner according to some collective idea of what is in the national interest.

J1 is a letter from the Department of Health and Social Security to the Conservative MP for Fareham, Peter Lloyd, explaining the government's policy on the NHS. The increased expenditure in the NHS from 1978/79 to 1983/84 was described as 'an all-time record and higher in real terms than in any year of Labour government' in *Four Years' Work*, a booklet published by the Conservative Central Office in May 1983. The same booklet pointed out that the Conservatives had abolished an entire tier of management (at Area Level), and reduced both the number of management teams and the number of circulars and notices sent out by the Department to the Health Service and local authorities, thus saving considerable expense. Increases in Health Service staff had been concentrated in the areas responsible for direct patient care (nurses, midwives, doctors and dentists).

Critics of Conservative policies relating to the NHS and health services have argued that the Conservative government came to power determined to destroy the public or State sector in medicine and health care, but the Conservatives have argued that in fact they have tried to make the NHS more efficient. You should try to assess the advantages and disadvantages of various policies pursued by successive governments over the years relating to the NHS, housing, education, race relations, industrial relations, and other major issues.

MPs, as a result of surgeries, correspondence, and informal contacts, discover what people think about actual or intended government policies. The government is able to assess the degree of popularity of its current policies and the likely response of the public to envisaged future measures as a result of inputs into the political system. Examples of this input process include the activities of pressure groups, questions raised by MPs at Question Time in the House of Commons, feeling among backbench MPs communicated to Cabinet Ministers, and articles and letters in the mass media. As a result the government may decide to change some intended measure before its implementation, abandon a particular line of policy, or revoke some legislation, all examples of output. Feedback from the public through various channels helps the government to perform its job more effectively, and J1 illustrates an aspect of this process of feedback and of output. If certain policies generate massive correspondence, or a public outcry, or opposition from key groups which the government needs to placate, then the government may have to change course. J2 and J13, for example, refer to popular disquiet over government economies in the NHS in 1983 and this may have contributed to the government plan to allocate an extra £800 million to the NHS in 1984.

J11–J13 illustrate a form of indirect participation in politics through the mass media, which not only give considerable publicity to opinion poll results, but also reflect various shades of opinion through editorials, letters, and articles on a range of current issues.

Certain issues cut across or relate to others. For example, the question of State control or ownership versus private enterprise or privatisation (for certain areas the issue is posed as nationalisation versus denationalisation), intermingles with controversies over opposing policies on housing, education, the Health Service, and major sectors of industry or services, e.g. coal, iron and steel, gas and electricity, and telecommunications. If governments do not pay sufficient attention to pressing problems relating to, say, housing (J6, J7), unemployment, education (J8A–J10), welfare services, the urban environment, race relations and ethnic minorities (J4, J5), this may lead to unrest, strikes and the growth of violence or serious crime, which also raises the issue of law and order, and the priorities the government has in public spending. These points should be borne in mind when studying the various documents in this section.

J1

DEPARTMENT OF HEALTH AND SOCIAL SECURITY
Alexander Fleming House, Elephant & Castle, London SE1 6BY
Telephone 01-407 5522
From the Parliamentary Under Secretary of State for Health

PO(4)4168/11

Peter Lloyd Esq MP

22 December 1983

Dear Peter,

Thank you for your letter of 3 October to Norman Fowler enclosing one from your constituent Mr N. Jones about the NHS.

I think the Government's record on the NHS speaks for itself. Over the last five years we have doubled expenditure in the NHS in Great Britain from £$7\frac{3}{4}$ billion in 1978/79 to some £15 billion in 1983/84. That represents an increase of more than 17 per cent compared with the Retail Price Index and has allowed substantial real improvements in services. It also means that the NHS is able to keep abreast of the increasing pressures which are on it as a result of the growing number of elderly people in the country. In fact, the Health Service is now treating more patients than ever before.

Another feature of the last five years has been the rapid increase in the number of staff working in the Health Service. Numbers increased by about 70 000, or almost 9 per cent, so that the National Health Service now employs over a million people in England alone — equivalent to 820 000 working full-time. But we have to ensure that all those extra people are being employed to the best effect. Over the last year or two we have been trying to make sure that health authorities scrutinise their use of manpower as carefully as every other area of expenditure. They need to review their use of *existing* manpower — to see whether each post still requires to be filled and that no part of the service is over-manned and wasting money required for other things.

This is why we asked authorities to work to specific targets for manpower by the end of this financial year. Those targets produced net increases in staff in some places* and reductions in others but nationally they only involved an overall reduction of just half of one per cent of Health Service manpower. They were settled in discussion with health authorities themselves and took account of the need for increases in manpower in some cases when new developments were due to come on-stream. I am confident that health authorities can meet these targets without affecting patient services. Moreover, by closer re-examination of their use of manpower, they will save money which they can spend on other things and be in a better position to develop services in the future.

For that is the Government's objective. Although we are looking to health authorities to modernise their management and embark on a major cost improvement programme, we are also providing a real increase in resources.

Next year we plan to spend £800 million more on the NHS in Great Britain as the Prime Minister pledged. In England we will be spending over £650 million more next year than this — an extra £400 million for current expenditure on hospital and community health services alone. After allowing for increased costs, it means that there will be room for real growth in services of some one per cent compared with this year. Any savings which health authorities can make in the costs of the services they already run will allow further developments of services in the future. We are also planning to increase NHS capital spending by £50 million, getting on for two per cent more than projected general inflation. Finally, we are budgeting for an increase in expenditure on the family practitioner services of some £190 million next year, after taking full account of this year's higher spending on these services. It is quite wrong to describe this policy as one of 'cuts' at all. Our policy and our record show the Government's continuing commitment to improve and develop the health service.

I am so sorry you have been kept waiting for a reply.

Yours ever,
John

* including our own Wessex area in which total NHS employees are increasing again — this year by 40. P.C.

Since the June 1983 election, the Tories' attack on the health service has intensified. They have:
● cut the cash for services in real terms.
● cut staffing levels for the first time in the NHS.
● forced health authorities to privatise ancillary services.
● continued their encouragement of the private sector.

Cash cuts

During the election campaign, Norman Fowler, Secretary of State for Health, claimed that spending on the NHS had risen by 7.5 per cent in real terms over the previous four years. What he didn't say was that spending of that order was needed just for services to stand still, because of increasing demands. [. . .]

Within a month of the Tories' election victory, Chancellor Nigel Lawson announced a new package of cuts, including £140m from the hospital and community health services budget:
● health authorities were faced with a one per cent cut in their budgets four months into the financial year.
● on the government's own calculations, growth of 1.2 per cent was reduced to just 0.2 per cent for 1983/84.
● taking account of growing demand and efficiency savings, services have been cut by 2–2¹/₂ per cent in 1983/84.

All the professions in the health service — the British Medical Association, the Royal College of Nurses, the Association of Health Service Treasurers, the National Association of Health Authorities — warned what the cuts would mean. Surveys by the Junior Hospital doctors and the Royal College of Nurses showed they were right. In a letter to *The Times* (21 March 1984), the Presidents of the Royal Colleges warned 'Without adequate funding the future development of preventive medicine, health care and improvements from advances in medicine will be threatened.' [. . .]

This year's budget

For the year 1984/85, there are signs that the Government has taken heed of the massive public and professional outcry about the cuts. An extra £800 million has been allocated to the NHS in Great Britain — a real increase of one per cent. That is an improvement on the long-term planning assumptions issued last June, which forecast a real growth of just 0.5 per cent next year.

But even the Government recognises that 1.5 per cent real growth is needed to keep pace with the rising number of elderly people and medical advances.

The Government's allocation will not even allow the health service to stand still. The one per cent growth they have allowed for is based upon:

● the 1983/84 budget *after* the Lawson cuts.

● a pay rise for health workers in 1984/85 of just 3 per cent — 2 per cent less than the expected rate of inflation.

If proper allowance is made for all these factors, the NHS would need almost half as much again to restore last year's cuts and maintain standards.

[from *Thatcher's Britain 1984* ed. Tony Manwaring and Jenny Pitkin (Labour Party and *New Socialist*, 1984)]

Private Medicine — It's a Leech on the NHS

PRIVATE PRACTICE has boomed under the Tories — 4.2 million people are now covered by some form of private health insurance.

The Government has:

● scrapped the last Labour government's restrictions on the use of NHS beds for private practice.

● relaxed controls on private hospital development and allowed the use of its Business Start-Up Scheme to help fund new hospitals in Harrow and Dorset.

● changed consultants' contracts to allow them more time for private work.

● given tax relief on employers' contributions to private health insurance.

● even encouraged health authorities to make use of private institutions for the care of NHS patients. A deal is being worked out for the Fylde Coast Private Hospital — £107 a day to lease 12 beds to the NHS.

But rapidly rising costs created a crisis for the medical insurance companies in 1982, forcing up subscriptions by 30 per cent. Government helped out by negotiating, on a voluntary basis, group discounts for medical insurance for over 650 000 civil servants. British Rail followed suit for its workforce. In both cases, the unions concerned vigorously opposed the proposals.

Private practice is fundamentally opposed to the principles of the NHS. The Health Service should be funded from general taxation and treatment should be free and available on the basis of medical need alone.

BLOOD MONEY: UNIONS WIN CHANGES

THE HEAD of the Blood Transfusion Service in Scotland warned that the demand for blood from private hospitals might threaten heart surgery for NHS patients. Scottish health unions delayed the opening in Glasgow of a new £10m private hospital by blocking supplies of blood from the service.

The Government was forced to act and announce that private hospitals would, in future, be charged for the administrative costs of the delivery, storage and processing of blood — approximately £20 per pint.

Private practice is a parasite on the NHS.

It depends on NHS-trained staff and facilities and techniques developed by public money. Its only interest is in the 'insurable' — the younger and fitter.

It can make no money out of the elderly, the handicapped and the mentally ill. They are left to the NHS to look after — 50 per cent of all Health Service beds are used by elderly patients.

Private practice undermines the NHS because, as more people provide for health care through private insurance, there will be increasing reluctance to fund the NHS properly from taxation.

[from *T & G Record* (journal of the TGWU), February 1984]

The Government is encouraging closer co-operation between the public and private health sectors. The development of private medicine eases the strain on the NHS and leaves more resources available for spending on groups like the elderly and handicapped.

[from *Four Years' Work — a summary of the achievements of the Conservative government since May 1979* (Conservative Research Department, 1983)]

Questions

1 What evidence can you find in Patten's letter to suggest that he is satisfied with the Conservative record concerning the National Health Service since 1979?
2 According to J2, Norman Fowler, Secretary of State for Health, made 'cuts' in the NHS during 1983. On what grounds is Patten able to say in J1 that 'It is quite wrong to describe this policy as one of ''cuts'' at all'?
3 How does Patten suggest that funds can be found for future growth in NHS services? (J1)
4 What reasons does Patten give to justify reduction in health service staff? (J1)
5 What evidence is there in J1 and J2 to suggest that the government made a U-turn in an aspect of its health policy in late 1983? Suggest reasons for this. (See also J13.)

Class Discussion

1 Discuss the criticisms which have been made of the NHS since its reorganisation in the early 1970s. Have Conservative policies since 1979 helped to make the NHS more efficient?
2 Comment on the opposing views expressed in J3A and J3B concerning: (a) the value of private medicine to the NHS; (b) the effect of private medicine on the elderly and handicapped.

Extension work

1 Distinguish between current and capital spending in the NHS.
2 Give examples of ancillary services of the NHS which have been privatised.
3 Assess the advantages and disadvantages of private medicine vis-à-vis the National Health Service as the position is likely to be seen by members of the Thatcher government and the Shadow Cabinet respectively.
4 Explain what is meant by the phrase '1.5 per cent real growth is needed'. (J2)

J4

STOP SHOUTING, START TALKING

THE spectacle of British working men taking to the streets in protest at Mr Enoch Powell's sacking for his explosive speech on race has produced a deep sense of shock. Because the term racist has become the most hateful in our vocabulary, many people have deluded themselves that nothing of this sort could happen here. Last week's events compel us to think more deeply. [. . .]

Over a short period, the flow of Indian, Pakistani, African, Cypriot, Maltese and West Indian immigrants produced a highly charged situation in Bradford, the West Midlands and parts of London. But because 'race' had become a taboo subject, there was almost no public discussion of the possibilities of tension that were being created. It was without any conscious act of volition that Britain found itself becoming an increasingly multi-racial society.

The Observer, a paper that has played an active part in campaigning against racist attitudes, did not react to the initial legislation in 1961 and 1962 to restrain the numbers of immigrants in the way that the leadership of the Labour and Liberal parties did. *The Observer supported* the Tory

proposal to limit the flow. Our reason for this, given at the time and since repeated, was that the native population here was unlikely to retain its traditionally tolerant attitudes if suddenly presented with a substantial intake of immigrants. We feared that coloured families could not hope to have welcoming neighbours if permitted to arrive in large numbers.

Why liberals go wrong

Since that time, we have published studies of the bitter distress of young coloured people who grow up here and find themselves snubbed and cold-shouldered. And we have publicised examples of discrimination by individual local authorities against coloured people. But we have paid relatively little attention to how opinion has been developing among the British public.

The citizens of Bradford and Birmingham are neither enlightened philosophers nor political extremists. But what few liberals have dared to face quite frankly is that these people are no more inclined to welcome a crowd of black people (as distinct

from an occasional individual) into their clubs and pubs than liberal intellectuals would be to admit a lot of people holding a blatantly different set of values into whatever they regard as their social group. It may be argued that skin colour and matters of opinion are utterly different. But both generate powerful feelings of identity. In Northern Ireland a man's religion is treated like a racial difference. Anti-semitism itself is based more on cultural prejudices and beliefs than on physical differences. Skin colour is only the most irreducible, inescapable, senseless but probably strongest of our own means of recognising a group identify. And only if we are conscious of our own sense of group identity can we gauge the strength of feeling that infringement of that sense arouses.

What has been happening in this country is that two experiences have collided at a time of great change and uncertainty in British history to produce a host of grievances, both real and imaginary. Housing problems, wage standstills, unemployment, rising living costs, uncertainty about Britain's future place in Europe and in the rest of the world have combined to produce unsettling economic and psychological pressures. At the same time, large numbers of British workers have found themselves living beside large numbers of coloured immigrants. The fact that the coloured immigrants have, on the whole, helped to reduce Britain's problems — notably in hospitals, and in those lower-paid jobs rejected by white workers — is too little recognised; instead the immigrants have come to be regarded by some as the cause of unemployment — even in the docks where there has been hardly any influx of coloured workers at all.

In times of change and confusion, it is usual that people feel their security and sense of identity is threatened: often, as in Germany in the 1930s, they look for a scapegoat to explain their difficulties. The accidental arrival of many coloured people at this time in our history has confused the problems of colour with the unrelated frustrations and grievances widely felt among both the workers and much of the middle class.

A sense of betrayal

The early-warning signs of racial ill-feeling in Notting Hill, Nottingham and Smethwick were largely written off as local aberrations. Parliamentarians, the press, radio, TV and the Churches all tended to minimise the underlying possibilities of racial tensions. The workers found themselves lectured at, rather than argued with. They found the Labour Party adopting policies that they did not expect from their representatives; and much of the middle class seems to have felt the same way about the Tory leadership. Despite Labour's change of policy on the race issue — which dismayed many of its own supporters who thought that the Government

had become altogether too restrictive — many of the rank and file felt that the party was not representing them properly.

It would be a great mistake to write off all these people as racists, or merely to disapprove of them and seek to correct their attitudes by legislation alone: they should be heeded and admitted to have problems that most people would find straining, if in their situation. It would be a mistake because, if we simply ignore their feelings, they will probably develop powerful emotional drives resulting in action which might then become unmanageable.

It would, also, be unfair. For in many ways the British circumstances are even less favourable to multi-racial harmony than are those in South Africa and the US. Even the wildest Afrikaner nationalists must concede that the Africans belong in South Africa: even Governor Wallace must admit that the Negroes were brought to America. But a lot of white Britons feel that the coloured immigrants are interlopers. Whereas Americans of every sort are all Americans, it is much harder for our people to see a turbanned Sikh or African as an Englishman, or even quite convincingly as British, though British citizens they are.

How, therefore, are the white Britons to be persuaded to accept coloured immigrants as part of their community? There is, of course, no simple answer to this question: but in seeking answers we should, at least, remember that British racial policies must essentially win the understanding, if not the entire agreement, of the white citizens of Bradford and Birmingham. If the policies are not accepted, it is the immigrants and their children who will be the victims, as well as the temper of British society.

Much can and must be done by the

gradual process of education and the raising of living standards. But we will be deceiving ourselves if we believe that these slow processes alone are adequate to meet as emotionally charged a problem as this one: there is little evidence from any part of the world to support such a hope.

In addition to pursuing the gradual processes, we must face certain issues that are both more immediate and also more fundamental. The first is the evident popular demand that all immigration should be stopped and that the total number of immigrants should be reduced by encouraging some to return to their previous homes.

In considering this demand, there are several principles to bear in mind. One is that every community has, indeed, the right to control its own immigration policy: therefore the demand for a complete stop is not, in itself, disreputable. Another is that promises must be kept and people must not be rendered stateless: therefore, the Kenyan Asians, who possess no other nationality than that of this country, cannot be refused admission, even if their arrival should be spread over a period. A third — and the most important of all — is that nobody should ever be made to leave this country by harassing him: to do that would be a disgrace and we must try to persuade our fellow-citizens to see harassment as an utter disgrace. A fourth is that genuine dependants should be allowed to join their families — because of past pledges on this score, because we as a nation cannot decently stand for the break-up of families, and because it is socially healthier for all concerned that the newcomers should be established as family groups. But, beyond these exceptions, there is a clear case for a standstill in other types of immigration, until we have managed to sort out the aftermath of our past decade of ill-considered policies.

It would also be perfectly proper for the Government to offer travel subsidies to those immigrants who want to get out — if only to convince the resident Britons that this is not an answer to the problem, since it is probable that only relatively few immigrants would be tempted to return to their former homes (the South Africans have quite failed to induce their Indian population to accept subsidised tickets to India).

The real question is how best to accommodate those who wish to stay.

We should start by recognising some realities. First, waves of immigrants have always initially produced 'ghettos' with all their attendant by-products — overcrowding, shabbiness, frustration, and some degree of antagonism with the older-established communities in their neighbourhood. Second, full integration is usually a slow business. In the case of the American Negro, it has not yet been achieved. It is common sense to acknowledge this and to plan for a long period of transition.

Integrating the newer communities into our social and political system (as distinct from trying to *force* them all into assimilation, which is not desirable) must be our objective. But it would be wise to expect that there is going to be a considerable period during which the host community and the strangers in their midst will be awkwardly engaged in accommodating themselves to each other.

If these are the realities, what is the right policy to adopt? Segregation is plainly unacceptable, but there can be little wrong in the possibility that some of the immigrant communities may wish to build their own lives in their own communities, at least in the early stages while they grow new roots. This is what happened with all the ethnic groups arriving in the US.

It might well be right that those who prefer to send their children to schools where the teaching and the atmosphere offer better chances to prepare them for integrated education should be helped to do so — provided this is not made an excuse for permanently segregated classrooms. If there is a real desire for these

communities to establish their own amenities (as the Southall Indians have done by acquiring their own cinema) they should be helped to do so. Football teams and even regiments have proved useful in maintaining Celtic dignity — provided people are not confined to them or denied admission to the big league. To compel people to integrate at every point in their social life is just as wrong as to try to prevent them from preserving what they choose to retain of their own cultural traditions.

If the newcomers choose to build up their own separate institutions they are entitled to be helped by financial and other means to ensure that their social conditions will be the same as those of the rest of the community.

Remedy for grievances

The other side of the coin, however, is that those newcomers (perhaps the majority) who do not wish to separate themselves from the host community should have the right (backed by law) to enter the wider community.

[from *The Observer* (editorial), 28 April 1968]

To be selective, to say that red totalitarians are better than black, or that it matters by whose politics a child is murdered is a betrayal of conscience, which makes conscience itself merely an instrument of propaganda. (Editorial, *The Times,* 30 May 1970)

The bomb goes off

On an April weekend, 13 years ago, Mr Enoch Powell, a member of Edward Heath's Shadow Cabinet, said in Birmingham: 'As I look ahead, I am filled with foreboding. Like the Roman, I seem to see the River Tiber foaming with much blood.' He was discussing the consequences of coloured settlement in this country and the creation of ghettoes in our main cities. For expressing this fear — in language which could have been more carefully chosen — Mr Heath dismissed him from the Shadow Cabinet, casting him out of the inner councils of the Conservative Party. In the eyes of the country's political establishment, he had become a leper. Last month, in Ashton-under-Lyme, Mr Powell, still an English Tory, but officially Ulster Unionist MP for South Down, said he saw no reason to depart from his view that, at some point in the growth of the New Commonwealth and Pakistan ethnic population in London and in other cities, 'there lies the certainty of violence on a scale which can only be described as civil war'. Of the ominous features in the present scene, he says that 'the most striking, which forms a link with the classic pattern of urban violence throughout the world in modern times, is the increase of deliberate attacks, both moral and physical, upon the police. It is part of the mechanism of escalating violence that the reaction of playing down, condoning or ignoring these attacks causes a loss of confidence on the part of the public at large and encourages repetition on an ever increasing scale. Recent events in Birmingham and London are uncannily typical.' This was said a fortnight before last weekend's Brixton riots, which are clearly the worst we have seen yet. Mr Powell argued that, due to their birth rate and other factors, and quite apart from further immigration, the New Commonwealth and Pakistan component of our cities 'is destined to double and to treble as the years go by. "We haven't seen nothing yet" is a phrase we could with advantage repeat to ourselves whenever we try and form a picture of that future.'

[from the *Spectator* (editorial), 18 April 1981]

'The next riots will take place in Birmingham and Manchester's Moss Side', said Mr Jeff Crawford, Harringey's Community Relations Officer, on Sunday, in a lull between the second and third nights of Brixton's rioting. 'Repressive police behaviour will make young blacks riot', he added, in a commentary as appropriate to Powell's prophecy as to Brixton's evidence. 'The war is now on. There's going to be no regret and no apology from us. We have been disrespected, humiliated and insulted by the police too long.'

It may be noted, but in most quarters it is more likely to be ignored or condoned, that Mr Crawford's language is more offensive, more specific, more bellicose and more inflammatory than anything Mr Powell has ever uttered, and almost exults in the future which fills Mr Powell with foreboding. Yet Mr Crawford's words attract little if any abuse or considered criticism; they are, apparently, unobjectionable or at any rate understandable. 'The war is now on. There's going to be no regret and no apology from us', is the message the country is given by a Community Relations Officer — as much a public servant as any policeman — after nights in which 150 policemen were injured, schools and houses burned to the ground, dozens of cars overturned and set on fire, shops and pubs looted and destroyed, and organised gangs armed with Molotov cocktails roamed almost at will searching for police to attack.

There were white youths as well as black among the rioters, looters, arsonists and common-or-garden thugs. It has been said that the riots were not racial but were directed against the police. It has been argued that the causes lie in deprivation, in lack of employment opportunities, in hostility from the police. No doubt there is some truth in this, but we should not be fooled or falsely comforted by such explanations. This was racial rioting, and there is almost certainly more to come.

Questions

1 'As I look ahead, I am filled with foreboding. Like the Roman, I seem to see the River Tiber foaming with much blood.' Why did Powell use this expression in April 1968? What were the immediate results of his speech? (J4, J5)

2 For what reason did *The Observer* support legislation passed in 1961 and 1962 to restrict immigration into Britain? (J4)

3 Explain how *The Observer* links problems in race relations with economic and social hardships. (J4)

4 Explain *The Observer*'s view on the following policies regarding race relations: (a) voluntary repatriation of immigrants; (b) forced assimilation; (c) separate development; (d) voluntary integration.

5 Why did rioting take place in Brixton and other cities in 1981, according to the *Spectator*? (J5)

Class Discussion

1 Discuss the possible causes of ethnic minority deprivation. Assess the contribution of affirmative action programmes and other policies in improving race relations.

2 Comment on the interpretation of the problems and events described by *The Observer* and the *Spectator* in the light of their known political leanings.

Extension Work

1 List the recommendations of the Scarman report after the Brixton riots, and assess the extent to which they were implemented.

2 Give details of the various Race Relations Acts. Why do racial disadvantage and racial discrimination continue?

3 Investigate policies followed by successive governments since 1970 to improve race relations, urban conditions, and employment opportunities, and to help the poor get properly housed. Why are these problems closely related?

4 Why did Crawford feel justified in saying 'Repressive police behaviour will make young blacks riot'? (J5)

J6–J10   *Housing and education*

RESPONSIBILITY AND THE FAMILY

Freedom and responsibility go together. The Conservative Party believes in encouraging people to take responsibility for their own decisions. We shall continue to return more choice to individuals and their families. That is the way to increase personal freedom. It is also the way to improve standards in the State services.

Conservatives believe equally strongly in the

duty of Government to help those who are least able to help themselves. We have more than carried out our pledges to protect pensioners against price rises and to maintain standards in the National Health Service. This rebuts the totally unfounded charge that we want to 'dismantle the Welfare State'. We are determined that our public services should provide the best possible value both for people they seek to help and for the taxpayer who pays the bill.

A free and independent society is one in which the ownership of property is spread as widely as possible. A business which is partly or wholly owned by its workers will have more pride in performance. Already firms like the National Freight Company, where managers and workers joined together to take over the business, are thriving.

Under this Government, the property-owning democracy is growing fast. And the basic foundation of it is the family home.

Housing: towards a home-owning democracy

We have given every council and New Town tenant the legal right to buy his or her own home. Many Housing Association tenants have been granted the same right, too. This is the biggest single step towards a home-owning democracy ever taken. It is also the largest transfer of property from the State to the individual. No less than half a million council houses and flats were sold in the last Parliament to the people who live in them. By our encouragement of private housebuilding and our new range of schemes to help first-time buyers, there are a million more owner-occupiers today than four years ago.

The Labour Party has met these proposals with vicious and prolonged resistance and is still fighting a rearguard action against wider home ownership. A Labour government would take

[from the Conservative Party Manifesto, 1983]

away the tenant's right to buy his council house, would prevent councils selling even voluntarily at a discount, and would force any former tenant who wanted to sell his house to sell it back to the council.

In the next Parliament, we will give many thousand more families the chance to buy their homes. For public sector tenants, the present 'Right to Buy' scheme will be improved and extended to include the right to buy houses on leasehold land and the right to buy on a shared ownership basis. The maximum discount will be increased by one per cent a year for those who have been tenants for between twenty and thirty years, taking the maximum discount to 60 per cent. We shall also help first-time buyers who are not council tenants through our various low-cost home-ownership schemes: 'homesteading', building for sale, improvement for sale, and shared ownership.

Britain needs more homes to rent, too, in the private sector as well as the public sector. For years, the blind prejudice of the Labour Party has cast a political blight on privately rented housing. But our assured tenancy scheme has encouraged builders to start building new homes to rent again, and our shorthold scheme is helping the private sector to meet the needs of those who want short-term rented accommodation.

We shall extend our Tenants' Charter to enable council tenants to get necessary repairs done themselves and be reimbursed by their councils. Housing Improvement Grants have been increased substantially in the last two years and will continue to play an important role.

We shall conduct early public consultation on proposals which would enable the building societies to play a fuller part in supporting the provision of new housing and would bring up to date the laws which govern them.

Our goal is to make Britain the best housed nation in Europe.

No home . . . what hope?

by John Pilger

IF ONE *image represents the reign of Margaret Thatcher as 1984 draws to a close, it is not from any of her spectacular meetings around the world; it is a homeless British child, confined in a vermin-ridden unsafe room in a bed-and-breakfast 'hotel'.*

For 1984 has been the year the Thatcher Government made history of a kind by virtually abandoning a national housing programme for Britain.

From next year local authorities will not be allowed to spend on new buildings money they receive from the sale of council houses. This will effectively cut the housing programme by a billion pounds. It will also add another 150 000 building workers to the half million made redundant since 1979, the year Mrs Thatcher came to office.

Indeed, since 1979 fewer houses have been built in Britain *than in any similar period* since World War Two, a remarkable fact when you consider that for many ordinary British people one of the reasons for fighting World War Two was to create a society which built homes for its people in need.

The economics of the present 'housing policy' are these:

In 1984 the Government spent an estimated £120 million in bankrolling those who run often squalid and unsafe bed-and-breakfast 'hotels' and 'hostels' where local authorities — denied the right to build homes — are forced to place their mounting homeless.

BUT now even this form of accommodation is, in today's jargon, being 'clawed back'.

The weekly limit on what the Department of Social Security will allow on accommodation for a homeless person is to be cut by as much as half.

The effect of this will be that many hotels and hostels will either close down or refuse to take the homeless, who will be forced to pay the extra out of their meagre meals and living allowance — for a single person that's only £21.40 a week.

The alternative will be to doss down in the cheapest and worst places, many not much better than workhouses, or on the streets.

Already, in London, there are at least 50 000 people living rough. Under the new 'clawback' of supplementary benefits, most people aged sixteen and seventeen will receive nothing with which to get a bed for the night.

These facts are translated into melancholy reality with a visit to the arches at London's Charing Cross, or to the car park beneath magnificent Queen Elizabeth Hall on the South Bank.

These are the centres of perhaps the fastest growing community in Britain: 'Cardboard City' and 'Box City'.

People, young, middle-aged and old live here like the not-yet-dead in flimsy coffins, the covers closed or a head peering out through a flap. Not surprisingly, they tell you to sod off.

A twenty-six-year-old I know, called Mick, had taken to living in Cardboard City because he reckoned it was cleaner than the vermin-infested cubicles of the few night shelters available in the West End of London.

'You've got a choice', he said. 'In one of those places you wake scratching. Out in the open you seize up with the cold; but at least there you feel free.'

Mick at present has graduated to a private place in West London calling itself a 'lodge'.

He shares with two old men a room 19 feet by 15 feet. There are no locks on any of the doors, and no keys. Until recently the linen was seldom changed.

There is no furniture in the room, unless you count a mostly blocked-up sink. He sleeps on a camp bed. There is a shower, which doesn't work.

There are no meals, no cooking facilities, not even a token breakfast. By the standards of some 'hotels' this is not the worst.

Earlier this year, in a similar place, another unemployed lad told me: 'You know, to lie down here you sort of surrender something of yourself.'

Mick spends his days in libraries, unemployment day centres and 'popping into the job centre for a laugh'. He is now struggling not to drink cheap booze.

At Christmas he had a couple of pints and a £2.50 cafe fry-up.

He is the sort of person some newspapers like to call a 'scrounger'; after he has paid the 'lodge' and the cafe and the launderette, his giro is finished with the week not half over.

What it costs the Government just

to keep Mick alive would secure a £20 000 mortgage.

Or, put another way, what it costs the Government to keep Mick in squalor is more than double the total average cost of housing an unemployed person in a one-bedroomed flat — a mere £17 a week.

Those like Mick are unseen in a society where most of us are not doing too badly, or are doing well, and the prevailing ideology is simply not to

care.

Kathy and her baby are also unseen in the streets around London's Bayswater except by curb crawlers who solicit her when, baby in arms, she walks from the squalor of her 'hotel' to buy half a pizza for her main meal.

Three and four children confined in a room 15 feet by 12 feet is not uncommon.

MICK and Kathy and all the others

like them have been described by an aide to the Prime Minister as 'single mobile people'.

That sounds much better than 'down and outs' just as 'social security' sounds much better than dole. And 'youth training scheme' sounds much better than cheap labour. And 'hotel' and 'hostel' sound much better than workhouse.

No words have yet been coined that sound much better than a home.

[from the *Daily Mirror*, 27 December 1984]

J8A

The people who can solve the class riddle

Inequality is the price we pay for living in a free society. The dilemma we face, in education as in other things, is that we do not find it easy to judge when the price is too high.

Are the various freedoms associated with private education — the freedom to operate a school independent of the state, the freedom to spend your earnings as you wish within the law, in the case of a few schools religious freedom — worth the cost in terms of a divided society and unequal access to opportunity?

The Labour party proposes to respond to the dilemma by making it illegal to charge fees for education; the dilemma will be removed rather than resolved. Twenty years ago such a policy (which is in effect abolition) would not have commanded widespread support in the party. Now it

does.

The failure of the Public Schools Commission in the late 60s, and more recently the misguided support which independent schools have given to the Conservatives' assisted places scheme, have persuaded even Labour moderates that private education should be outlawed. They argue that in this case the price of freedom is too high and that society should have the courage not to go on paying it.

The Conservative Party takes the opposite view. The freedoms involved are well worth the cost in inequality, not least because they encourage the independence, thrift, competition and excellence that society needs. Some Tories, imbued with the Disraelian vision of an unfragmented society, are uneasy about the divisive effect of private education

but their voices are seldom heard. For most Tories, private schools are no more of a problem than home ownership and private industry. [. . .]

But if we break the mould of our present view of how secondary education should be organised it is possible to conceive of a system that embraces both local and national schools, the former administered by local education authorities and serving the needs of the mainstream of secondary education, the latter administered by central government and serving needs that cannot be met locally.

So the national schools might, for example, be specialist mathematical or language schools, or high-powered sixth form colleges either serving a wide urban catchment area or offering residential sixth form education.

In some areas there is an urgent need to provide access to minority subjects; at one time that would have meant classics but now it also means physics, further mathematics and some modern languages.

Once we start to think in these terms the riddle of what to do about the public schools looks much less formidable. As soon as some of the schools were convinced that they could play a part in a national (not a local) education system, while retaining the degree of independence enjoyed by national universities, we should be well on the way to resolving the public school dilemma.

The SDP is in an ideal position to explore this way forward. Uncluttered by previous commitments it can take a fresh view of how secondary education might develop. It is not inhibited by political dogma or vested class interest. Above all it is the only party that can inspire the trust of the independent sector while at the same time convincing that sector that the public school dilemma has got to be resolved.

John Rae
The author is Head Master of Westminster School.

[from *The Times*, 2 June 1981]

J8B

Private schools are a major obstacle to a free and fair education system, able to serve the needs of the whole community. We will abolish the Assisted Places Scheme and local authority place buying; and we will phase out, as quickly as possible, boarding allowances paid to government personnel for their children to attend private schools, whilst ensuring secure accommodation for children needing residential education.

We shall also withdraw charitable status from private schools, and all their other public subsidies and tax privileges. We will also charge VAT on the fees paid to such schools; phase out fee charging; and integrate private schools within the local authority sector where necessary. Special schools for handicapped pupils will retain all current support and tax advantages.

[from *The new hope for Britain* (Labour Party Manifesto), 1983]

J9

Deep shame of our class bias
by Richard Hoggart

In spite of all the intended reforms of recent decades, 'no significant reduction in class inequalities has in fact been achieved'. We are not becoming much more open, socially or educationally.

Even the meritocracy, about whose human thinness and unforgivingness T. S. Eliot and Michael Young warned us, is not emerging. The new 'service class,' which does to some extent recruit from the working class — some bright fish jump the rapids — looks after its own in much the old manner. The social-educational links remain massively firm.

Put it another way. The 'to-him-that-hath' law still runs strong in this country. Create a new social benefit because it is badly needed, especially by the working classes, and the 'service class' will take best advantage of it. Such reforms usually mean 'increased subsidies to the affluent'. They will fill the Arts Council subsidised theatres; they will take better advantage of the National Health Service because they know how to make their wants articulate and will not be easily bullied or ignored; they will get most from the billions of extra money poured into education, and especially into higher education, in the last 20 years.

[from *The Observer*, 13 January 1980]

UNITED KINGDOM — Education Bill — Provisions and Enactment

The Education Bill, which was introduced in the House of Commons on 17 December 1975, and enacted on 22 December 1976, required local education authorities (LEAs) in England and Wales to submit proposals for reorganising secondary education on comprehensive lines.

A similar bill, introduced by a previous Labour Government in February 1970, was overtaken by the dissolution of Parliament in the following May, and in June 1970 the incoming Conservative Government issued a circular (Circular 10/70) to LEAs giving them freedom to determine the shape of secondary education in their areas. This circular superseded an earlier one (Circular 10/65), issued by the Labour Government in July 1965, which had requested LEAs to submit, within one year, plans for reorganising secondary education on comprehensive lines; however, Circular 10/70 was in turn superseded by Circular 4/74, introduced in April 1974 by Mr Reginald Prentice (then Secretary of State for Education and Science), which outlined measures to implement the Labour Party's election promise to end selection for secondary education and to introduce a fully comprehensive system.

The main provisions of the 1975 bill, which had been foreshadowed in the Queen's Speech of November 1975, were as follows:

1 LEAs were required to have regard to the general principle that secondary education was to be provided only in comprehensive schools, with the exception of schools for the physically and mentally handicapped and for music or dancing.

2 LEAs which had not yet completed secondary school reorganisation along comprehensive lines might be required by the Secretary of State for Education and Science to submit proposals, and the latter might also require governors and managers of voluntary grammar schools to submit proposals for any changes to their schools which appeared to him to be necessary to complete LEA reorganisation plans. However, such pro-

posals would not be approved if the managers or governors satisfied the Secretary of State that they could not meet their share of the cost of implementing them. [Voluntary schools are those which although founded by voluntary bodies — e.g. churches — have all or most of their costs met by the relevant LEA.]

3 LEAs would require the Secretary of State's permission before taking up places at independent schools.

4 The Secretary of State would be empowered to make regulations enabling LEAs to charge less than the economic cost for school milk.

At the time of the bill's enactment 46 of the 105 LEAs in England and Wales were fully comprehensive, although 19 of them still had some voluntary schools in their areas which operated selection. The seven authorities referred to by Mr Mulley in the second reading debate as refusing to go fully comprehensive were Buckinghamshire, Essex, Trafford (Greater Manchester), and the London boroughs of Bexley, Kingston upon Thames, Redbridge and Sutton. Kingston was the only LEA without any comprehensive schools.

While the Education Bill was before Parliament, action was taken in the courts over the decision of the Tameside metropolitan district council (Greater Manchester) not to implement a scheme for the introduction of comprehensive secondary education in their area on 1 September 1976; the eventual outcome was that the House of Lords effectively upheld the council's action.

The comprehensive scheme had been submitted to the Secretary of State for Education and Science in March 1975 by the then Labour-controlled council and approved by him on 11 November 1975, but control of the council had passed to the Conservatives in the local elections held on 6 May 1976, in which the question of the introduction of comprehensive education had been a major issue in Tameside.

Mr Mulley on 11 June directed the council to give effect to the proposals approved on 11 November

1975, and to 'implement the arrangements previously made for the allocation of pupils to secondary schools for the coming school year on a non-selective basis', and a week later, on 18 June, he was granted leave by the High Court to seek an order compelling the council to comply. The High Court on 12 July ruled that Mr Mulley had been justified in issuing his directive and granted the order which he sought, but the Court of Appeal on 26 July allowed an appeal by Tameside council against this order, on the grounds that the council had not acted 'unreasonably', and the House of Lords on 2 August dismissed an appeal by Mr Mulley against the 26 July ruling.

Delivering judgement on 21 October, explaining the Law Lords' decision, Lord Wilberforce concluded that

Mr Mulley had 'fundamentally misconceived and mis-directed himself' in respect of the Tameside case, and that however much he might have disagreed with the new council's proposed action there were no grounds on which he could properly have found that the council were acting or were proposing to act unreasonably.

Following enactment of the Education Act, Mrs Shirley Williams, who had succeeded Mr Mulley as Secretary of State for Education and Science in September, wrote on 24 November to the seven LEAs listed above and also to Tameside, requiring them to submit to her within six months proposals for the abolition of selection in their areas — (*Times* — *Daily Telegraph* — *Guardian* — Hansard).

[from *Keesing's Contemporary Archives* for 4 February 1977]

Questions

1   State how the Conservative Manifesto justifies giving every council tenant the legal right to buy his or her own home. (J6)

2   Explain how the government's housing policy, according to J7, has made it difficult for local authorities to house the homeless properly.

3   What types of freedom (normally advocated by right wing supporters) does Rae mention regarding private education? (J8A)

4   Why do most of the Labour Party now support abolition of the public schools? What methods have they proposed to use to achieve this? (J8A, J8B, J9)

5   Suggest reasons why the service (or middle) classes have benefitted more than the less well-off from the Welfare State. (J9)

6   Explain how secondary education became a political football between the two main parties in the 1960s and 1970s. (J10)

7   Which political party probably controlled the LEAs that refused to go fully comprehensive? (J10)

Class Discussion

1   Discuss the pros and cons of allowing council house tenants the right to buy their homes.

2   Comment on the plight of the present houseless poor as revealed by Pilger. (J7)

3   How do the details revealed in J7 reflect on the Conservative 1983 manifesto proposals 'to make Britain the best housed nation in Europe'? (J6)

4   Explain what is meant by: (a) 'social-educational links'; (b) ' "to-him-that-hath" law'; (c) 'merito-cracy'; (d) 'service class'. (J9)

5   Comment on Rae's proposal for the reorganisation of secondary education. (J9)

6   Discuss the significance or importance of the Tameside Case. (J10)

Extension Work

1   Describe how Conservative policies have helped the private rented sector of housing since 1979.

2   What is the Assisted Places Scheme? When and why was it introduced? What is the role of local education authorities?

3   How have the Conservatives encouraged private education since 1979?

4   Name the Act on which the Law Lords based their judgement that Mulley had 'fundamentally misconceived and misdirected himself'. (J10)

J11–J13   *Popular opinion on key issues*

J11

DEFENCE AND THE 1983 BRITISH ELECTION

Bruce George, MP, and Curt Pawlisch

For perhaps the first time in British political history, defence, and in particular Britain's policy on nuclear weapons, was a major issue in the June general election campaign.

However, the results of the election have given rise to varying interpretations of the importance attached to defence issues by the British electorate. Bruce George, Labour MP for Walsall South, and Curt Pawlisch, a post-graduate student at the University of Wisconsin, here provide an overview of the role of defence and disarmament issues in the campaign and an assessment of their part in Labour's downfall.

Political observers have long insisted that defence issues are of little concern to the British electorate. A closer review of history would call this simplistic view into question, although in recent years defence has not figured prominently in campaigns, nor has it appeared to have had much effect on their outcomes.

Clearly, however, defence emerged as one of the most important issues in the 1983 British election. Labour's defence policies, especially its endorsement of unilateral nuclear disarmament, proved to be a major reason for Labour's worst defeat in 50 years. Its share of the popular vote sank to 28 per cent, only two per cent higher than the total received by the SDP/Liberal Alliance and well below the Conservatives' 44 per cent. Britain's first-past-the-post electoral system did cushion the blow to Labour in terms of Parliamentary seats. The results are shown below:

9 May 1983		10 June 1983	
Con.	332	Con.	397
Lab.	238	Lab.	209
SDP	29	SDP	6
Lib.	13	Lib.	17
Other	23	Other	21
Total:	635	Total:	650

(Note: the 1983 election was the first to be fought under the new boundary changes which had added 15 seats to the House of Commons.)

The limited poll data and analyses which have appeared after the election confirm the unpopularity of Labour's defence policies. According to Ivor Crewe, for instance, defence was second only to unemployment as an issue which influenced electoral choice. Because, Crewe says, Labour could not capitalise on the issue of unemployment, defence loomed even larger in its impact.

MORI poll data confirm that the election increased the number of people who said that they would take defence and disarmament into account when deciding

how to cast their vote. (Note: MORI, in their poll work, divided the question of defence into two questions, one for defence generally and one for disarmament.) Those mentioning defence increased from 15 per cent to 29 per cent from April 21–25 to June 1–2. Those mentioning disarmament increased from 16 per cent to 25 per cent. Not only were more people paying increased attention to the defence debate by the end of the campaign, but the Conservatives were increasing their approval rating to 48 per cent for their policies on nuclear arms.

On the question of nuclear disarmament, voters overwhelmingly rejected the unilateralist approach. A Harris poll conducted for *The Observer* during the campaign found that 74 per cent of those surveyed agreed with the statement that Britain should keep its own nuclear weapons (20 per cent disagreed, six per cent did not know).

Non-defence factors

Defence was, of course, not the sole reason why Labour lost the campaign. As the chart prepared by Ivor Crewe indicates, other issues also had an effect upon electoral choice. Numerous other factors should also be considered. Certainly the gradual erosion of the class-party nexus since 1974 among skilled workers has hurt Labour. The organisation of the 1983 campaign is now under close scrutiny — allegations have been made that Labour's Central Office was tied in knots of disorganisation. Party disunity was another factor. Since 1979 Labour had been at war with itself on policies and internal organisation, a war which resulted in numerous reforms such as the mandatory reselection of sitting MPs, and a byzantine electoral college system for the election of its Leader and Deputy Leader. The divisive race for the Deputy Leadership position between Denis Healey and Tony Benn, the Militant Tendency controversy, the Gang of Four's decision to launch the SDP, were all factors which certainly must have raised suspicions in the minds of the electorate that Labour was too disunited to govern. Nevertheless, given the fact that the Conservatives' defence policies were preferred by 54 per cent of those citing defence as an issue influencing their vote, there can be little doubt about the significance of the defence issue to the final outcome.

The issues that mattered

Percentage mentioning an issue as one of the two most important influencing their vote*

	All %	Change 1979–83	Con. loyalists %	Con. defectors %	Lab. loyalists %	Lab. defectors %	Party preference on issue (among those citing it as important)	
							in 1983	in 1979
Unemployment	72	(+45)	54	73	84	75	Lab. +16	Lab. +20
Defence	38	(+36)	46	41	33	42	Con. +54	not asked
Prices	20	(−22)	27	15	15	13	Con. +40	Lab. +13
NHS/Hospitals	11	(+7)	4	12	20	16	Lab. +46	not asked
Pensions	8	(+1)	4	7	14	10	not asked	Lab. +27
Education	6	(−2)	6	11	4	9	not asked	not asked
EEC	5	(+1)	7	4	2	9	Con. +50	Lab. + 8

* This was an open-ended question. No prompt card was given to respondents. The issues above were those most frequently mentioned.

Which party has the best policies?

On nuclear arms	April 21–25	June 1–2	Net change
Con.	43	48	+5
Lab.	24	21	−3
Alliance	9	15	+6
No opinion	25	16	−9

On defence generally	April 21–25	June 1–2	Net change
Con.	49	53	+4
Lab.	22	19	−3
Alliance	8	14	+6
No opinion	22	14	−8

Source: Market and Opinion Research International.

[from the *Armament and Disarmament Information Unit Report*, July/August 1983]

THE PRIORITY ISSUES

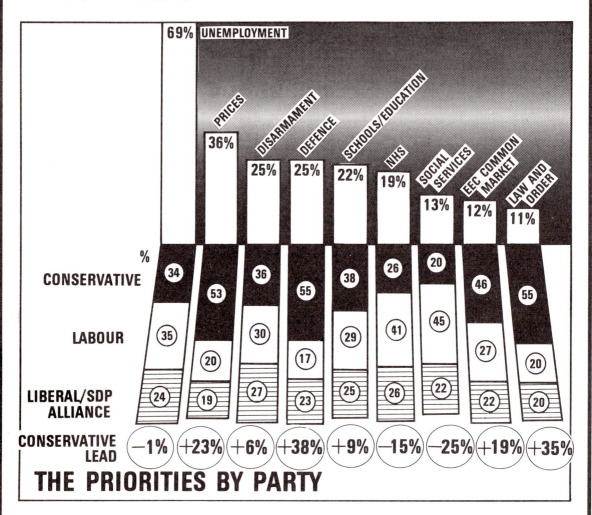

69% UNEMPLOYMENT

PRICES 36%

DISARMAMENT 25%

DEFENCE 25%

SCHOOLS/EDUCATION 22%

NHS 19%

SOCIAL SERVICES 13%

EEC COMMON MARKET 12%

LAW AND ORDER 11%

%

CONSERVATIVE — 34 · 36 · 38 · 26 · 20 · 46 · 55

LABOUR — 35 · 53 · 30 · 55 · 29 · 41 · 45 · 27 · 20

LIBERAL/SDP ALLIANCE — 24 · 20 · 19 · 27 · 17 · 23 · 25 · 26 · 22 · 22 · 20

CONSERVATIVE LEAD — −1% · +23% · +6% · +38% · +9% · −15% · −25% · +19% · +35%

THE PRIORITIES BY PARTY

● The panel was asked which issues they would take into account when deciding how to vote. The top chart shows the nine issues most frequently mentioned, with unemployment still far ahead. The lower chart divides each of the panel-groups who nominated each issue into their party affiliations. Thus, 34 per cent of those naming unemployment were Conservative supporters, 35 per cent Labour, 24 per cent Alliance. The Tories' strongest issues are defence and 'law and order'. Those concerned with the social services and the NHS were markedly more likely to support Labour. But the most striking conclusion is that of the five issues that people in general care most about — unemployment, prices, disarmament, defence and education — the Tories dominate in four. Labour finds most support among those concerned with minority issues.

[from the *Sunday Times*, 29 May 1983]

Gallup Poll

Nine out of ten say put more money into the NHS

THE overwhelming majority (90 per cent) of the public think it is important to put more money into the Health Service and only five per cent take the opposite view.

Given the choice between tax cuts and expanding public services, they opt for the latter by a margin of three to one.

This emerges from further questions in the latest Gallup Poll conducted exclusively for *The Daily Telegraph.*

People were asked how important they felt it was that the Government should or should not act on each issue.

The following table shows scores for each issue by party, where the score is the percentage favouring the policy less the percentage disapproving. Comparisons are shown for February 1981 for nine of the issues.

	Total	Cons.	Lab.	Lib./ SDP	Feb. 1981
Putting more money in the Health Service	85	69	97	93	78
Giving council tenants the right to buy their own homes	72	83	65	63	67
Spending more money to tackle pollution of the air and rivers	72	71	72	77	74
Increase measures to promote equal opportunities for women	68	63	72	75	na
Government should set firm guide-lines for wage and price rises	66	72	60	68	na
Increase public spending to reduce unemployment	63	41	80	79	na
Bringing back the death penalty	39	48	37	29	47
Redistributing income and wealth in favour of poorer people* (*read 'ordinary' people in 1981)	39	10	64	52	37

Take measures to reduce the amount of sex and nudity on TV and in films and magazines	37	42	30	40	na
Introduce stricter laws to regulate trade unions	33	70	−4	31	na
Shifting power from London to the regions and local authorities	29	16	37	39	34
Cut down public spending to reduce inflation	26	47	15	−4	na
Re-establishing grammar schools as an alternative to comprehensive schools	26	54	1	11	na
Withdrawing British troops from Northern Ireland immediately	14	−11	40	14	26
Make abortion widely available on the National Health Service	11	8	19	4	na
Giving more aid to poorer countries in Africa and Asia	1	−4	−7	17	−7
Spend as much money as is necessary to maintain a strong defence in the Falkland Islands	−4	33	−6	−23	na
Take Britain out of the Common Market	−15	−48	20	−16	na
Sending coloured immigrants back to their own country	−16	−14	−13	−33	6
Giving up Britain's nuclear weapons, whatever other countries decide	−45	−75	−19	−36	na

[from *The Daily Telegraph*, 28 October 1983]

Questions

1   Suggest reasons for the importance of disarmament and defence issues in the 1983 election. (J11)
2   What reasons do George and Pawlisch give for the defeat of the Labour Party in the 1983 elections? (J11)
3   Find the phrase in this article which refers to the phenomenon of 'partisan dealignment'. Give specific reasons why this has taken place. (J11)
4   Mention one issue listed in J12 which gains more support among Labour voters and which would help decrease unemployment.

5 On which of the issues listed in J13 do the supporters of the main parties appear to differ most about what the Government should do?

6 On which of the issues in J13 do Labour supporters favour the private sector?

7 Mention one important political issue noticeably absent from the list chosen by the Gallup Poll which is a matter of acute difference of opinion between the two main political parties. (J13)

8 On which issue in J13 does it appear likely that a moderately left-wing position is being taken by less well-off or aged Conservative supporters?

Class Discussion

1 Why do Conservatives rate price stability (or the fight against inflation) as a higher priority than unemployment, while Labour supporters focus most on the unemployment problem?

2 Which two of the issues listed in J13 are specifically associated with the economic ideas of John Maynard Keynes (deficit-financing) and Milton Friedman ('monetarism') respectively?

3 Which proposals in J13 relate to race relations and law and order?

4 On which issues in J13 does public opinion suggest that some sort of 'incomes policy' should be implemented?

5 Suggest reasons why Conservatives appear more favourably inclined towards keeping troops in Northern Ireland than Labour supporters.

6 Comment on the major issues likely to influence voting according to the *Sunday Times* MORI poll. Are there other important issues missing from this list? (J12)

7 Compare and contrast the results and format of the MORI poll data as described in J11 and J12 respectively. Suggest reasons why differences and divergences appear.

8 Suggest reasons why housing was not an electoral issue in 1983. Refer to J6 and J7.

Extension Work

1 Which of the points in J11 are connected with the Labour Party's 'alternative economic strategy', put forward in its 1983 manifesto?

2 What do the writers of J11 mean by 'a byzantine electoral college system'? (See also E2.)

3 Why specifically does the Labour Party, as stipulated in its 1983 manifesto, want to take Britain out of the Common Market?

4 Explain how the issue of the death penalty (capital punishment) for murder cases was more or less resolved or decided for the immediate future in late 1983.

5 Outline the main proposals or suggestions which have been made since 1969 concerning the political future of Northern Ireland.

Section
K

Party beliefs and political attitudes

Introduction

In many respects there is a large measure of agreement across the broad middle belt of British politics from the left wing of the Conservatives, across the Centre ground held by the Alliance, to the right wing of the Labour Party. In the past this common ground has been expressed in such terms as support for consensus politics, for the mixed economy of Keynesian demand management, for 'Butskellism'. In this section the documents represent views from the far Right (K2), the right wing of the Conservative Party (K3, K4), and the left wing of the Labour Party (K5, K6). According to its outlined programme the Communist Party, perhaps the most influential of the far left groups, appears to support similar ideas to those of activists in the Labour Party concerning grassroot participatory democracy in a future Socialist Britain. However, they also stress the goal of moving towards a higher form of society — Communism. [1]

K1 is a survey of certain left wing and right wing attitudes, and on this subject reference can be made to the differing approaches to human rights outlined in A6 and A7. Broadly speaking, right wing views stress the importance of law and order issues, of defence of private property and individual rights (e.g. private education, health and enterprise), while the Left puts more stress on moving towards equality, with collective access to amenities such as education, health and social services, and adequate protection for the less fortunate.

Although the 25 per cent electoral support for the Alliance in 1983 virtually made Britain a multi-party system, Britain still experiences one perhaps inevitable tendency characteristic of a system where two parties predominate. Extreme groups (holding views that are not politically respectable) try to use the tactic of entryism by penetrating the parties which are closest to them in terms of politics but which are regarded as legitimate.

Often, minority extremist parties have influence out of all proportion to their active membership support. According to Peter Shipley, who on behalf of the Conservative Research Department claimed to have uncovered various left wing groups which aimed to subvert the Labour Party, the Communist Party (with a membership of about 20 000) along with some of the smaller groups 'can take the credit for the leftward drift of the Labour party'.[2] The Labour Party, at the end of 1981, investigated the influence of the Revolutionary Socialist League (better known as the Militant Tendency) within the party, which aimed to turn Britain into a Trotskyist state. In October 1983 five leading members of this group were forced to leave the Labour Party. A report prepared by the Young Conservatives in 1983 expressed their view that certain Conservative politicians retained links with extreme right wing groups or had formerly been members of such groups.[3]

Francis Pym criticised the terms left wing and right wing, especially as this implied that the extremes of Marxism and Fascism were as far away as possible from each other 'when both experience and common sense suggest that the two extremes are almost inseparable'. A more apt visual image, he believed, would be a heart, in which both extreme views met at the bottom point, 'moderating gradually as they travel round their respective sides and finally pouring together into one point at the centre.'[4] Within the heart, he suggests that all manner of subtle differences can be concealed. In contrast to the style of confrontational politics which has characterised the conflict between the Thatcher government and certain local authorities (see K6), Pym makes in his book a powerful plea for 'consensus politics'.

The right wing of the Labour Party, weakened by losses to the Social Democratic Party since 1981, believes in social democracy and the 'mixed economy' along lines not unlike the tenets of the left wing of the Conservative Party. The Old Left of Labour, the Tribune Group, which believes in a gradual parliamentary road to socialism, has been personified in recent years by Michael Foot. The New Left, which developed in the early 1970s, believes in extra-parliamentary measures, and various forms of community participation or workers' co-operatives rather than the growth of nationalised industries under State control. K5 and K6 are two examples of this thinking. (See also F7.) On the other side of the political spectrum, Thatcher represents the laissez-faire or Free Market school or wing of the Conservative Party, which for the first time became influential within the party when she became leader in 1975. For different reasons this group is also disenchanted with the 'mixed economy', and this explains the move towards privatisation, as in the case of privatising the telecommunications part of the Post Office under the name of British Telecom in 1984 (referred to in B1 and K6), and the increased support for private enterprise. Pym and other critics of Thatcherism (called 'wets' by Thatcher) belong to the paternalist, one-nation-State, interventionist wing of the Conservative Party, which influenced Conservative policies from 1945 to 1974, and is also known as 'Left Toryism'.

[1] *The British Road to Socialism*, Programme of the Communist Party (March 1978).
[2] 'Tories name 25 extremist groups' by Charles Laurence, *The Daily Telegraph*, 19 July 1981.
[3] *Thatcher's Britain 1984* ed. Tony Manwaring and Jenny Pitkin, (Labour Party, 1984), p. 5.
[4] *The Politics of Consent* by Francis Pym, (Hamish Hamilton, 1984), p. 175.

The great leap right

Crack down on crime • cut back on the dole • peg welfare services • support the whites in Rhodesia • reduce 'planning'

Table shows, in descending order of 'right-wingness', public opinion on the questions asked (figures in percentages):

	'RIGHT'		'LEFT'	
CRIME In general do you think that punishment given to people convicted of crimes in Britain is too severe, not tough enough or about right?	Punishment not tough enough 83 Twelve per cent think the current situation is about right		Punishment too severe	1
UNEMPLOYMENT BENEFITS Do you think it would be better or worse if it was more difficult to get unemployment benefits — the 'dole'?	Better if 'dole' more difficult	79	Worse if 'dole' more difficult	13
TAXATION AND SOCIAL SERVICES Which do you think is more important — to reduce taxation, or to increase and improve the social services?	Reduce taxes	67	Increase and improve social services	20
ECONOMIC AFFAIRS Some people say the Government should have a bigger say in the control and planning of industry, other people think the Government already interfere too much. Which do you think?	Government interfere too much 66		Government should have bigger say	20
RACIAL DISCRIMINATION Do you think it should be against the law to refuse a job to someone because of his race or colour?	Should not be against the law	53	Should be against the law	42
RHODESIA If there was a civil war in Rhodesia between white Rhodesians and black Rhodesians which side would you want to win?	Support white Rhodesians	44	Support black Rhodesians	17
ELITIST/POPULIST GOVERNMENT Which do you think is more important in a government — education and experience of governing, or understanding how ordinary people feel and think?	Education and experience	26	Understanding ordinary people	54
	The balance of percentages is made up by 'don't knows'			

[from the *Sunday Times* (poll by Opinion Research Centre), 25 August 1968]

188

Proportional representation: a political red herring

by John Tyndall

Much has been spoken in defence of the 'pluralism' that is regarded as essential to the maintenance of a democratic order of things. But what is the nature of the pluralism of which we are speaking? Does it mean a tolerance of differing opinions within a broad consensus of patriotism and commitment to vital national interests? Or does it mean the acceptance within the body politic of separate and warring factions whose interests are fundamentally incompatible with each other and often incompatible with that of the nation itself?

If it means the first, then pluralism has a place in politics which is probably essential if those politics are not to become inbred and to stagnate. But if it means the second, then it is difficult to see how under such circumstances strong and wise government can ever be possible. Ultimately, every act and policy of government has to be subject to a highest law, which must be the good of the nation. For government and political life to be conducted in accordance with that principle, no other 'highest law' must be allowed to exist — which means, put in the bluntest terms, that no other interest must be allowed to exist. This means that not only government but every other institution within the nation — the mass media, education, the machinery for industrial relations, industry and commerce, the armed forces, cultural life and religious life — must be placed at the service of the national community and in the service of the national idea. Such freedoms as these institutions enjoy cannot be absolute but must be circumscribed by the requirements of patriotic duty.

Common goal

Proceeding from this, the debate over national issues which takes place in the political and all other arenas must be a debate which assumes from the start the existence of a common goal, a national goal, and is about ways and means of reaching this goal; it cannot be a debate between two fundamentally opposite and conflicting goals, two fundamentally opposite and conflicting interests. We see this in microcosm in Northern Ireland in the conflict between the Loyalist and Republican factions. No argument or persuasion can ever resolve the essential division between those two factions; the triumph of one has to mean the extinction of the other. On the wider panorama of British politics, the same may be said of the conflicting ideals of nationalism and internationalism, race preservation or racial surrender, national independence or 'one world', national defence or pacifism, cultural integrity or cultural mongrelisation and the descent to the cultural jungle. Between these philosophies and goals there can be no 'debate', and to suppose that a body politic can accommodate them simultaneously, leaving to the interplay of 'democratic' forces the task of working out choices or compromises betwixt them, is to succumb to the kind of mental paralysis that is the hallmark of the progressive 'liberal' everywhere who has presided over the eclipse of Western civilisation.

No proper British recovery can be possible until the first named of the aforementioned alternatives are elevated far beyond their positions as mere 'points of view', and made into essential foundation stones of national existence, any threat to which is no more 'tolerated' than we would tolerate terrorism, rape, fraud or armed robbery.

If we return for a moment to the question of the 'fairness' and 'justice' of political systems, it may be accepted that the PR system is 'fairer' and more 'just' than the present British system in the representation it gives to parties, but in terms of fairness and justice to the electorate — who still vote under basically the same conditions — the difference in the two systems is purely marginal.

But the main point on which we must take issue is the

189

question of whether 'fairness' or 'justice' to the respective players of the game of party politics should in any way come into the reckoning when we are considering the efficacy of methods of government. I proceed in this debate from the premise that no form of government is a substitute for good government; it should be good government, in the last analysis, that should be our first objective, and indeed it might be claimed that the greatest fairness or justice to the people of a country is best promoted by that government which bestows on them the greatest benefits in those things that are most important to the people: good houses, ample opportunities for employment at decent wages, good care for the elderly and the very young, a good environment and a safe and secure country to live in. To the average man such things are far more important than any theoretical 'rights' he may have in the way of parties to vote for or the apportionment of 'power' among the parties once he has voted for them. There is absolutely no reason to believe that such benefits will be better secured by a PR system than by the existing system, given the basic rules under which the game is played and given the places where true power resides once the razzamataz of elections is over and real politics resume their course.

[from *Spearhead* (publication of the British National Party), April 1984]

K3

The role of the Monday Club

The Conservative and Unionist Monday Club is the largest pressure group in the Conservative Party. Situated on the centre-right of the Party, the Club fully supports the general political strategy of the Prime Minister, the Rt. Hon. Mrs Margaret Thatcher, MP. The Club's political role is to monitor various aspects of Government policy and action and to make detailed presentations of policy to ministers and the public at large in an attempt to modify and change, where it considers necessary, Government legislation in specific areas. The Monday Club sees its central purpose as being to maintain pressure on the Party leadership to stick to Conservative principles and carry out the promises contained in the Party's election manifesto.

The Monday Club opposes the politics of concensus which have failed the nation for the past twenty years. At the present time the Club is placing particular emphasis on the economy, with particular regard for privatisation and the encouragement of free enterprise and more competition, the removal of trade union immunities and industrial relations reform, an end to mass immigration from the New Commonwealth and Pakistan and a better-financed scheme for voluntary repatriation, the repeal of race relations legislation, fundamental reform of the Common Market to make it work more for Britain's interests, and maintaining and strengthening the Union with Northern Ireland. The Club is also well known for its stand in demanding the effective and efficient defence of the UK, the improvement and preservation of law, order and authority within society, and closer defence and trading links with the Republic of South Africa.

[from 'The aims of the Monday Club' (Monday Club, September 1982)]

PRIME MINISTER Margaret Thatcher has spelt out the underlying theme of her Government in a forthright new statement revealing her basic philosophy.

She presented her message in a speech on how she would like her governments remembered in the history books and chose as the occasion a gathering of some of Britain's most influential and respected journalists.

Mrs Thatcher was addressing the centenary lunch of the Parliamentary Lobby at the Savoy Hotel, London. And she laid into vested interests which had been untackled, among which she noticeably included local government.

'I would like the governments I led to be seen as those which decisively broke with a debilitating consensus of paternalistic government and a dependent people; which rejected the notion that the State is all-powerful and the citizen as merely its beneficiary; which shattered the illusion that Government could somehow substitute for individual performance.

As governments which tackled the vested interests which had been immune for years — the trade unions, the nationalised industries, local government, the monopolies in the professions.

As governments which were strong to do the things that only governments can do, but strong enough to leave the rest to the character and initiative of the British people.

[from *Conservative Newsline*, February 1984]

'. . . Bless us with unity, Save us from tyranny . . .'

[from the *Daily Mail*, 3 August 1982]

Common ownership

by Eric Heffer

Calls for common ownership have always been attacked by opponents of socialism. They argue that when industries are nationalised, they fail, thereby demonstrating that socialism is a failure.

Nationalisation exists in many countries, none of which are socialist. The so-called 'mixed economy' is a means of preserving the capitalist enterprise system. It may not please doctrinaire Friedmanites or Thatcherites. But it pleases those more enlightened capitalist economists who recognise that a degree of government intervention in economic affairs is essential if the free enterprise system is to be preserved. Government intervention in such circumstances is seen as a way of under-pinning the private sector.

The truth is that a totally free enterprise system simply does not work. Since the capitalist system came into existence there have been periodic booms and slumps. With increased technology the prospect of unemployment has increased.

Is it not an absurdity that people need houses, yet building workers are unemployed; that families need all kinds of machines, yet engineers are out of work? That despite food surpluses many people, mainly in the Third World, are hungry? The fact is that our economic system is based on the concept of 'production for profit and not for use'. Labour's socialist concept is the reverse. To achieve our aim it will be necessary to plan the nation's resources. However, in any national plan for production, it is essential that it does not become bureaucratic. Democratic procedures are essential at all stages. There is always a danger that 'the plan' will become everything — that society could be sacrificed to 'the plan'. There is the potential conflict between efficient centralised control and possibly less efficient, democratic decision-making.

As most big corporations are owned by private individuals, or groups of individuals, the class system is perpetuated. Public schools exist only because of the finances created by private enterprise. If class society is to be ended, therefore, it is essential to get rid of the private ownership of industry and finance.

Labour can only really plan the nation's resources and ensure that investment is undertaken where required if the banks and finance houses are brought into public ownership. That is why a new Labour government must act quickly to publicly control the banks and finance houses. Otherwise its task of building a new society will be made much more difficult, if not impossible.

Public ownership, however, does not have to be solely in the form of nationalisation. That can be one method, especially for service industries, where competition is practically non-existent and where natonalisation is undoubtedly the best method. Where a measure of competition can exist, there are many and varied possible forms of public ownership, such as municipal ownership and co-operation. However, if socialism is to be created then forms of democratic management must be developed, otherwise a 'new class' could develop with State bureaucracy supreme.

State ownership and State control are not synonomous with socialisation. State ownership and control exist in the Soviet Union, but that country is not socialist. There has to be a proper balance between State ownership and personal and collective initiative.

[from 'Why you should support Labour: the party of democratic socialism' (Labour Party, 1981)]

Rate cap Resistance

Interview with David Blunkett

David Blunkett is the Leader of Sheffield City Council. He is one of the key figures in the new generation of local Labour leaders. He has lived in Sheffield all his life and has served on Sheffield City Council for 15 years. He is a member of the Labour National Executive Committee and is chair of the Local Government Campaign Unit, an organisation representing trade unions and some 70 local authorities, which was formed in October 1983 in response to the attack on local government. Here he is interviewed by Mark Page.

[. . .]*How do you see the fight between local councils and central government over rate capping in relation to the overall struggle against Thatcherism?*

We're in an historic battle about dissent. It's been with us ever since people came together and had any kind of body politic. And we are fighting for the right to dissent, the right to tolerance of differences of view, for the kind of society that people take for granted. Above all we're fighting against a restructuring of the economic and social life of the community. Thatcher is intent on creating the 'property-owning democracy', where the market place and not the ballot box is the way in which we will distribute our wealth, order our society and control our resources. The pound in your pocket rather than the cross on your ballot paper will determine your vote in this new, restructured, so-called 'democracy'. The battle for collective public service is a key element in all this. We must start debating as a movement our values and the ways in which we will extend democracy, parti-cipative democracy, as well as defending what we've got; because it is partly the inadequacy of, and the alienation from, the way in which the system is worked that has enabled Thatcher to take the steps she has with such success.

Why do you think local councils have become centres of opposition to the power of national government?

First, it's because opposition within the Palace of Westminster has been so ineffective over the last six years. Secondly, Thatcher herself has elevated local government to a new political importance by recognising that collectivism is as much her enemy as any traditional parliamentary opposition and seeking to destroy it, be it the provision of collective community services through local government or people coming together in traditional industries and resisting her restructuring. To her, social democracy, socialism, radicalism, just simple collectivism, are all much of a muchness. They are what she dislikes and is determined to smash. And from her point of view the operation of market forces, the creation of privatisation as an alternative to social provision, clearly demands that she does indeed take those steps.

What do you think is the significance of the campaign around local government services for the Labour Party more generally?

We have to win people for a vision of the future, not just against Thatcher. Therefore people's participation in democracy, in their own lives, is a key question now being raised. That's why housing sales, and the flotation of shares to the workers in British Telecom, evoked such a response from ordinary people. They need a new way of being able to find some expression for their desires. We need to recognise that and develop a socialist response, to win them to what we want in a world where people work and pull together and share their talents and resources.

Secondly, a Labour government can't simply run things from Parliament. Parliament is important, it helps to gain power for people, but State socialism, in the form that people formerly envisaged it, is frankly dead. Whilst we want Parliament to concentrate on the great problems of international finance and international affairs, and to extend control by using its legislative power to give back to people that which is theirs, we actually need at local level instruments to make it a reality. I don't think local government can do it all, but it can act as a catalyst to support and help people to take control over their lives, whether it's by municipal ownership in the economy, extending democracy in the social provision of social services, education, leisure, housing, the environment, transport, or whether it's putting resources at the disposal of people. It's a partnership between a socialist government struggling with the problems of international politics and finance, and the local State mobilising people behind the objectives of the government and at the same time providing an instrument for carrying out those detailed policies that make a reality out of all the slogans and the jargon. In the past we've expected State socialism and State sectors of the economy to turn people on, and they haven't. We've relied on nationalised bureaucracies which have frankly alienated people. We've got to ask ourselves in the 1990s and the 21st century what role will we in the individual communities be playing in making socialism work, not how we will be criticising the failures of a Secretary of State for Industry or the Chancellor of the Exchequer of a socialist government.

Do you think there is such a thing as a new kind of municipal socialism?

We ought to be clear that much of what we stand for is not new at all. It is really a return to the early days of local government and the notion that people wanted to control and have a say in their own lives rather than simply hand over to parliamentarians who would do it on their behalf for five years and if you did not like what happened you could get rid of them. We have drifted away from that, we have drifted towards a centralised paternalistic democracy where we have expected and relied on solely parliamentary action to resolve difficulties and that has failed to mobilise people. We are going back to that. The radical local authorities have also been trying to show that democracy is not confined to spending money on services, democracy is about our lives and therefore it is about the local economy, industry and commerce, it's about where we are going.

[from *Marxism Today* (publication of the Communist Party of Great Britain), March 1985]

Questions

1 What evidence is there in the table in K1 of a preponderance of right wing attitudes amongst the public in 1968?

2 Give the probable reason why present-day issues such as the level of unemployment and the rate of inflation did not feature in the ORC poll in 1968. (K1)

3 What does Tyndall mean by the following: (a) the 'highest law'; (b) 'good government'; (c) 'cultural mongrelisation'; (d) 'progressive "liberal"'? (K2)

4 What would you deduce are the main aims of the British National Party from a reading of K2?

5   In what way does Tyndall suggest that economic rights are more important than political rights? (K2)

6   What indications are there in K3 that the Monday Club is concerned about race relations and race issues?

7   In what respects can it be argued that Thatcher and Blunkett have similar ideas on politics according to K4 and K6? (See also J6.)

8   What arguments does Heffer offer against: (a) the 'mixed economy' system; (b) the nationalisation form of public ownership; (c) continued existence of big private corporations? (K5)

9   Suggest one key reason why Heffer thinks the Soviet Union is not socialist. (K5)

10   In which passage in K5 does Heffer suggest an answer as to how to obtain 'a proper balance between State ownership and personal and collective initiative'?

11   Point out how Blunkett argues that Thatcher's aims are not really democratic. (K6)

12   Suggest reasons why the policies of the Conservative government since 1979 have been partly the cause of the development of the Labour Party's interest in the municipal or decentralised forms of socialism. (K6)

Class Discussion

1   What is meant by privatisation? Does this policy incorporate the three main themes mentioned by Thatcher in the extract from *Conservative Newsline*? (K4)

2   Define: (a) 'paternalistic government'; (b) 'vested interests'. (K4)

3   Compare and contrast the results of the *Sunday Times* Poll (K1) with the results of the Gallup Poll given in *The Daily Telegraph* (J13), particularly in relation to crime (law and order issues), public expenditure and welfare.

4   Comment on Heffer's belief that: (a) private ownership of industry and finance should be ended; (b) production should be subject to a national plan. (K5)

5   Define and explain the meaning of the following terms: (a) 'property owning democracy'; (b) 'radicalism'; (c) Thatcherites; (d) 'municipal socialism'; (e) 'collectivism'. (K5, K6) (See also J6.)

Extension Work

1   To what extent are the aims of the Monday Club being implemented by the present government? (K3)

2   Give a full definition of the term 'Parliamentary Lobby'. (K4)

3   From research into the early days of British socialism, find justification for Blunkett's comment that 'what we stand for is not new at all'. (K6)

Index

Also available from Stanley Thornes (Publishers) Ltd:

A.D. Burgen   *Comprehension Exercises in Sociology*
J.R.S. Whiting   *Politics and Government: a first sourcebook*

199